To Carrick,
with love from Sara.

MAINSTREAMS OF *MUSIC*

by David Ewen

Opera

Orchestral Music

Solo Instrumental and Chamber Music

Vocal Music

MAINSTREAMS OF

MUSIC

Volume One

1972

Opera

Its Story Told Through the Lives

and Works of its Foremost Composers

by David Ewen

Franklin Watts, Inc. 845 *Third Avenue · New York, New York 10022*

Illustration Credits

The Bettmann Archive: pages vi, 84, 115, 133, 135, 235, 252
The Pierpont Morgan Library: page 8B
Photographie Giraudon: (Musée Condé): pages 38 (Musée de l'Opéra): 23, 39; 48B (Bibl. du Conservatoire): 49
The Mansell Collection: pages 24A, 25A, 26, 81
Louis Mélançon: pages 1, 50, 51, 66, 67, 69, 82, 83, 97A, 98, 99, 116, 136, 137, 138, 149, 151, 180, 181, 182, 196, 209, 232, 233
The Library of Congress: pages 4, 68
Culver Pictures, Inc.: pages 96, 97B, 114, 117, 118A & B, 119A & B, 120, 121, 152, 153, 179A & B, 195, 210, 230, 236
Ullstein Bilderdienst: pages 134, 150, 176, 177, 178, 199, 231, 234
Don Hunstein, Courtesy Columbia Records: page 198
Sovfoto: page 208B
Staatsbibliothek, Berlin: page 80

Jacket photos by Don Hunstein, courtesy of the Metropolitan Opera Association.

Photo research by Wesley Day

Copyright © 1972 by David Ewen
Printed in the United States of America

Typography and binding design by Diana Hrisinko

Library of Congress Cataloging in Publication Data

Ewen, David, 1907–
    Opera; its story told through the lives and works of
its foremost composers.

    (His Mainstreams of music, v. 1)
    SUMMARY: Traces the history of the opera discussing
important composers and their works from the sixteenth
century to the present day. Includes a glossary of
operatic terms.
    1. Opera—History and criticism. 2. Composers—
Juvenile literature. [1. Opera—History and criticism.
2. Composers] I. Title.
ML1700.E94   782.1'09   75-185687
ISBN 0-531-02578-0

Contents

Introduction

You are an opera *aficionado*. Nobody can shake you from your conviction that this is the most exciting, absorbing, spellbinding of all the arts: a wondrous union of music and drama, dance and spectacle, scenery and costume. No matter how many times you enter the opera house, you begin to hold your breath as the lights fade, the conductor makes his way to the podium, he gives his downbeat, and the first measures of the overture change an auditorium into a place filled with magic. No matter how many times you may have seen the opera you are attending, or how many times you have heard it over the radio or on recordings, you never fail to respond with supercharged emotion each time the big arias or the exciting ensemble numbers are sung by supreme artists; whenever stirring choruses resound through the opera house; whenever eye-filling ballet sequences are danced. Until the final curtain descends and the crash of applause and the "bravos" bring the principal singers in front of the curtain to break the spell, an opera performance for you is a world of enchantment removing you completely from reality.

The music of an opera can lift a rather weak story to a high level of art, providing moments of soaring beauty as in an aria like "Celeste

Aida" or "Un bel dì" or "Casta diva" or "Che gelida manina." The dramatic weaknesses found in a number of opera texts, called librettos, are forgotten during the glittering, glistening vocal exhibitions like the *Lucia* "Mad Scene." Spectacular scenes like the ball in *Don Giovanni,* or the march of the knights into Wartburg Castle in *Tannhäuser* or the "Triumphal March" in *Aida,* although they may slow the plot, do carry the audience along in enthusiasm by the strength of their music. As a matter of fact, a good many librettos (particularly those since the middle nineteenth century and quite a few in the eighteenth century) are thoroughly credible in their plot development and characterization and represent excellent theater in their own right.

The capacity of a text to tell a story is heightened and intensified through the power of music to convey emotion, create moods, suggest atmosphere, build climaxes—in a way that words alone can never accomplish. Above and beyond the fact that so many of the individual numbers in operas are so beautiful to listen to (just as are the speeches in Shakespeare), the union of music and words makes for a totally unique stage experience.

The history of opera, virtually from its beginnings, represents an endless struggle between the music and the drama to gain the upper hand. There have always been composers (and the cliques surrounding them) who, regarding opera simply as elaborate entertainment, favor only those works glorifying singing, melody, dance, and elaborate scenes. On the other hand there have been opposing forces who insist that opera can only be a great and noble art when equal emphasis is placed on drama and music, integrating both inseparably. Such a concept had been the goal of composers as far back as Rameau and Gluck. The battle between opera as entertainment and opera as drama has been fought in many different countries with many different protagonists over a period of many years.

There are those today who adore the conventional Italian and French operas of the nineteenth century with their magic outpouring of melody and emotion, just as there are others who, when they enter the opera house, seek a vital, compelling human experience even at the expense of melody. Fortunately, most operagoers are neutral. There is much to enjoy in either type of opera. Even when they are formal and routine in their musical format, and often devoid of conviction in their text, many nineteenth-century operas have established themselves permanently in the repertory because of their capacity to evoke a kind of

magic no other theatrical form can duplicate. And musical drama, as opposed to formal opera, contributes a different kind of pleasure—forceful, compelling, throbbing theater.

Serious operas versus comic operas? Italian operas and French "grand" operas versus the German musical drama? National drama versus modernistic operas? The wonder of opera lies in the great variety of style, subject matter, and depth of expression it has to offer.

These varied attractions of opera are the reasons why it has survived for more than three hundred and fifty years and flourishes today. This is why the major opera houses sell out as never before; why there are so many opera festivals both in America and Europe; why so many opera companies have sprung up from the grass roots; why colleges and universities devote so much effort to opera productions; why opera has even invaded our public parks, motion picture theaters, and our homes through the phonograph, the radio, and television.

By using "facts only as vehicles by which to enter its own dream world," as Herbert Graf, the distinguished opera director, once wrote, and by treating "in terms of music not only the story but, more basically, the emotions arising from the story," opera is an art form able to stir the heart and the imagination of those ready and willing to accept it on its own terms. This evaluation holds true for the opera of yesterday, despite its stereotypes. It holds even more true after most of those stereotypes have been replaced by fresh new approaches. And this is why opera means so much to you.

It is for you, the opera lover, that this book has been written—to describe what you may know either vaguely or not at all: how opera came into being; how it grew and developed and changed through the years at the hands of its foremost masters; what the most important operas are like. But I would not be truthful if I did not admit that this book is also intended for the skeptics, with the hope that knowledge may bring tolerance, and tolerance may in turn inspire appreciation. Then you, too, my dear skeptic, may join the ever-growing army of opera *aficionados*.

DAVID EWEN

ŒUVRE IV.e

L'ARBRE ENCHANTÉ

Opéra Comique, en un Acte de Mr. Vadé

Dédié

A MONSIEUR

FRERE DU ROY.

La Musique

PAR Mr. LE CH.lier GLUCK

Mis en Vers et en Ariettes par Mr. Moline.

Représenté à Versailles devant leurs Majestés le
lundi 27 Février 1775. pour la Fête que Monsieur
à donnée à l'Archiduc Maximilien,

Par Mrs. les Comédiens Italiens Ordinaires du Roy.

PRIX avec les Parties Séparées 18.tt

Gravé par Mme. Lobri

A PARIS.

Chez Mr. Lemarchand Éditeur et Md. de Musique, Rue
Fromanteau, a l'Opéra

Et aux adresses ordinaires

A.   P.   D.   R.
Écrit par   L. Aubert

I

Opera Is Born

Opera came into existence during a period in music history known as "baroque." The word baroque was borrowed from art and architecture to describe the ornate, overornamented, extravagantly decorative designs favored in the seventeenth century. The baroque era in music began roughly in the last years of the sixteenth century and ended with the death of Bach and Handel in the middle of the eighteenth. It was succeeded by the classical period of Haydn and Mozart. One of the reasons the term baroque came to be applied to the music of this era was the ornateness of the music, the ornament, the decoration (particularly in the shaping of a melody). A second reason was this period's love for magnificence and splendor. Still another was the spirit of exaltation we encounter in baroque art that was frequently carried over into music—particularly in oratorios and cantatas.

The age of baroque music had been preceded by the age of polyphony. Polyphony, meaning many tones or voices, was unaccompanied choral music (principally for the church) in which several independent melodic lines were sung simultaneously. The greatest single contribution made by the baroque era was the transformation in musical style from polyphony to homophony. Homophony emphasized a *single* melody (or voice) supported by an accompaniment of chords (harmony). This change did not mean that polyphony was discarded during the baroque era. After all, were not oratorios and cantatas born during the baroque age and did they not abound with polyphonic writing? But what did happen then was that composers were discovering a new way of writing music. This new approach—the way of combining sounds, really—meant that some of the composers could now begin writing instrumental music and developing the early instrumental forms, like the sonata. From this development would sprout the orchestral, chamber, and solo instrumental masterworks that so enthrall us today.

But the changeover to homophony made something else possible too, something hardly less valuable: the invention of opera.

Culture owes a great debt of gratitude to that wonderful city of Florence, which lies at the foot of the Apennines in Tuscany, Italy, between Rome and Bologna. The glory of Florence was perhaps at its height in the sixteenth century, when, with bountiful cultural generosity, it contributed to the world probably the two greatest artists of all time: Michelangelo and Leonardo da Vinci. It was then, too, that the influence of the Renaissance (which had first come to being in this very city) was still strongly felt. And it was then that this city evolved one of the greatest and most widely admired mediums the art of music knows—opera.

It is no coincidence that both the Renaissance and opera should have been cradled in Florence, for opera is a child of the Renaissance. The word Renaissance means "rebirth." What had been reborn in Florence was the art, spirit, and culture of ancient Greece. The influence of the Renaissance had first been felt in Florence as far back as the fourteenth century. It flourished there before spreading throughout Western Europe.

By the end of the sixteenth century, the Renaissance had become such a vital force in Florentine life that a group of intellectuals was inspired to try reviving Greek drama. This group (known as the *camerata,* or "men who meet in a chamber") gathered regularly in the 1580s at the palace of a dilettante nobleman—Giovanni Bardi, the count of Vernio. They came together to talk about poetry, art, and drama. Since the spirit of the Renaissance hovered over the city like an omnipresent star, they discussed Greek culture most often. Besides Count Bardi, the group

comprised men of no small consequence in Florence's intellectual life.

Among them were the poet Ottavio Rinuccini; the composers Giulio Caccini, Jacopo Peri, and Emilio de' Cavalieri; the gifted performer on lute and viol Vincenzo Galilei (father of the world-famous scientist, Galileo); and the nobleman and patron of the arts Jacopo Corsi.

Again and again a single theme sprang up in their discussions: Why could not the grandeur and majesty of Greek drama be revived in the same way that Greek art and Greek culture had already been reborn? Jacopo Peri pointed out "in the opinion of many, the Greeks *sang* their tragedies on their stage." This conclusion was more or less true. Until about the fourth century B.C., Greek drama used choral songs and choral dances extensively. The chorus, comprising about a dozen or so, sang declamatory passages in unison. Sometimes the actors would improvise declamations for their noblest lines where speech approached toward singing.

The members of the *camerata,* then, felt strongly that if sixteenth-century Florentine poets were to write plays in the true spirit of Greek dramas, the texts must be supplied with music. This addition posed no small problem. After all, the prevailing music style of the time was still polyphony, and polyphony was cumbersome and ineffectual in a theatrical format presenting an individual text. You cannot have several people sing at the same time throughout a work and have the audience comprehend the words.

And so, the *camerata* devised a new music style of one solo voice singing in a form of exaggerated speech. (The ancient Greek writer Aristoxenus had written that song must be patterned after speech inflections.) Thus the *camerata* invented the monophonic, or monodic, style, which involved one voice reciting or declaiming in almost a speaking style. This singing-speaking style, called *stile rappresentativo,* was probably close to what we hear in opera today as recitative. In 1581, Vincenzo Galilei clarified what this new music should sound like in his book *Dialogue of Ancient and Modern Music.* In 1590, Emilio de' Cavalieri put theory into practice by devising recitatives, or declamations, for two fables performed in Florence in 1595. In both works a simple instrumental accompaniment was used as a background for recitatives. By 1601 the style officially came to be known as "the new music" (*le nuove musiche*), a term Caccini used as the title of a series of madrigals, explaining that the new technique was devised to permit the performer "to speak through music."

It fell to the composer Jacopo Peri (1561–1633), at the urging of Corsi and Rinuccini, to apply this new manner of writing to classical

A view of Florence, showing the Piazza Santa Trinità.

Jacopo Corsi's palace (left) in Florence, the setting for the first performance of an opera in 1597.

drama. Rinuccini prepared a text based on Greek mythology, and Peri
set it in the new monodic style with simple instrumental accompaniment.
The result was *Dafne,* in prologue and six scenes, which its authors
called a "fable in music" (*favola in musica*), a descriptive term long used
for a work with a text based on a legend. A more popular designation,
and the one most frequently employed, was "drama through music"
(*dramma per musica*), covering all fields of drama utilizing music. Regardless of what it was called, *Dafne* was an opera, the first opera in
music history—even though the word *opera* would not be used for this
type of composition for another few years.

The score of *Dafne* has been lost. Documents of the period enable us
to recreate more or less what took place at the premiere of the world's
first opera. That performance took place during the carnival of 1597.
The auditorium was a brilliantly lit salon in Jacopo Corsi's palace. The
splendor of this setting was hardly more awesome than the social position of the audience, all of whom were of the nobility, come by invitation. Backstage, the composer was putting on his costume, for in his
opera he was assuming the role of Apollo.

The curtains parted. An old Greek legend, its theme the last word in
ingenuousness, came to life. Dafne (or Daphne) is pursued by the god
Apollo. To protect Dafne, her mother transforms the girl into a laurel
tree, which then becomes sacred to Apollo. That's the whole story.

Surely the production would have been unremarkable, but for one
important fact. The three characters—Dafne, Apollo, and Dafne's
mother—*sang* rather than spoke their lines. The monotony of continuous recitatives was occasionally relieved by a dance or a brief choral
number, the latter also in a monodic style. Further interest was contributed by the fact that the voices and the dances were accompanied by instruments: a harpsichord (the precursor of the piano) or organ, lutes,
old-time flutes, and a bass viol (forerunner of the cello).

This new art form for the stage made a profound impression on its
first audience. During the next two years *Dafne* was performed at the annual carnivals. Each time it was received with the greatest enthusiasm.
The members of the *camerata* could no longer doubt that their artistic
brainchild was a healthy offspring. What they could not suspect was that
they had *not* revived ancient Greek drama by any means, since *Dafne*
had no kinship whatsoever with the kind of tragedies the Greeks had
written. What the *camerata* had achieved was something far more important. They had invented an altogether new kind of theater: opera.

If any testimony be needed to prove how strong an impact this new art form had upon its listeners, that testimony came as early as 1600. On February 9 of that year the marriage of Henry IV of France to Maria de' Medici was celebrated. For this event, Peri was commissioned to write a new work similar to *Dafne*.

Once again Rinuccini provided a text lifted from Greek mythology: the story of Orpheus and Eurydice, a subject that would remain a favorite with numerous librettists and composers for the next century and more. It is easy to see why this legend was so popular with composers. Orpheus was a Thracian musician who had such a gift for playing the lyre (an instrument he is supposed to have invented) and for singing that he could tame animals with his music. Orpheus, then, was a hero for whom composers could write affecting music, and his poignant story could inspire such music.

The tale is by now thrice familiar. Orpheus, mourning the recent death of his wife, Eurydice, is permitted by the gods to retrieve her from the other world. The persuasive power of his eloquent singing gains him admission to Hades. He finds his beloved Eurydice there and leads her back to earth. You probably remember that in the myth, until they had escaped from Hades, Orpheus was not to look back at Eurydice, and when he did so she fell dead. The writers of operas have all tried to avoid this tragic ending. Rinuccini's text had no condition placed on Orpheus at all, and so a happy ending was assured.

Peri's *Euridice* ("Euridice" is the Italian form of Eurydice) was performed at the Pitti Palace in Florence on October 6, 1600, with the composer appearing as Orpheus. This is the first "drama through music" to survive, having been published in 1601. *Euridice* is primitive by any standards. The text is naïvely conceived. Most of the action takes place offstage, a messenger serving to inform the characters of the play (and the audience) what has happened. No less ingenuous and elementary is the music. There is no overture. *Euridice* begins with a prologue in which a character representing Tragedy reveals to the audience that this work had been written for the royal wedding. (Using a prologue to describe to audiences what they are about to witness, or to point up the fact that the principal character represents a nobleman for whom the work was written, was a practice that would continue for a number of years.)

Then the drama unfolds. Most of the singing is in a declamatory style that is little more than stylized speech. The opera has some choruses, some of them recitatives, others imitating the kind of madrigal writing prevalent during the polyphonic era. The accompanying instruments (hidden behind the scene) included a harpsichord or organ, a lyre, two types of lutes, and gambas; their main function was to provide simple chords as a background. To an audience of today *Euridice* can have no possible interest other than historic. But the Florence of 1600 was enchanted.

Another member of the *camerata,* Giulio Caccini (1546–1618), was so interested in Peri's *Euridice* that he contributed a few numbers of his own to it. Then, still captured by the story of Orpheus and Eurydice, he wrote his own version. Caccini's opera was also called *Euridice;* it was also published in 1601; and it was also introduced at the Pitti Palace, though not until December 5, 1602. Caccini's musical treatment is not much different from Peri's in its reliance on recitatives. But a short step forward in the development of opera—a very short step, indeed—is made when some of the recitatives are embellished with ornamentations that help extend the style and technique of monodic writing for the first time.

Notwithstanding this slight advance, the Florentine method of writing dramas through music soon became a bore. The novelty of having a drama sung throughout had begun to wear off. The nobility, which made up the opera audiences of that day, were discovering that a long succession of recitatives made for stilted, artificial drama as well as for monotony; that the music slowed down the action to a snail's pace; that the kind of music Peri and Caccini were capable of producing aroused little emotion.

2

Creative Transformation

Claudio Monteverdi, Alessandro Scarlatti,
Henry Purcell, George Frideric Handel

It is not beyond the realm of possibility that dramas through music, as conceived by Peri and Caccini, might have faded completely from favor and lapsed into permanent oblivion—but for one singularly significant development: the emergence of a genius at this propitious moment in opera's history. This genius transformed a stylized and contrived kind of musical theater into something more vital by both utilizing all the musical resources available to him (other than recitatives and choruses) and inventing techniques and methods that were altogether new. This genius was Claudio Monteverdi (1567–1643).

Monteverdi was only fifteen when he published his first volume of music, a set of motets in the then prevailing polyphonic style. After that he published many more volumes of polyphonic music: eight volumes of madrigals, together with masses and motets and magnificats. All revealed remarkable technical skill in writing counterpoint—but much more than that, too. A striking independence of musical thinking compelled him to sidestep the strict rules of counterpoint when his artistic conscience felt that a better effect could thereby be achieved. Monteverdi used discords when discords served him. Slowly he evolved a musical language of his own that was far ahead of his times.

In 1600 he heard Peri's *Euridice*. Its impact on him was overwhelming. Up to that time, in his polyphonic music and with his new idioms, Monteverdi revealed a strong bent for drama and sentiment. The new art form from Florence provided him, he realized at once, with a medium far more suitable for his artistic personality than the vocal polyphony he had previously used. In *Euridice* a new world had suddenly opened up for him, a world he was restless to explore for himself.

A post at the ducal court at Mantua headed by Vincenzo Gonzaga, which he had assumed in 1590, offered him his first opportunity to experiment with this new art form, since Vincenzo Gonzaga's two sons commissioned him to do so. The court poet Alessandro Striggio fashioned for Monteverdi a new text, again based on the Orpheus and Eurydice legend. Monteverdi's opera, *La Favola d'Orfeo* (*The Fable of Orpheus*)—now most frequently just called *Orfeo*—was first publicly produced in Mantua on February 24, 1607. It was a triumph. The audience could not fail to be stirred by the drama, made so compelling through Monteverdi's music.

Striggio's libretto was no improvement over Rinuccini's. It is in the music that we enter a world Peri and Caccini never knew. It was quite true that Monteverdi followed the lead of his predecessors by emphasizing the monodic style. But with what a difference! Through great tonal leaps in the vocal line (sometimes to express grief, sometimes excitement), Monteverdi intensified the emotions. To increase musical interest further he broadened his phrases, or stretched out the sounds, beyond the brief ones previously employed by Peri and Caccini. Passages like "Tu se' morta," in which Orpheus expresses his grief at his wife's death and "Possente spirito," where Orpheus pleads to be allowed to cross the river Styx and enter Hades to find his wife, have such intensity of feeling that we can sense the recitative is beginning to edge toward operatic melody. The chorus "Ahi, caso acerbo," which follows the announcement by the messenger that Eurydice is dead, has such emotional intensity that a modern concept of choral writing in opera begins to take shape.

His concern for drama led Monteverdi to alter his tempi and rhythms frequently, and to interpolate chromaticisms (sharps and flats), the better to suit every changing mood or emotion. He used sudden changes of harmony, even discords, to suggest tension or conflict. He assigned a far greater importance to the chorus than Peri and Caccini had done, and he wrote for it, as we have indicated, with far greater expressiveness.

The musical dramatist in Monteverdi made him refuse to accept the limited number of instruments Peri and Caccini had used for their accompaniments. Monteverdi used an orchestra of forty instruments (twelve violins, five viola da gambas, two basses, three muted trumpets, a piccolo, a high trumpet, two trombones, two small organs, two harpsichords, harps, and so forth), because he needed more colors to his tonal palette and more instrumental effects to project atmosphere, suggest emotional nuances, and build up climaxes. The orchestra was used not only as a support for the voice with simple chords but also, for the first time, to provide recitatives with a richly orchestrated background.

We now have two kinds of recitatives instead of one: "dry" (*secco*), in which simple statements or verbal exchanges are accompanied by elementary chords, and "accompanied" (*accompagnato* or *stromentato*) recitative for emotional or dramatic episodes, where the accompaniment is given a fuller and richer treatment. For the next two centuries, composers would generally use only the harpsichord for the dry recitative and the orchestra for the accompanied.

Other epoch-making innovations are found in Monteverdi's use of his orchestra. For the first time something anticipating the overture is utilized: a little fanfare preceding the prologue, played by the entire orchestra but emphasizing the trumpets. The orchestra is used throughout the opera for various interludes, for passages introducing or concluding a vocal number or separating one vocal number from another, and for the dances, one of which ends the opera in a joyous mood. The way Monteverdi wrote for the orchestra—and in certain places for individual instruments as an obbligato, or a persistent motif, to accompany the voice—was something completely new in the early seventeenth century. In fact it is no exaggeration to say that the modern symphony orchestra first came into being with *Orfeo* and that Monteverdi was the first composer to understand the science of instrumentation.

Orfeo, then, is the first such work to hint at how far the drama through music could develop. The French musicologist Henry Prunières went so far as to maintain that Monteverdi "turned the aristocratic spectacle of Florence into modern musical drama overflowing with life and bearing in its mighty waves of sound the passions which make up the human soul."

The celebration for the marriage of Francesco Gonzaga (the son of Vincenzo) to the infanta of Savoy led Monteverdi to write his second opera, *Arianna,* to a libretto by Rinuccini. It was produced in Mantua in 1608. The only music to survive from it is a single melody: "Lasciatemi morire," the heroine's lament. Here she bemoans the fact that she has been abandoned by her lover and berates a fisherman for having saved her from drowning when she tried to commit suicide. This is the most moving melody for single voice with accompaniment written for opera up to this time, its tragedy heightened by discords in the harmony and the intervallic leaps in the melody. When *Arianna* was first produced, the audience is reputed to have wept when the lament was sung. Monteverdi apparently also thought highly of this music, for in 1614 he used it for one of his greatest madrigals, and in 1641 he borrowed the melody for a sacred text.

By 1613, Monteverdi was deservedly esteemed as one of Italy's most distinguished composers. It was to be expected that he received one of the most desirable musical appointments in the country—that of *maestro di cappella* at the cathedral of San Marco in Venice. He stayed at this post for the rest of his life, always working long and painstakingly in meeting the exacting demands of directing the music for the church services and in composing numerous madrigals and dramas through music. He kept growing artistically all the time, his dramatic powers strengthening, his musical resources perpetually being enriched with techniques of his own invention.

One of his most important dramas through music written in Venice was *Il Combattimento di Tancredi e Clorinda,* produced in 1624. The text was a silly one, even if it was the work of one of Italy's foremost sixteenth-century poets, Torquato Tasso. In this opera Monteverdi introduced some new orchestral techniques, such as plucked strings and tremolos, or trembling tones. Monteverdi invented these effects (now such elementary devices in string performance) to emphasize agitation and passion. This is why his style in this opera was described as "agitated."

In Venice, Monteverdi eventually found a new incentive for writing dramas through music, other than commissions from noblemen. In 1637 the first public opera house was opened in Venice, the Teatro San Cassiano. Venetian nobility rented the box seats by the season, but the general Venetian public was admitted into the lower parterre for the nominal admission price of about twenty cents.

Monteverdi's first opera written not for private performance in palaces but for the public stage took place in this theater: *Adone,* in 1639. After that, Monteverdi continued creating dramas for public consumption. When in 1642 still another public opera house came to Venice—the Teatro SS Giovanni e Paolo—Monteverdi created for it

L'Incoronazione di Poppea. This is the first opera based on a historical rather than mythological theme—the coronation of Poppea (or Poppaea). The main historical characters are Nero, the Roman emperor, his wife, Octavia, and his mistress, Poppea. Through her scheming Poppea succeeds in getting Nero to marry her and make her empress.

This was Monteverdi's last drama through music, completed when he was seventy-four years old. Here, as earlier, he is still the bold innovator. He introduced comic scenes as temporary relief from the tragic ones. And so lyrical is some of his monodic writing that we are now at last beginning to get true melody in place of just recitatives. One of the most beautiful melodic pages in the score comes toward the end of the opera, a love duet by Nero and Poppea.

Since Monteverdi lived in Venice so long and wrote so many dramas through music there, the city of canals replaced Florence as Italy's center of opera. So popular had the musical theater become in Venice that during the sixty-three years separating the opening of the Teatro San Cassiano and the end of the century, sixteen public opera houses had been founded in that city; and they had presented 358 operas.

It was in Venice that the term *opera* was used for the first time in connection with a musical stage production instead of *drama through music.* This happened in 1639, when one of Monteverdi's most significant successors—Pier Francesco Cavalli (1602–76)—referred to his *Le Nozze di Teti e di Peleo* as an *opera scenica,* or "scenic work." (The Italian word *opera* means "a work," any kind of a work.) Some of Cavalli's contemporaries preferred calling their own musical stage composition *opera in musica,* or "a work in music." Within a brief period, Venetian composers and their public began using simply the single word, *opera.*

A generation of opera composers appeared in Venice after Monteverdi's death. All used texts based on mythological or historical subjects. All were influenced by Monteverdi.

Among these composers Cavalli deserves special attention. Even more sharply than Monteverdi had done, Cavalli achieved a distinction between recitatives and full melodies, which now can be referred to as arias. Each of these forms he endowed with the character it would possess for many years with subsequent Italian composers. Cavalli even went an additional step beyond Monteverdi in using the orchestra to dramatize situations tonally. Together with Monteverdi before him, Cavalli was the one whom most Venetian composers used as a model for their own operas.

Cavalli was also the composer who introduced Italian-made opera into France, in 1660, when he came to Paris to help produce his *Serse* as part of the celebration of the marriage of Louis XIV. Cavalli made another trip to Paris in 1662 to introduce there his opera *Ercole amante* to inaugurate the hall of the Tuileries on February 7.

Another Venetian composer, Antonio Caldara (1670–1736) carried Venetian opera into Austria, visiting that country several times to present some of his works. When, in 1716, Caldara received a permanent appointment to the royal court in Vienna, he expanded the importance of Venetian opera in Austria. Germany also profited from the Venetians. A German-born composer, Heinrich Schütz (1585–1672), visited and studied in Venice, an experience that led him to write *Dafne,* Germany's first opera, for the wedding of Princess Sophie of Saxony. The work was produced at the Hartenfels Castle in Torgau on April 23, 1627.

Some of the methods that later became basic to Italian opera writing had been evolved or suggested by the Venetian school of composers headed by Monteverdi. Others came out of the city of Naples, which succeeded Venice as the capital of opera. What Monteverdi had meant to Venetian opera, Alessandro Scarlatti (1660–1725) became for Naples: the fountainhead of new methods; the source of inspiration; the object for imitation.

Scarlatti (not to be confused with his son, Domenico, famous for his harpsichord sonatas) began his career as an opera composer in 1679 at the Teatro Capranica in Rome. At that time the auditorium was reserved exclusively for nobility, but in 1695 it was opened to the masses to become Rome's first public opera house. In 1682, Scarlatti established himself in Naples. Working until his death, while serving a good deal of that time at the Royal Chapel, he still completed over one hundred operas, many of which were first produced in Naples. They were presented at the royal palace and at various royal entertainments and celebrations, as well as in public opera houses. The first presentation of an opera in a public theater in Naples had taken place at the Teatro di San Bartolomeo, in 1654.

Scarlatti became such a towering musical figure in Naples that numerous composers there were influenced to write operas the way he did. Through the years, a large receptive audience was built up in Naples for these operas. In order to meet the demand, two new houses came into existence in Scarlatti's lifetime: the Teatro dei Fiorentini and the Teatro Nuovo. A third opened after Scarlatti's death: the still-renowned Teatro di San Carlo, or the San Carlo Opera House.

It is not necessary to name Scarlatti's early or even most successful operas since, with negligible exceptions, they have lapsed into total oblivion. Certain developments in his works that the opera structure would henceforth absorb, however, deserve our attention.

Scarlatti progressed beyond Monteverdi in giving the orchestra importance. No longer was the overture a brief preface; with Scarlatti it became a fully developed, self-sufficient composition made up of three parts (a fast section, a slow one, and a fast one). This form came to be known as the "Italian Overture," but it would be more accurate to dub it the "Neapolitan Overture" since it is found in the works of numerous Neapolitan masters during the century following Scarlatti.

Scarlatti also extended the potential of the two forms of recitatives. But with Scarlatti, the accompanied recitative acquired a depth of feeling that at times came close to passion, and a dramatic strength new to opera. Scarlatti accomplished this by using varied orchestral colors, timbres, and sonorities with the kind of ensemble available to him at that time, and by trying to make the orchestra a partner to the voice rather than merely serve as an accompaniment. The dry recitative passed to disuse early in the nineteenth century, but the accompanied recitative as Scarlatti helped to develop it became an essential element in opera from his time on.

Perhaps the greatest vocal contribution by Scarlatti was his development and perfection of the *da capo* aria form. This melodic structure is a three-part form. The middle section is a melody contrasting with the opening and the closing—the closing part repeating the opening, but trimmed with ornaments and embellishments to allow the singer to exhibit his virtuosity. The *da capo* aria was an indispensable part of Neapolitan opera until Niccolò Jommelli (1714–74) abandoned its formalized structure for an aria more closely tied in to the text of the opera. This flexible style of aria proved more useful and became an operatic fixture.

Operas on a tragic theme, following the format originating in Naples, then amplified elsewhere in Italy, came to be known as *opera seria.* This term and the rigid tradition it represented persisted until the end of the eighteenth century. Another and far different type of opera was born

in Naples: *opera buffa,* or comic opera. *Opera buffa* (opera in a broad comic vein) evolved its own rules and conventions even as did the *opera seria*—but this took place some years later outside Naples.

Comedy and comic characters had intruded into serious operas in random scenes beginning with Monteverdi and Cavalli in Venice. A comic episode in an opera is one thing; *opera buffa* quite another. The new type of opera came about because early in the eighteenth century a major reform in libretto writing took place. This change was initiated by Apostolo Zeno, who eliminated from his texts all elements of the comic and emphasized tragedies based on historical or mythological themes written in a flowery poetic style.

His style was carried on and extended in Vienna in the same century by Pietro Metastasio, the most prolific and the most highly esteemed and influential librettist of his generation. For years, this tradition of writing librettos dominated Italian opera. Those who wished to write operas in a comic vein, therefore, had to work out a genre of their own; that genre achieved fulfillment with *opera buffa.*

The earliest predecessor of *opera buffa* was the *commedia dell' arte,* a form of stage entertainment popular in sixteenth-century Italy. The example set and established by *commedia dell' arte* led librettists of comic operas to avoid historic and mythological figures as characters and replace them with everyday people who get themselves involved in romantic complications, usually one involving an elderly master and his young maidservant.

Another ancestor of *opera buffa* was a short comic scene known as an *intermezzo,* originally performed at Italian festivities as far back as 1539. Frequently, an intermezzo was presented between scenes of serious operas to provide a change of mood, even though no possible relationship existed between the opera performed and the intermezzo interpolated between its scenes.

To one of the early Italian composers, Nicola Logroscino (1698–1765), goes the credit for inventing extended finales in which the entire cast participated and with which each of the acts ended.

Scarlatti marked the transition between the intermezzo (a form in which he was singularly prolific) and *opera buffa.* In this transition, Scarlatti's comedy *Il Trionfo dell'onore (The Triumph of Honor)* is a milestone. It was produced in Naples in 1718. Not yet *opera buffa,* it does come close to being one. Its main character is a young rake, a wild young man, who gets involved with two women, both of whom he abandons. He is wounded in a duel, leading him to repent his evil ways and to marry one of the two deserted women. Throughout, the opera is light and engaging, suggesting the comic touch both in the text and in some of the arias, styled like those that would later characterize *opera buffa*. But the conventions of *opera buffa* are not yet clarified here.

These conventions were finally established sixteen years after the premiere of Scarlatti's comedy by a Neapolitan composer whose lifespan consisted of just twenty-six years. He was Giovanni Battista Pergolesi (1710–36). When he was sixteen he came from his home in a small town near Pergola to Naples. His first opera, a serious work in the style of Scarlatti, was produced at the Teatro di San Bartolomeo in 1731. Between the acts Pergolesi interpolated a one-act intermezzo, his first try at comedy. The comic style suited him so well he continued writing intermezzi. In 1733 he produced his masterpiece, an intermezzo with which *opera buffa* makes its official entry into the musical theater. It was *La Serva padrona* (*The Maid Mistress*), in one act, interpolated between the acts of one of Pergolesi's serious works at San Bartolomeo on August 28, 1733.

It would hardly be possible to devise a plot simpler than the one Pergolesi used. The play has only three characters, one of whom, the valet, is mute. Uberto is upset because his servant, Serpina, is hot-tempered and capricious. To extricate himself from her clutches, Uberto decides to get married. He asks his valet to find him a wife. Since Serpina wants to marry her master, she arouses the old man's jealousy by inventing the fiction that she has a lover (the valet disguising himself to play the part of the lover). The trick works. Uberto finally proposes. He soon discovers he has been duped, but is so delighted at becoming Serpina's husband that he forgives the two conniving culprits.

Pergolesi's score is made up of four arias and two duets (an aria for each of the two principal characters and a duet for both in each of the two parts in which the single act is divided). The music is typically *opera buffa* in its mockery, gaiety, and liveliness. There is a jovial aria for the victim and a tender one for the servant in love with her master. Each is of a type henceforth to be encountered in *opera buffa*. The form would soon abound with stories about scheming servants, and deceived, lecherous old men (all of them recognizable people moving about in familiar settings and getting entangled in simple, everyday problems). The text of *La Serva padrona* became the mold from which most of the texts of later operas of this type would be shaped.

La Serva padrona proved such a sensation in Naples that its popularity spread like contagion throughout all of Italy and after that in many parts of Europe through performances by a touring Italian company. The *opera buffa* now became a medium of artistic importance equal to that of *opera seria*.

As finally crystallized, the *opera buffa* structure consisted of two acts, instead of the three usually found in *opera seria*. Originally, the dialogue and the texts for the vocal numbers were in local dialect. Peasants were featured as characters, with peasant settings as a favored surrounding, and the text indulged in a good deal of vulgarity. In time, however, the broad vulgar farce was reduced to a more discreet kind of humor, with tender episodes providing contrast. The peasant setting was replaced by one representing the middle class. Always there was a busybody—a schemer, a conniver—who set the plot spinning, who instigated the trouble among the principal characters, and got them enmeshed in mock marriages and mock legal proceedings. The plots invariably dealt with frustrated love affairs, which were always neatly resolved by the time the final curtain descended. Characters (scheming servants, cuckolds, deceived wives, frustrated lovers) were often made to appear in disguises; mistaken identity was a favored device to get these characters into more complications.

As for the music, *opera buffa* overflowed with lilting tunes—some gay, some sentimental—with some fast-paced patter songs for solo voices, vocal duets, and trios of varying moods, and several chattering choruses. Each act ended with a finale, more extended in structure than any preceding musical episode, in which the entire cast joined to bring the first act to a climactic point in the story and to conclude the second act in carrying that story to its happy ending.

The most celebrated *opere buffe* in the half century separating *La Serva padrona* and Mozart's *The Marriage of Figaro* are the following: *La Cecchina* or *La Buona figliuola* (1760) by Niccolò Piccinni (1728–1800); *The Barber of Seville* by Giovanni Paisiello (1740–1816) which, since it was produced in 1782, preceded the now far more famous masterwork of the same name by Rossini by a quarter of a century, and, in 1792, *Il Matrimonio segreto* by Domenico Cimarosa (1749–1801). All represent steps leading us to the techniques, style, and form of Mozart's *The Marriage of Figaro* and Rossini's *The Barber of Seville*. These two works tower like castles over the comic-opera edifices of the eighteenth century. But we shall have much more to say about them in later chapters.

As *opera seria* developed in Italy—and as its popularity spread throughout Europe—it was forgetting the ideal that originally had guided Monteverdi to write his dramas through music, namely that text and music should share equal responsibilities in creating an art work. The librettos of *opera seria* were filled with characters who seemed more like overstuffed puppets than human beings and who moved about in stilted, hard-to-believe plots. With each successive decade, opera became far more a feast for the eye than for the mind—with its preference for lengthy scenes of pageantry and with extended dance sequences impeding the dramatic action. And a feast for the ear, as well—music increasingly taking over command to the point where the text served just as an excuse for presenting the musical passages. At the same time, writing for solo voice was becoming overdecorated with intricate embroidery: runs, trills, cadenzas, leaps to the highest possible register, all intended to delight audiences with the extraordinary virtuosity of the day's famous singers.

Indeed, the voice was becoming such a focal point of importance in opera during this period that a cruel practice came into being in the seventeenth and eighteenth centuries whereby voices were artificially developed to produce remarkable vocal feats. *Castrati* were the idols of the opera-going public. They were men who were emasculated early in life to prevent any change of voice during puberty. These male sopranos then had a vocal range equal to that of a woman—but with a flexibility, power, delicacy, sensuousness of tone, and a technique that not even the foremost female singers of the age could rival.

As the popularity of Italian opera kept growing, leading to the opening up of so many public opera houses, the abuses perpetrated by librettists and composers in writing operas kept mounting. Opera now entertained the masses and not exclusively a select nobility as had once been the practice. And librettists and composers stood ready to cater to the tastes and prejudices of the masses, who doted on the trite and the superficial.

Once in a while, rare though it was, we come upon an opera in the seventeenth century that defies prevailing tastes by reaching for dramatic credibility and allowing the music to serve the drama. One such rarity occurred in England with *Dido and Aeneas* by Henry Purcell (1659–95).

Poetry and drama have always been favored by the English, and poetry and drama, therefore, had to play a significant role in English opera. The earliest form of English opera was of the "chamber" variety —a form more intimate than *opera seria,* requiring limited musical and

stage resources and using texts and music of comparative simplicity. A

L ORFEO

FAVOLA IN MVSICA

DA CLAVDIO MONTEVERDI

RAPPRESENTATA IN MANTOVA

l'Anno 1607. & nouamente data in luce.

AL SERENISSIMO SIGNOR

D. FRANCESCO GONZAGA

Prencipe di Mantoua, & di Monferato, &c.

In Venetia Appreſſo Ricciardo Amadino.

M D C I X.

The title page of the first edition of Monteverdi's Orfeo, printed in Venice in 1609.

Henry Purcell.

George Frideric Handel.

An engraving by William Hogarth of a production of The Beggar's Opera
*in 1728. A satirical ballad opera, it ridiculed the conventions of the
Italian opera being given in London at that time.*

*A contemporary
English
caricature of Handel,
captioned
"The charming brute."*

A Hogarth engraving commenting on the popularity of masques and operas with the public of eighteenth-century London, while literature and art were neglected.

pioneer among such chamber operas was *Venus and Adonis,* in three acts, produced in or about 1685, with a text by an unidentified author and music by John Blow (1648–1708). Blow's melodies and duets were written with such sparing strokes, and with so few embellishments, that the poetry could be articulated distinctly—something the English public demanded. To give still greater importance to poetry, many chamber operas used spoken dialogue, usually in verse, instead of recitatives.

Henry Purcell became the most significant composer of chamber opera. *Dido and Aeneas* is his masterpiece. It was first produced at a girls' school in Chelsea, England, in or about 1689. Nahum Tate's text was based on the fourth book of Virgil's *Aeneid,* a classic of Roman literature. The story describes the love of Aeneas, the Trojan hero who had been dispatched by the gods to found a new empire following the sacking of Troy, and Dido, the queen of Carthage, a country to which Aeneas had been driven during a storm. Through the diabolic powers of a sorceress and some witches, this love affair is frustrated. Aeneas leaves Carthage to fulfill his mission. So terrible is Dido's grief that she takes leave of life. (The story of Dido and Aeneas was used by over sixty composers, but only the treatment by Purcell, and, almost two centuries later, by Hector Berlioz (*Lez Troyens à Carthage*) are remembered.)

Dido and Aeneas is a work extraordinary for its emotional force, atmospheric interest, and theatrical strength—even when listened to today. The logical progress of the plot line is unimpeded by irrelevant, ornamented arias, extended ensemble numbers, or scenes of pageantry. There are, indeed, beautiful arias, expressive choruses, and intriguing dances. But these are so well integrated into the drama that they add to rather than detract from the audience's interest in the play. Purcell's recitative writing is often more dramatic than that found in even the best Italian operas of the same period. In addition, seventeenth-century opera can find few parallels for Purcell's gift at tone painting in music—be it a storm, or the mystery of a witch's cave, or the stir and bustle of sailors preparing ships for sea. And when Purcell is at his lyrical best, he is as eloquently songful as even the Italians. This happens particularly in the closing scene: with "Dido's Lament," sung just before her death (one of the noblest melodies in all English opera). The opera then closes with the elegiac chorus "With Drooping Wings." Dido's aria followed immediately by the chorus is of a poignancy to pierce the heart like a knife blade.

Unfortunately, *Dido and Aeneas* made no impact on the opera of its time, which preferred to remain true to Italian ways. No operas were

OPERA written by English composers to follow the new route mapped out by Purcell. Instead, beginning in 1706, the English preferred to import their operas from Italy rather than encourage their own composers to write as Purcell had done. London, then, like the rest of Europe, became infected with the virus of the artificialities and superficialities of conventional Italian opera.

When Londoners finally found a composer of their own to admire, he was a man capable of writing in the Italian style they had come to adore. Strange to say, this man was not Italian, nor was he of English birth. He came from Halle, Germany. He was George Frideric Handel (1685–1759).

Handel's operatic apprenticeship had taken place in the German city of Hamburg, whose first opera house had opened in 1678. Its director, in 1703, was the most important (and most prolific) German opera composer of his time: Reinhard Keiser (1674–1739). All of Keiser's 125 or so operas were thoroughly Italian in style, although written in German. The Hamburg Opera produced four or five of these a year, together with the most favored Italian operas of that period.

Handel came to Hamburg in 1703 to advance his own musical career by finding employment in this famed opera house. First he played the violin in its orchestra. It was not long before he tried his hand at writing operas. His first, *Almira,* produced in 1705, was so successful that it is the belief of more than one historian that this was the reason that Keiser began making things extremely unpleasant for Handel in the opera house. Eventually Handel had to leave Hamburg.

Handel's success in Italy with two new operas in 1708 and 1709 brought him the post of *Kapellmeister* (the German equivalent of *maestro di cappella*) at the court of the elector of Hanover in Germany. Handel took a brief leave-of-absence in 1711 to go to England to help produce there his latest opera, *Rinaldo,* which sold out the Queen's Theatre for fifteen performances. In 1712, Handel returned to England—this time for good. Fifteen years after that he officially became a British subject.

He was extraordinarily prolific in England in many areas of music, but it is only to the field of opera that we must here devote ourselves. In this field, his career at times knew the Alpine peaks of success, at other times the darkest valleys of failure. In spite of the fact that Handel's first new operas for England, in 1712 and 1713, failed to duplicate the success of *Rinaldo,* his popularity did not diminish perceptibly, since other compositions proved successful. He was appointed music master to the royal family and was given an annual pension by King George I (his one-time employer in Hanover, who had mounted the British throne in succession to Queen Anne in 1714).

The ups and downs of Handel's fortunes as an opera composer in England have few parallels. His direction was definitely upward when in 1719 he became director of the then newly founded Royal Academy of Music, for which he wrote *Radamisto,* which took London by storm. This did not mean that, together with enthusiastic admirers, he did not also collect enemies—very powerful enemies. The sad truth was that Handel was an objectionable person—gruff, ill-mannered, tyrannical in his treatment of those working with him, given to explosive tempers, and capable of hurling the most vulgar curses at those who irritated him. Gathering their forces under the leadership of the Earl of Burlington, his enemies set out to destroy Handel's popularity. The maneuver they decided upon was to import to London one of the period's most famous Italian opera composers, Giovanni Bononcini (1670–1747), some of whose works had already been greatly admired in London.

Bononcini came with an armful of new operas. The London audiences were beside themselves with delight, for Bononcini was a master in writing in the accepted Italian format. But so was Handel. To counter Bononcini's successes, Handel wrote *Ottone*—following all the tricks of the trade with which Italian opera composers wooed their audiences. *Ottone* was so well received at its premiere in 1723 that Bononcini was thrown into the shade, while Handel basked once again in the sunlight of fame. This bitter rivalry between the Italian master and the German-born English composer was actually not one of style or principle but of personalities. An opera by Bononcini? An opera by Handel? They were virtually the same product—Italian in style. A Londoner, John Byrom, pointed this up during the Bononcini–Handel rivalry by writing the following verse, which became extremely popular in its own day and brought the phrase "tweedledum and tweedledee" into the English language:

> Some say, compared to Bononcini
> That Mynheer Handel's but a ninny.
> Others swear that he to Handel
> Is scarcely fit to hold a candle.
> Strange all this difference should be
> 'Twixt Tweedledum and Tweedledee.

Handel retained his popularity for a few years. Then suddenly and virtually without warning he toppled from the heights. In 1728 there was produced in London John Gay's *The Beggar's Opera*—a topical satire on English society and corruption set to a score filled with popular tunes and take-offs on some of the pomposity of opera arias. Londoners fell in love with *The Beggar's Opera* because it was timely, amusing, and satirical. Besides, most Londoners were becoming tired of the sameness of texts and musical methods in Handel's operas, which continued to follow the all-too-familiar Italian groove. The attendance at Handel's Royal Academy of Music became so depleted that the opera house had to go into bankruptcy. So, a few years later, did a second opera house, the King's Theater, which Handel had opened with a partner. Nevertheless, Handel continued writing operas for eight more years, hoping to recapture his audiences. His last opera, *Deidamia,* was produced in 1741.

But the glory of Handel the opera composer just could not be recaptured. For all his inherent musical greatness, Handel simply had refused to accept the proposition that the stilted historical subjects he treated in his operas in the conventional Neapolitan manner had become a bore.

He had done nothing to advance opera in any way. This was his great fault. He had failed to achieve a single major success in the opera house between 1731 and 1741. Following his death, his forty or so operas went into total oblivion until early in the twentieth century, when some of them began to be revived. Later in the century, recordings of his operas were made as well. The most successful of these revivals—and possibly the best opera Handel ever wrote—was *Giulio Cesare* (*Julius Caesar*) (1724).

When listened to today, Handel's operas are fascinating only because, being a genius, he could work within highly traditional forms and yet occasionally scale heights. His operas, with negligible exceptions, are far more interesting to us in parts than as a whole. They are little more than staged and costumed song recitals for the various solo voices (Handel having made only sparse use of ensemble numbers, chorus, or orchestra). The dramas that served as the frame for these songs were as artificial as the characters who sang them.

But there can be no question of the elevated quality of his best arias. Time and again he brought to the *opera seria* (a dying tradition by Handel's time) a sublimity of melody with few equals in the opera of his generation. Those arias will live as long as music will. "Ombra mai fù" from *Serse* (1738) is undoubtedly the one that is best known—

frequently presented under the title of Handel's "Largo," because of its instrumental transcription in that tempo. But there are many equally wonderful melodies in other operas. We need name only a representative few: "Cara sposa" and "Lascia ch'io pianga" from *Rinaldo;* "Care selve" from *Atalanta* (1736); "Alma mia" from *Floridante* (1721); and "Dove sei?" from *Rodelinda* (1725).

Handel finally realized that he was through as an opera composer. And so, in 1741, he gave up opera for good to concentrate on another medium, the one in which he was destined to become one of the greatest composers of all time—the oratorio. From the depths in which he languished in 1741 he once again rose high—higher, in fact, than he had previously done. With the sublime choral works of his last years he finally arrived at the immortality toward which he had been heading with his operas without ever arriving at this goal.

Had he been able or willing to outgrow the rapidly dated *opera seria* formula of his time—had he been less willing to bend the knee to popular success—he might have become one of opera's greatest composers. As it is, the best that can be said of him is that he was a composer of some great moments in opera.

3

Opera Develops in France

Jean-Baptiste Lully, Jean-Philippe Rameau,

Luigi Cherubini

Outside England and Italy, there appeared two composers who refused to conform to Italian formulas. Perhaps they remembered that the original goal of the *camerata* had been to "let the text be the master of the music and not its servant." Perhaps they recalled that the first operas, culminating with Monteverdi, had been named "dramas through music." In any event, these two composers—each in a different country—were dissatisfied with the way opera was developing. Each decided that the time had come for a major upheaval. One of these composers was Rameau, in Paris; the other, Gluck, in Vienna. Before considering the work of Rameau, let us glance at the development of opera in France.

The first operas given in France were composed by Italians, one of the earliest being (once again) a setting of the Orpheus and Eurydice legend, produced in Paris in 1647 with music by Luigi Rossi (1597–1653).

The French people were partial to eloquent dramas in harmonious-sounding verses and long, flowing lines, as found in the works of such distinguished writers as Corneille and Racine. Another favorite form of entertainment for the French was ballet. Not until opera in France favored the three elements so close to French hearts (drama, poetry, and ballet) did it finally find an admiring public. Curious to say, this happened first with the works not of a Frenchman but of an Italian: Jean-Baptiste Lully (1632–87), who, despite his Italian birth, is the father of French opera.

Lully, like opera itself, was born in Florence. He came to Paris as a boy to work in the household of a female cousin of Louis XIV. His employer took note of his talent for music and placed him in her court orchestra. Later on, Lully was appropriated for the orchestra of Louis XIV at the royal court. In 1653, Lully composed music for a ballet produced at court, and the work was so well liked that from then on he was frequently commissioned to write ballet scores, many of them to accompany plays by another of France's highly esteemed playwrights, Molière. Louis XIV responded so enthusiastically to Lully's ballet music that in 1661 he appointed Lully "composer to the king" and a year later made him music master to the royal family (the latter post bringing with it the rank of nobility).

Opera and Lully crossed paths in 1672 when, through scheming and double-dealing, Lully managed to get royal permission to take over the management of France's first public opera house, the Académie Royale de Musique (ancestor to the present-day Paris Opéra). The Académie had been founded in 1669 by the Abbé Perrin and Robert Cambert. An opera, *Pomone,* by Cambert had opened the theater in 1671.

As head of the opera house, Lully inevitably directed his gifts to composing for the theater. The same guile and shrewdness that made it possible for Lully to take the opera house away from Cambert also came into play when Lully started writing operas. He had lived long enough in France to have learned what the French people favored on the stage; and his collaboration with Molière had taught him a good deal about the French theater. Lully realized at once that a successful opera composer in Paris would have to forget his Italian birth and disassociate himself from the Italian-type operas of composers like Cavalli, for whose productions in France Lully had already written ballet music.

Lully set himself to develop an operatic formula more in tune with French tastes. As preparation, he spent hour after hour at the Comédie Française (Paris's famous theater of classic drama), listening and studying how the great performers delivered their poetic lines. Lully soon evolved a recitative whose changing meters lent themselves naturally to French poetry. He discovered from French plays, ballets, and music that elegance of style and a courtly grace were basic French traits. And so, he developed arias avoiding the gaudy for the sake of elegance and emotion. Knowing only too well how fond the French were of ballets and pastoral scenes, he decided to use plenty of them in his operas. He became the first composer to introduce the minuet into opera.

Lully was also aware of France's admiration for classical dramas. Consequently, he chose as his favorite librettist Philippe Quinault, a French dramatist capable of providing him with a thoroughly French type of poetic play serving as a model for French composers for many years. Lully's music to Quinault's texts was responsible for bringing to being a *new* kind of opera: "tragedies in music" (*tragédies en musique*), they were called. With them—the first being Lully's *Cadmus et Hermione* in 1673—we have the real beginnings of French opera.

Lully wrote some twenty operas in fourteen years. The best came toward the end of his life, and the most famous of these probably is *Armide et Renaud* (1686). Lully's operas follow a set pattern. First comes an overture of a particular pattern (referred to as a "French overture" to distinguish it from the "Italian" type devised by Alessandro Scarlatti). The Lully overture opens with a sedate slow part. This is followed by a lively section written in "imitation." (This is a technique familiar to you as a "round," in songs like "Three Blind Mice" or *"Frère Jacques."*) The overture ends with a graceful dance.

There follows a staged pastoral prologue in which the characters sing the praises of their king, and perform dances in honor of his achievements. Only then does the five-act tragedy begin. Henry Prunières explained that the theme of the tragedies invariably concerns "love thwarted by the jealousy of a god or sorceress who raises supernatural powers against the lovers, thereby providing the stage-setter with an opportunity of raising a tempest, of changing a radiant grove into a hideous desert inhabited by monsters, or of showing his audiences scenes from the Underworld." Most of the story is told through recitatives neatly fitted out to suit the swelling, rolling lines of Quinault's poetry. Several arias, choruses, orchestral interludes, and ballets are allowed to intrude into the story. Dramatic interest is heightened by the descriptive, pictorial way in which Lully uses the orchestra to depict storms and battles through a harmony and orchestration far more advanced and varied than those previously employed.

Four years before Lully died, there was born in Dijon, France, on September 25, 1683, the man destined to become his immediate operatic successor in France: Jean-Philippe Rameau (1683–1764).

Rameau's name shines brilliantly in French music for many reasons.
He was one of the earliest composers in France of harpsichord music, in
which he devised new techniques in writing for the keyboard. He was
one of music's earliest theorists, his volume on musical theory published
in 1722 being the foundation stone on which the science of harmony
rests. He was one of the first masters of French chamber music. But it is
with his operas that we are here exclusively concerned. His operatic
work brought to France a golden age that not only resulted in several
striking stage works but also introduced new ideas on how opera should
be written and what its aesthetic goals should be.

Rameau, the son of the cathedral organist in Dijon, started studying
music early (violin, harpsichord, and the organ), developing his musical
education further while receiving his academic schooling at the Jesuit
College in Dijon. When he was eighteen, he traveled to Italy, playing the
organ at various church services and the violin in orchestras. It is of no
small significance—in view of his later development—that the Italian
operas he heard made almost no impression on him. This was not his
kind of music—and he knew it.

By 1702 he was back in France, working for a while as church organist in Clermont-Ferrand. Three years later he moved to Paris, where
he published his first book of harpsichord pieces. From 1709 to 1723 he
was an organist for cathedrals in Dijon, Lyons, and Clermont-Ferrand.

Finally back in Paris, where he would remain for the rest of his life,
he made his first attempt at writing for the theater, beginning, as Lully
had done, by writing music for ballets. In 1727 he was engaged as the
household music master for a powerful patron of the arts, Le Riche de
la Pouplinière. His job was to play the organ, to teach the children
music, and to conduct the palace orchestra. It was while thus employed
by La Pouplinière—and at his employer's advice—that Rameau turned
to writing operas.

His first was *Hippolyte et Aricie,* based on a drama by Racine, heard
in Paris on October 1, 1733. Rameau here diligently followed in Lully's
footsteps by choosing a classical subject for his text and pursuing Lully's
musical methods by adopting a French identity. But Rameau represented important progress over Lully. His recitatives—like those of
Lully in the way they followed the patterns of inflection in French
poetry—had greater dramatic strength. Rameau's writing for orchestra
was enriched with a far more original harmony than that used by Lully
(not at all surprising when we recall that Rameau was a scholar on the *35*

A contemporary engraving of a production of Lully's Alceste

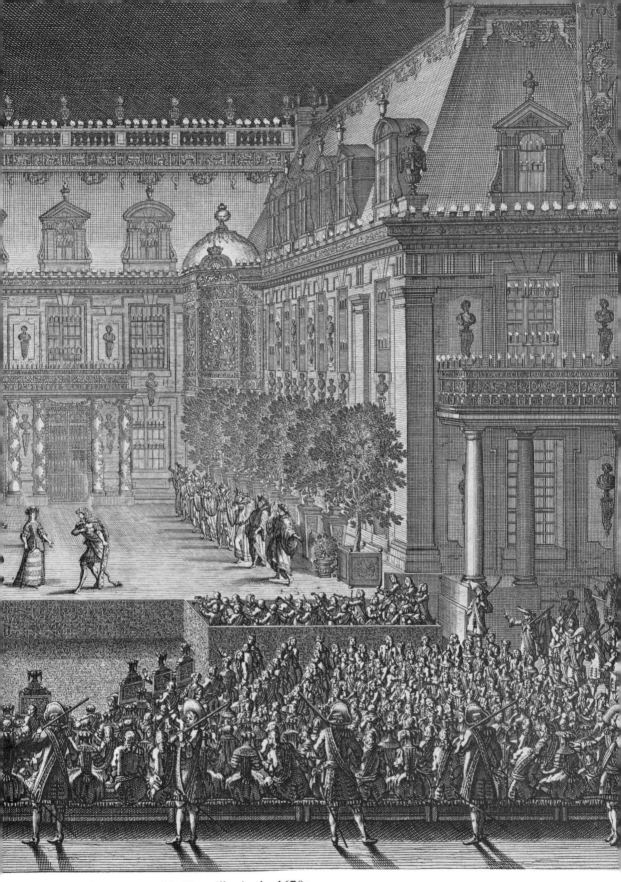

given in a courtyard in Versailles in the 1670s.

An announcement of a production at the Académie Royale (the Paris Opéra) of Rameau's Castor et Pollux.

Jean-Philippe Rameau.

subject) and was even more vivid and realistic in its tone painting. His arias were more melodious, his dances more graceful, his choruses more majestic.

Rameau rose to a place of first importance in eighteenth-century French opera. *Les Indes galantes* (*The Indigo Suitors*)—called a "ballet-opera" because ballet was so important in the unfolding of the plot —was a sensation when introduced in Paris on August 23, 1735. This drama was a lavish spectacle with four separate stories, each a tale of love transpiring in four different parts of the world: Turkey, Peru, Persia, and a North American forest. More and more beautiful have Rameau's melodies become. Even more realistic is his orchestral writing, as tonally he re-creates a raging storm, a festival of the Sun God, or an erupting volcano. Increasingly entrancing and picturesque is his writing for an exotic type of ballet.

Rameau's most famous opera, *Castor et Pollux*, followed on October 24, 1737. This work shows the Lully tradition carried to such heights of musicodramatic expression that Lully's own operas now begin to sound old-fashioned. Enlisting the help of the full flowering of his remarkable gifts in lyricism, harmony, and orchestration—as well as his sound dramatic instincts—Rameau here produces a score of a grandeur and nobility without rival in French opera up to this point. The text is a simple one, a variation of the Orpheus and Eurydice legend. Castor and Pollux are twin brothers. When Castor dies, Pollux is beside himself with grief. The gods are willing to revive Castor if Pollux is ready to take his place in the lower regions. Pollux consents. For this act of self-sacrifice, both Pollux and Castor are deified and placed permanently in the heavens as a constellation. The lovely airs and dance pieces that flow through the opera are still able to stir our emotions.

By the time Rameau wrote *Dardanus* (which sold out all its box seats eight days before its premiere on November 19, 1739) there were few in France to deny that he was its greatest opera composer. Louis XV bestowed on him an honorary title and a generous annual pension. Rameau's audiences worshiped him. His musical colleagues held him in the highest esteem—not an easy thing to do since there was much in Rameau's personality, as in Handel's, that was abrasive. Rameau was miserly, avaricious, rude, egotistical. But he was a genius, for which his fellow workers at court and in the opera house were willing to tolerate his many personal frailties.

Rameau was at the peak of his influence and fame when suddenly a
major attempt was made in France to discredit him. This resulted in a

historic battle in Paris between two opposing forces, the outcome of which had far-reaching repercussions in opera's evolution. The struggle has come to be known as "the battle of the buffoons" (*la guerre des bouffons*).

This is how the conflict started. In 1752, a traveling Italian opera company visited Paris and performed Pergolesi's *La Serva padrona.* Its simple, everyday theme and characters, its zestful humor, its lightness of touch captured the enthusiasm of many French opera lovers, including some redoubtable French intellectuals, among whom was the famous philosopher Jean-Jacques Rousseau. Rousseau, as a matter of fact, was so taken with Pergolesi's comedy that he, too, wrote the text and music of an *opera buffa: Le Devin du village,* produced in 1752. He also published a letter in 1753 expounding his belief that Pergolesi and his Italian colleagues were the true representatives of opera. "There is neither melody nor measure in French music," he said—and by "French music" he was thinking specifically of Rameau. The queen herself and a number of other powerful Frenchmen echoed Rousseau's contention that Rameau was too cerebral to the point of being dull and lifeless. But there were also powerful forces on Rameau's side, headed by the king and his mistress, Mme de Pompadour, and also by Voltaire, one of France's most brilliant literary figures. Voltaire said, "Rameau has made of music a new art."

The arguments, pro and con—Pergolesi versus Rameau, Italian opera versus French opera—continued heatedly for a few years. During the battle a fraud was perpetrated that strengthened Rameau's position. A little Italian comic opera was produced, said to be the work of a Viennese Italian. The queen and many other admirers of Pergolesi were delighted with it, pointing to it as further proof that Italians knew how to write opera far better than the French.

Only then did the manager of the opera house reveal that this little comic opera was the work of a French composer using a French libretto. Above and beyond ridiculing the efforts of the "buffoonists" to destroy French opera and exalt the Italian brand, this little trick unexpectedly played a highly important part in making many French people, heretofore antagonistic to Pergolesi and *opera buffa,* become enthusiasts of comic opera. Thus a French variety of Italian *opera buffa* came to life. It was called *opéra-comique,* and its first great exponents were Pierre Monsigny (1729–1817) and André Grétry (1741–1813).

Then, in the early 1760s, Rameau's *Dardanus* was revived. Such was its triumph that the French Academy officially acclaimed its composer.

All opposition to Rameau now collapsed; the victory of French opera was decisive.

Rameau died in Paris on September 12, 1764, a victim of typhoid fever. If there were few to weep for the passing of a man who had always been sharp-tongued, cruel (even to his own family), and boorish, there was hardly anybody in France who did not mourn the death of a great composer. As Karl Nef, a historian of our own century, said of Rameau, he was one of "the most original discoverers of all time," whose operas are "to be reckoned among the greatest achievements in the field of musico-dramatic arts."

The mantle of Rameau fell on Luigi Cherubini (1760–1842). Like Lully, Cherubini was born in Florence; and, once again like Lully, Cherubini spent most of his life in France, where he assimilated its culture, art, and national traits so that in time he became more French than Italian. Cherubini had written his first opera in Italy when he was nineteen—an *opera seria*. He continued in this vein for the next few years, occasionally setting texts by Metastasio. Some were failures, some successes. Four more *opere serie* flowed from his pen while he spent a year in England, but not even the personal honors showered on him by the king and the prince of Wales could make the English people respond favorably to his operas. And so in 1788 Cherubini decided to find a new permanent home—in Paris.

Rameau's influence made all the difference. Once and for all Cherubini discarded *opera seria* to adopt the now fully developed and widely appreciated French type of opera, that of Rameau. No longer was Cherubini the fastidious embroiderer of decorative melodies; no longer did he rely so heavily on splendiferous scenes; no longer was he satisfied to work with the spineless, heartless librettos of the Metastasio variety. And, in his music, he revealed how much he had learned from Rameau's operas by producing arias of a noble beauty, writing with dexterity for two or more voices, and also by depending heavily on harmony and orchestration in projecting the drama. Cherubini's two most famous operas are *Médée* (*Medea*), written in 1797, and *Les deux journées* (*The Water Carrier*), in 1800.

Medea, in the tradition of Rameau, was based on a Greek legend that Corneille had used for one of his poetic dramas. The central character is a queen who becomes demented when her husband decides to marry another woman. Tortured by jealousy, and mentally unbalanced, 42 she murders her children and her husband's intended wife.

In *Medea* Cherubini used spoken dialogue as well as accompanied recitatives to unfold the narrative. (Many years later Franz Lachner replaced the spoken drama with recitatives, and this is the way this opera is usually given today.) Cherubini, however, did not avoid melody. Some of his arias (such as "Deo tuoi figli la madre") are as elevated in spirit and soaring in emotion as his orchestral writing is filled with original invention. The overture is a solid masterwork, well capable of standing on its own feet apart from the opera. Some historians believe that Beethoven was inspired by it in writing his *Egmont Overture*.

The greatest artistic importance of *Medea* lies perhaps in the way the title character is developed more convincingly and more penetratingly in the music than in the text. Discords, chromaticisms, dynamics, and orchestral colorations are all used to penetrate a bit more deeply into Medea's heart and psyche, to point up her tragedy, to describe the disintegration of her reason.

Les deux journées is one of the first operas in which the rescue of a principal character is the core of the plot. This is why it is known as a "rescue opera"—a term used for several other operas of the early nineteenth century, including Beethoven's *Fidelio*. In *Les deux journées* Count Armand is the one who is saved, and the humble water carrier is his rescuer from possible death at the hands of Cardinal Mazarin. An important aria in this opera, "Un Pauvre Savoyard" is the prototype of tender romances and ballads found in many later operas. Wagner studied it well, was influenced by it, and remembered it when he wrote "Senta's Ballad" for *The Flying Dutchman*. Another Cherubini opera is still remembered, but only for its remarkable overture: *Anacreon*, produced in 1803.

Besides becoming famous for his operas, Cherubini exerted considerable musical power in Paris by holding many posts, the most significant being that of director of the Paris Conservatory for twenty years. Toward the end of his life, Cherubini deserted opera for sacred choral music. He died in Paris, having provided a major transition in French opera between Rameau and the French opera masters of the nineteenth century, beginning with Meyerbeer.

4

Baroque Reform

Christoph Willibald Gluck

For years, *opera seria* had been solidly established at the court of Austria and in the heart of its nobility. Then in Vienna, too, there took place a revolt against the status quo in opera. Christoph Willibald Gluck (1714–87) was the revolutionary there. In a bitter struggle between operatic ideals (not much different from that which had taken place in Paris with the "battle of the buffoons"), Gluck's adversary was the renowned and powerful librettist, Pietro Metastasio.

Metastasio had come to Vienna from his native Italy in 1730. Soon thereafter he became the favorite poet and dramatist of the court, and as such, without a rival or adversary, he ruled over the operatic destinies of Austria through the writing of the most popular opera librettos of his time. All of Metastasio's texts for *opere serie* treated biblical or historical subjects, which symbolically glorified the rulers of Austria and its political and social structures. Metastasio loved rhetoric for its own sake: long-flowing speeches; florid verses; euphemistic figures of speech. His characters are all stereotypes. His plots are so complicated that it is often difficult to unravel the many developments or untangle the involvements of the characters in those developments. He had a rigid formula and he stuck to it.

Nevertheless, composers everywhere were only too ready and willing to follow the route mapped out for them by the poet. So sought after were Metastasio's librettos that any one of them was frequently used by sixty or seventy composers. One composer, Johann Hasse (1699–1783), wrote the music for *every* Metastasio libretto (and Metastasio had written over sixty!).

Even the young Gluck wrote music for some of Metastasio's texts. But in time Gluck had a vision of an opera far different from the *seria* variety: an opera that refused to accept such tyrannical methods; an opera that did not exert its every effort to glorify virtuoso singing; an opera calling for a text with dramatic value and flesh-and-blood characters; an opera where the chorus was not just an ornament or a commentator but an essential part of the plot; an opera, in short, where the drama set the rules for the music and not vice versa. What Gluck was aiming at was musical drama—the beginning of the long, tortuous road that eventually led to Wagner.

He was born a Bohemian—in Erasbach, the Upper Palatinate, on July 2, 1714, the son of a forester on Prince Kaunitz's estate. In 1732 young Gluck went to Prague to concentrate on music study while supporting himself by singing in church choirs and playing the violin in orchestras and dance music at fairs. Then, four years later, he came by foot to Vienna to make his mark there as a musician. With his big, large-boned frame, square jaw, high cheekbones, and rugged complexion, he looked more like a peasant than a musician. He found employment as a chamber musician at Prince Lobkowitz's palace. Playing there, Gluck made such a good impression upon Prince Melzi, an Italian nobleman, that the prince convinced Gluck to leave his job and serve him at his own palace. Gluck was delighted to go. In Italy he could learn a good deal about opera at its source. He did. His first *opera seria, Artaserse* (text by Metastasio), was produced in Milan in 1741. During the next four years he completed eight more *opere serie,* which aroused such admiration that in 1745 he was invited to London to write and help produce two new operas for the Haymarket Theatre.

By 1748 he was back in Vienna, now a composer with an established reputation, and with the skill and talent to compete with the highly esteemed Italian composers on their own terms. And so, selecting a Metastasio text, Gluck wrote *Semiramide riconosciuta,* with which the Burgtheater was reopened after a year of darkness because of lack of funds. Maria Theresa, the empress (in honor of whose birthday the opera was given), and her court were delighted.

45

But Gluck's popularity in Vienna was short-lived. The Italian opera master, Niccolò Jommelli, was visiting Vienna to attend the premiere of one of his operas. Fickle Vienna turned sharply from Gluck to focus its adulation on this famous visitor. Disheartened, Gluck went off traveling again—to Hamburg, Prague, Copenhagen.

By 1750 he was back in Vienna, where he married the daughter of a successful merchant and later acquired the post of court composer. Security brought self-assurance, and self-assurance permitted indulgence in experimentation. For Gluck was not the kind of musician content to stand still in his work. He was now less and less inclined to imitate the florid and artificial work of the Italians. At the same time he was becoming increasingly inventive and original in his own musical thinking and writing. "He is somewhat mad," Metastasio now said of him, adding that Gluck's music was full of "noise and extravagance." Little could Metastasio guess that what Gluck was now creating was but a faint warning of what he would soon be doing: bringing about a revolt in opera which, when consummated, would open up an entirely new avenue for that art form.

Gluck found two important allies whose ideas on opera paralleled his own. One was Count Giacomo Durazzo, director of Vienna's theaters. The other was Ranieri de' Calzabigi—by profession, chamber councilor to the exchequer; by cultural interests, a poet and playwright. Both men were ardent admirers of French art and poetry and the operas of Lully and Rameau. Both men agreed that the time had come to rid Vienna of the ridiculous abuses perpetrated by Italian opera composers. A major reform was needed—and in Gluck both Durazzo and Calzabigi found the composer with the talent, intelligence, will, foresight, and courage to come to grips with an opponent as formidable as Metastasio. They had taken a true measure of their man. They realized he had pride bordering on arrogance; a complete conviction that his musical gifts were far superior to those of his Italian rivals; a singleness of purpose once he understood what his musical destiny should be. Durazzo and Calzabigi were convinced that not powerful enemies nor bitter feuds, not crushing defeats nor personal humiliation would divert a man like Gluck from his self-appointed mission.

Gluck later clarified both his position as opera composer and his aims in one of the most remarkable documents in the early history of opera. In the preface to his opera *Alceste* he wrote, in part: "I resolved to avoid all those abuses which had crept into Italian opera through the mistaken vanity of singers and the unwise compliance of composers, and which had rendered it wearisome and ridiculous, instead of being, as it once was, the grandest and most imposing stage work of modern times. I endeavored to reduce music to its proper function, that of seconding poetry by enforcing the expression of the sentiment, and the interest of the situations, without interrupting the action, or weakening it by superfluous ornament. . . . I also thought that my chief endeavor should be to attain a grand simplicity, and consequently I have avoided making a parade of difficulties at the cost of clearness; I have set no value on novelty as such, unless it was naturally suggested by the situation and suited to the expression; in short, there was no rule which I did not consider myself bound to sacrifice for the sake of effect."

To set this operatic revolution into motion—to attack everything for which *opera seria* and Metastasio stood—Calzabigi chose for his libretto the thrice-familiar theme of Orpheus and Eurydice. Was not this the subject of the very first opera to survive, and the one used by Monteverdi for his first experiment with drama through music? Calzabigi and Gluck were aiming for another drama through music, one like Monteverdi's, but taking advantage of all the developments and techniques that had been perfected in music during the intervening years.

On October 5, 1762, Gluck's *Orfeo ed Euridice (Orpheus and Eurydice)* was produced by Durazzo at the Burgtheater. The audience, which included the social elite of the city, was taken aback by what it saw and heard. Gluck's *Orfeo* represented to them a starvation diet of bread and water compared to the succulent gourmet delicacies *opera seria* had to offer. Where were those intricate, meretricious runs, decorative roulades, and fancy embellishments to test the remarkable vocal ability of the castrato Guadagni, who appeared as Orpheus? Where were those scenes of pageantry to stun the eye? Where was the plot multiplying one thrilling piece of action by another? Where were the exciting mob and battle scenes and overpowering climaxes? None were found in *Orfeo*. The Viennese nobility looked, listened—and yawned. Metastasio's position and influence seemed more firmly secure than ever.

It is not difficult to understand why Vienna so completely rejected *Orfeo* at first hearing. The stark simplicity of the music, the reduction of stage action to essentials, the avoidance of anything superfluous to the text represented to them naïveté and lack of invention rather than imagination and eloquence. There are four characters in all (with the chorus so vital to the progress of the drama that it might well be considered a fifth character). The familiar story unfolds simply and naturally, with more concern for genuine emotion than for histrionics. It has the static

Christoph Willibald Gluck.

An announcement of a production of Gluck's Alceste *at the Académie Impériale (the Paris Opéra) during the nineteenth century.*

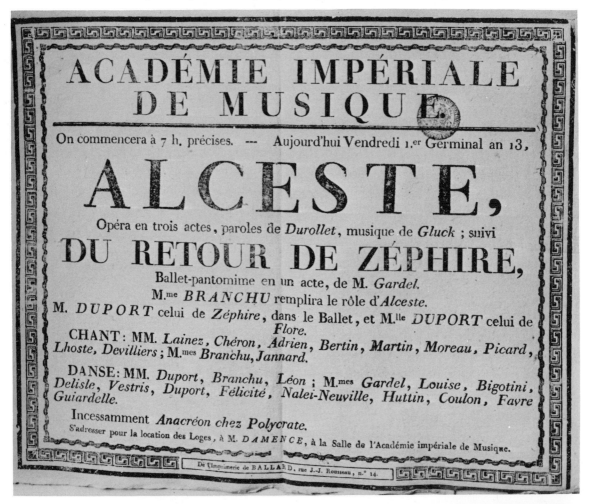

ACADÉMIE IMPÉRIALE DE MUSIQUE.

On commencera à 7 h. précises. --- Aujourd'hui Vendredi 1.er Germinal an 13,

ALCESTE,

Opéra en trois actes, paroles de *Durollet*, musique de *Gluck* ; suivi

DU RETOUR DE ZÉPHIRE,

Ballet-pantomime en un acte, de M. *Gardel*.

M.me *BRANCHU* remplira le rôle d'*Alceste*.

M. *DUPORT* celui de *Zéphire*, dans le Ballet, et M.lle *DUPORT* celui de *Flore*.

CHANT : MM. *Lainez, Chéron, Adrien, Bertin, Martin, Moreau, Picard, Lhoste, Devilliers* ; M.mes *Branchu, Jannard.*

DANSE : MM. *Duport, Branchu, Léon* ; M.mes *Gardel, Louise, Bigotini, Delisle, Vestris, Duport, Félicité, Nalei-Neuville, Huttin, Coulon, Favre Guiardelle.*

Incessamment *Anacréon chez Polycrate.*

S'adresser pour la location des Loges, à M. *DAMENCE*, à la Salle de l'Académie impériale de Musique.

De l'Imprimerie de BALLARD, rue J.-J. Rousseau, n.° 14.

A page from the French monograph score of Gluck's Orfeo ed Euridice
(*act 3, scene 1*), *given in Paris in 1774.*

Orfeo (Grace Bumbry) and Euridice (Gabriella Tucci) in a Metropolitan Opera production.

A scene from a Metropolitan Opera production of Alceste.

quality of a frieze. For what had concerned both librettist and composer most was not the story itself, but all the facets and nuances of emotion experienced by the two principal characters.

One would have imagined that at least some of Gluck's arias (for all their "noble simplicity," so exalted in melodic beauty they could melt a heart of stone) would have found favor: for example Orpheus' beatific reaction to the radiance of Elysium in "Che puro ciel"; his poignant plea to be allowed to enter Hades in "Deh placatevi con me"; and, most celebrated of all, his lament "Che farò senza Euridice," when Eurydice meets death a second time because he has defied the command of the gods. One would imagine that the first-night audience would have held its breath with wonder and awe at the otherworldly description of Elysium (with its wondrous flute melody) magically evoking a world of incomparable peace and calm ("The Dance of the Blessed Spirits").

But an audience so long inured to spectacle and vocal pyrotechnics let all these wonders pass by unnoticed. Besides this, the audience regarded Gluck's new richness of harmony and orchestration (for a far more greatly enlarged and varied ensemble than the Italians used) as just so much sound and fury signifying noise. "The Dance of the Furies," for example, with its piercing discords and crashing cymbals, seemed repellent to them.

What we marvel at, and what the Viennese nobility could not be expected to discern at first contact, was the way the words suited the theme, and the music suited the words, giving the legend a new life and meaning and emotion. This was the dawning of a new day for opera.

But Gluck was not discouraged, nor could he be dissuaded from further pursuing the direction he had chosen for opera. "No obstacles shall deter me from making new attempts to achieve my purpose," he announced proudly. "I would rather have one Plato on my side than all the populace."

He no longer had Durazzo as an ally; Durazzo had been dispatched to Venice as ambassador. Fortunately, Calzabigi was still on hand not only to provide moral support but to write another text as well, *Alceste,* also based on a Greek legend, and also a hymn to the triumph of love over death. Alceste (Alcestis) is a queen in ancient Greece ready to give up her own life to save Admetus, her dying husband—a bargain the gods accept. Alceste's death causes her husband such torment that he follows her. His friend Hercules goes to Hades to retrieve them both.

After a bitter life-and-death struggle at the gates of Hades, Hercules succeeds in bringing Alceste and Admetus back to the upper world. For his heroism Hercules is made a god.

From the first descending chords of the orchestra—sounding like the implacable voice of Fate—*Alceste,* even more than *Orfeo,* tapped altogether new veins in opera. The overture, for example! No longer is it a seemingly irrelevant piece of music with no emotional or atmospheric relationship to the drama that followed, as was the case with Italian operas (a convenience to allow the audience to make itself comfortable in their seats). In the original version of *Alceste,* Gluck did not use the term overture but introduction (*intrada*), planning it to "indicate the subject and prepare the spectators for the character of the piece they are about to see," as he explained. So bound up is this introduction with the opera that it leads right into the opening scene without a break, something without precedent.

Then in page after page, drama and music become one in reaching high moments of artistic realization: the "Chorus of the Spirits," which comprises only the single note F, a remarkable adventure in simplicity and force; or Alceste's dramatic aria where she pleads to the gods to permit her to die in her husband's stead, "Divinités du Styx," with its remarkable changes in tempo and tone colors.

No longer would Gluck avail himself of the use of a castrato; his simple kind of melody made the vocal gymnastics of a castrato superfluous. The drama, not the singing, had to seize the limelight. And the drama was emphasized by the greater responsibility Gluck assigned to the recitative and to his orchestra, and in the way in which the choruses were so completely integrated into the overall design.

Introduced on December 26, 1767, *Alceste* found the Viennese even more hostile to Gluck's revolution than before. The general reaction was tinged with bitterness, coated with the acidity of satire. Said one: "If that is the sort of evening's entertainment the Court is to provide, good-bye! We can go to church without paying two gulden." Said another: "For nine days the theater has been closed, but on the tenth it opens with a Requiem."

Gluck and Calzabigi made one more effort to convert the Viennese —on November 3, 1770, with *Paride ed Elena (Paris and Helen).* When this opera also proved a resounding failure, Gluck had to realize that it was impossible (at least for the time being) to change the operatic tastes of the Viennese. "I flattered myself," he said, "that the others would be eager to follow the road I had broken for them, in order to destroy the evil practices which have crept into the Italian opera and have dishonored it. I am now convinced my hopes were in vain."

He would seek out a more propitious battleground: Paris, the city where Rameau and his principles had triumphed. And so, in the fall of 1773, Gluck arrived in Paris to work on a new opera, *Iphigénie en Aulide (Iphigenia in Aulis)*, with a French text based on one of Racine's great poetic tragedies, in turn derived from ancient Greek legend. In ancient Aulis, King Agamemnon must sacrifice his daughter to the gods if he is to get winds favorable for the sailing of the Greek fleet to Troy. The protection of Achilles, Iphigenia's lover, postpones the fateful day of her death until the gods prove willing to release Agamemnon from his oath, since he had so convincingly proved to them he had been ready to do his grim duty.

For a time things did not go much more easily for Gluck in Paris than they had in Vienna. There were still "buffoonists" around to look upon Gluck as a new enemy of Italian opera. There were those who resented the invasion of an Austrian into the Académie Royale de Musique. And there were still others who preferred French opera over Gluck's developments. Members of the opera company did what they could to sabotage the premiere of Gluck's new opera. For a while it looked as if the opera would not get beyond rehearsals. Then the queen herself, Marie Antoinette, came to Gluck's support. From then on all obstacles and interferences evaporated.

Iphigenia in Aulis, produced on April 19, 1774, turned out to be a triumph after all. Rameau's many followers came to realize that this was the destination toward which Lully and Rameau had themselves been heading with their innovations. Many of those who had opposed Rameau (including Jean-Jacques Rousseau) sang Gluck's praises. The queen was ecstatic: "I was carried away by it. We can find nothing else to talk about. You can scarcely imagine what excitement reigns in all minds in regard to this event. It is incredible." Everybody in Paris was talking about Gluck's opera. The box-office receipts broke all records for the Académie. A new lady's hairstyle came into fashion known as *"à l'Iphigénie."*

When the first French production of *Orfeo* came in August of 1774 and caused a furore (in this performance a tenor, instead of a castrato, sang the part of Orpheus), Gluck could sit back with quiet satisfaction. His ideas had won out, at last. But he was completely unaware that behind his back a powerful clique had formed to diminish his successes.

The old-timers, the promoters of Italian opera, were back at their favorite game of indulging in intrigue!

What followed was not much different from what had once happened to Handel when *his* enemies tried to destroy his fame in London. Gluck's opponents brought to Paris one of the most popular, if not *the* most popular Italian composer of that day: Niccolò Piccinni, whose *La Cecchina* or *La Buona figliuola* had by now been established as a classic in *opera buffa* all over Europe. Gluck's enemies went further still. They knew that Gluck had been commissioned to write an opera, *Roland,* for the Académie. They commissioned Piccinni to write an opera on the very same text. When Gluck learned about this trickery, his fury made him tear up the manuscript of his opera and publish a letter in a Parisian journal bitterly expressing his feelings.

This letter proved to be the first shot in a new operatic war in Paris. Gluck was now the spokesman of those valuing the new dramatic way of writing operas; Piccinni became the leader of those devoted to the old Italian standards. "Such passion and fury were aroused," reported a baroness at the time, "that people had to be separated. Many friends and even lovers quarreled on this account." And another fine lady wrote to David Garrick, the famous English actor: "They are tearing each other's eyes out here, for or against Gluck."

Piccinni's *Roland* enjoyed a huge success; a French presentation of Gluck's *Alceste* did not. The pro-Gluckists were disheartened just as the pro-Piccinnists were exhilarated. Recognizing the full publicity value of this conflict of operatic ideas, the astute director of the Académie commissioned *both* Piccinni and Gluck to write an opera based on the Grecian drama of Euripides. The French title of the work is *Iphigénie en Tauride.* The director had in mind a kind of duel, fought not with rapiers, but with opera scores.

In *Iphigenia in Tauris,* Iphigenia is a priestess in Tauris, to whose temple are brought two victims fated for sacrifice—Orestes and Pylade. Just before the sacrifice, Iphigenia discovers that Orestes is her long-lost brother. Her plea to the king, Thoas, to save her brother's life proves in vain. It is up to Pylade to save Orestes, which he accomplishes.

Gluck's opera was heard first—on May 18, 1779. The reaction of Melchior Grimm, an influential commentator on musical and literary subjects, was characteristic: "I know not if what we have heard is melody. Perhaps it is something much better. I forget the opera and find myself in a Greek tragedy." (This statement is all the more remarkable since Grimm had been on the side of the Italians in the "battle of the buffoons.") So great was the acclaim accorded to Gluck's opera that Piccinni tried his best to withdraw his opera from performance. He failed, and so did the opera. (The fact that the prima donna was drunk on opening night did not help matters!) This marked the end of the feud. "The works of Gluck," summed up a writer in a French journal in 1781, "are about the only fortune of operatic music."

Gluck returned to Vienna to spend the rest of his days in the glory he so well deserved. Europe recognized him as one of its foremost composers. Most important of all, Gluck knew well (to use the words of Paul Bekker, a twentieth-century musicologist) that he had "thrust the doors open and allowed the daylight of human naturalism to fall upon the opera world of his time."

With Gluck we pass from the baroque to the classical era. During the classical era, the formula of *opera seria,* with the castrato, was jettisoned. In their serious and comic operas Italians would continue to cling tenaciously to some of the paraphernalia that had cluttered the stage and the music, such as vocal exhibitionism and visual display. But a greater variety of method and means and a more aristocratic type of lyricism were introduced to enhance emotionalism and theatricalism at the expense of artificiality.

In Austria, where Gluck had so carefully laid out the groundwork for a simpler, nobler, and more restrained kind of opera than that Italians favored, the classical age produced a mighty new voice for opera. Its surpassing eloquence and elegance would reverberate throughout the civilized world for the next two centuries without any diminution in its magic. It is the voice of Mozart, for which opera has produced few worthy challengers.

5

Classical Perfection

Wolfgang Amadeus Mozart

A well-known musical anecdote leaps to mind as I begin to write about Mozart in general and Mozart the opera composer in particular. A young student once asked a world-famous composer how he, the composer, went about the business of writing an opera, symphony, or concerto. "Why," the composer replied simply, "I just sit down and write music."

This is precisely what Wolfgang Amadeus Mozart (1756–91) did: he just sat down and wrote music. He did not theorize about music and then proceed to put theory into practice the way Gluck did. He followed no rigid formulas, be they of his own making or those of others in the manner of the Italians. He did not work and rework, refine and revise to get the results that satisfied him the way Beethoven would. (As a matter of fact, with Mozart most first drafts were also final drafts, with little or no alteration required.) Nor did he construct a musical edifice methodically from detailed architectural plans, stone by stone, until a cathedral had been built—the way Wagner would work.

Mozart sometimes gave the impression of working haphazardly. Parts of his great opera *Don Giovanni* were hurriedly scribbled down while he awaited his turn at bowling in a beer garden. He scratched out the whole overture of this opera the night before the world premiere, having neglected to write one during the rush of rehearsals. But do not for a moment assume that there was anything careless or slipshod about his work—the above incidents notwithstanding. He was unique, and his method of operation was unique. He had an entire score clear in mind down to the minutest details before he sat down to write. That is why he looked as if he were improvising spontaneously rather than composing. That is why he was able to perform the feat of sending to his copyist the string and woodwind parts of the *Don Giovanni* Overture before having written the parts for the horns, trumpets, and tympani. The whole score was perfectly clear in his mind.

He never concerned himself particularly with the type or style of libretto he was setting. He wrote *opera seria* and *opera buffa* early in his career, whose texts followed established styles. He wrote in the German-language comic opera form, called *Singspiel,* the equivalent of American musical comedy. It catered to the masses with a text that was in local dialect or slang filled with frivolous or farcical situations; and the musical numbers (separated by the dialogue) were made up of popular or folk-like tunes. He wrote tragic operas, and he wrote operas that are basically comic. One of his operas, *Don Giovanni,* is in a class by itself—"a gay drama" it was dubbed.

He wrote sixteen operas in all, eight between his twelfth and nineteenth years. He took to every existing species of operatic form indiscriminately and proved himself a master in all. Setting a text, whatever its subject or nature, Mozart wrote as he pleased. He did things in his music guided by seemingly infallible instincts and intuition rather than pursuing a preconceived, carefully thought-out plan, or copying somebody else's mannerisms. Musically he was always himself. That is the way it was when as a boy of twelve he wrote his first two operas, and that is the way it remained for the rest of his life. He acquired a text—and then he just sat down to write the appropriate kind of music for it.

That among his operas are some of the greatest the world has known arises from the fact that, combined with an imcomparable creative genius, he possessed an unequalled technical skill. There was not a single musical problem for which he could not find the solution. Thinking in terms of music came to Mozart as naturally as breathing. He always had the correct expression for even the most elusive effect. Through music he could say anything he wished in any way he wished, always realizing stylistic perfection. And he did it with such ease that even the production of a towering masterwork seemed like child's play. For far from being the painful process that it was to most other composers, creation for Mozart was a source of happiness, of genuine physical pleasure. The music just poured from him in copious streams. His kind of musical articulateness is one of the wonders of music history.

Mozart almost makes one believe in reincarnation. He was such a fabulous child prodigy that it seemed he might have learned everything there is to know about music in some previous existence. It is true he had a splendid teacher in his father, but Mozart needed little instruction. His childhood achievements in music are so unbelievable that they sound like legends or the fabrications of sentimental biographers; but they are all quite true.

He was born in Salzburg, Austria, on January 27, 1756. His father, Leopold, was a professional musician employed at the archbishop's court. Leopold was a musician of considerable attainments; he published what is probably the first textbook on violin playing. He was ideal, both as father and as teacher, to nurture and raise an incredible prodigy. Leopold and his wife had another child, too—a daughter, Marianne (Nannerl), born five years before Wolfgang. She, too, was highly musical, an excellent performer on the harpsichord who often appeared publicly with her brother.

As a child of four or five, the boy Mozart could already play both the harpsichord and violin well. He could perform any composition he had heard once. He could improvise on any given melodic subject for half an hour or more with a marvelous outpouring of fresh ideas. In Italy, when he was fourteen, he heard a single time Allegri's *Miserere* (an extended work of great polyphonic complexity); then back at his hotel he wrote down the whole score from memory. By then original compositions were gushing from him like water from an open faucet: sonatas, symphonies, yes, even operas. No wonder that Goethe, the great German poet, said of the boy Mozart: "A phenomenon like that of Mozart remains an inexplicable thing."

He wrote his first two operas in 1768 when he was only twelve. One was an *opera buffa, La Finta semplice,* which had been commissioned by the emperor of Austria. The other was a *Singspiel—Bastien und Bastienne.* It took the boy four months to write the twenty-one arias, the duet, the chorus, and the three finales comprising *La Finta semplice.* The musical powers in Vienna, however, saw to it that this little opera was kept from performance, maintaining it was below their dignity to have a twelve-year-old boy compete with them.

OPERA

Bastien und Bastienne did manage to be heard, however—not at a major theater or opera house or at court but in the private garden of a Viennese physician who specialized in a kind of mental therapy. (His name was Dr. Mesmer, from which we derive the word *mesmerize*.) This *Singspiel* was a parody of Rousseau's *opera buffa, La Devin du village,* and the sixteen tunes Mozart wrote for it are charming, skillful, and at some moments even sophisticated in the way the artificialities of Italian opera were burlesqued.

In 1770 Mozart was traveling in Italy. (This was the period when he wrote down Allegri's *Miserere* from memory.) His genius was readily acknowledged. The pope conferred on him the Cross of the Order of the Golden Spur. The Accademia Philharmonica in Bologna broke all precedent by electing him a member, something it had never before done to any musician under twenty years of age. Most important, the Teatro Regio Ducal in Milan commissioned him to write an *opera seria,* Mozart's first attempt at treating a tragic subject. The result was *Mitridate, Rè di Ponto.*

Here, as in Vienna, attempts were made to sabotage the performance. Here too, as in Vienna, the opera masters were insulted at competing with a boy, and were further infuriated when, after the first rehearsals, they heard arias of a beauty and aristocratic elegance they could not duplicate. They spread around the word that Mozart's opera was "poor and childish" (as Herr Leopold dutifully reported to his wife) and alleged that "so young a boy, and a German to the bargain, could not possibly write an Italian opera." But, in the end, their efforts to prevent the performance proved futile. *Mitridate* was performed on December 26, 1770. The audience was aroused to such a pitch of excitement that one of the soprano arias had to be repeated, and twenty performances of the opera had to be given.

But a prophet in his own land . . . For Mozart, triumph in foreign lands, but in his native Salzburg little but humiliation. A new archbishop had come to power who knew nothing about music and had little regard for Mozart. Though he employed him in the court orchestra, he treated Mozart as if he were a lowly servant and paid him a servant's salary. Now slowly growing into manhood—and producing masterwork after masterwork in every possible medium—Mozart chafed under the irritations of his humdrum existence, with a job he detested and personal insults he did not deserve. Fortunately for him, he was allowed short leaves of absence. On one of these, in 1772, he went to Milan to help in the

60

production of his latest opera, *Lucio Silla.* On another, in 1775, he attended the premiere of a new *opera buffa, La Finta giardiniera.*

But there were sad days ahead for Mozart. He revisited Paris, where as a child and a boy he had been deified, only to discover no further interest in him or his works. The critic Grimm, once one of Mozart's most ardent fans, now found him "too confident, too little a man of action, too much ready to succumb to his own illusions, too little *au courant* with the ways that lead to success." Frustration was followed by tragedy: the death of his mother, to whom Mozart had always been singularly attached. Mozart rushed back to Salzburg, once again to encounter personal indignities at the hands of the archbishop. He suffered this way for two years until a temporary avenue of escape opened up for him when his latest opera, *Idomeneo,* was being produced in Munich in 1781.

Though Mozart imitated nobody he was capable of being influenced. In *Idomeneo* his operatic thinking was molded partly by Gluck, whose *Alceste* he had heard in Paris. This accounts for the importance he now assigned to the chorus (in later operas Mozart used the chorus sparingly) and for the grandeur of style in so many of the arias. This also explains why the overture is in the vein of Gluck's, to put the audience into the proper frame of mind for the drama.

But Mozart always remains Mozart in the end, and it is Mozart and not Gluck whom we encounter in the recitatives, which have a more melodic character and profit from a more individual accompaniment than those of Gluck. Thoroughly Mozartean in its originality is the way in which the opening recitative quickly alternates between the dry and the accompanied form to suit the needs of the words. Original, too, is the expanded accompanied recitative in the last act, which uses so many changes of tempo, key, and accompaniment—and such alternations of style—that it seems to anticipate the extended narratives Wagner wrote many years later. Most daring of all: in the third act he insisted upon writing a vocal quartet in a place clearly calling for a showy aria, producing the first of his great ensemble numbers.

Mozart's innovations did not seem to bother the audience. The opera was an immense success. "I must own," said the first horn player in the orchestra, "I have never yet heard any music which made such a deep impression on me." He was reflecting the opinion of many.

This success convinced Mozart that the time had come for him to free himself from his bondage to the archbishop of Salzburg—indeed to make a permanent break with Salzburg itself. He soon found a pre- *61* text to do so. The archbishop was leaving for Vienna for the funeral of Maria Theresa, the Austrian empress. Mozart was asked to join him. When the archbishop refused to allow Mozart to give any concerts in Vienna, Mozart flew into a fury, in return for which the archbishop showered fiery insults on him. "I will have no more to do with a wretch," shouted the archbishop. "Nor I with you!" was Mozart's sharp retort. This was the end between them. The next morning Mozart sent in his resignation.

Mozart was finally finished with Salzburg—for good. He hoped to make a happier, more successful life for himself in Vienna. Things, indeed, looked promising. The emperor forthwith commissioned him to write an opera for the Burgtheater. Mozart decided to write a *Singspiel,* using a light German text that fluctuated between broad burlesque and gentle sentiment, and filling it with arias, some in a German folk style. He was frankly out to woo both the emperor and the Viennese public.

Things Turkish then being popular in Vienna (including Turkish coffee, Turkish candy, Turkish hairstyles, and music that sounded Turkish), Mozart used a sixteenth-century Turkish setting with a ruler, Selim the Pasha. The heroine, Constanza, has been kidnapped by pirates and made prisoner in the Pasha's palace. She spurns the Pasha's love overtures since she loves Belmonte, a Spanish nobleman, who has slipped into Turkey to rescue her. They escape, but are caught. Magnanimously, the Pasha forgives Constanza, gives her her freedom, and blesses the union of the two lovers.

This *Singspiel* is *Die Entführung aus dem Serail* (*The Abduction from the Seraglio*). Once Mozart's musical imagination was set aflame, the triteness of *Singspiel* gave way to a comic opera with music of surpassing originality, sentiment, wit, and tenderness. The rapturous arias follow one after another, interrupted from time to time by lighter musical moments that glisten and sparkle like precious jewels. Though he had planned to write a popular theatrical piece for mass consumption, Mozart ended by creating a German comic opera elevated to the status of great art. In fact, he produced the first important opera in the German language and the first comic opera in German to be remembered.

Once again we find the road that stretches from the writing of an opera to its production is not always paved smoothly. Enemies appeared almost out of thin air to block Mozart. They were headed by Antonio Salieri, the court composer, possibly the most powerful musician in Vienna. Salieri knew full well how good *The Abduction* was, and how truly extraordinary were Mozart's gifts. This represented a serious threat to his own position. He pursued Mozart with poisonous resentment, aided by the fawning coterie that always surrounds people in power. Every possible method was used to delay the premiere and create embarrassments for Mozart. Then the emperor stepped in and ordered that the Mozart opera be given without further interference. Introduced on July 16, 1782, *The Abduction* was a triumph. The emperor went so far as to say that the music was much too good for Viennese ears.

Mozart had good reason for self-satisfaction. The enthusiasm of the emperor and nobility, Mozart felt, would surely now bring him a high-paying post. Confident of his future, he married his sweetheart, Constanze Weber, on August 4, 1782. Evidence of his growing importance came when a baroness offered her home for the wedding feast. With the woman he loved now his wife, Mozart waited impatiently for some attractive job to come his way.

But none came. Salieri's machinations were constantly operating behind the scenes. The emperor, who could be generous with praise but niggardly with money, could not find the funds for a major musical appointment. Mozart had to give lessons, which paid so little that he could never make ends meet.

But a creative demon in him made him incapable of permanent despair. While waiting for his moment to come (and it never did) he consoled himself with his extramusical interests: dancing, bowling, billiards. At the same time he worked harder than ever, producing some of the greatest music the world has known, the music of his next opera, for example—*Le Nozze di Figaro* (*The Marriage of Figaro*). The emperor had grudgingly commissioned it at the behest of the newly appointed poet of the imperial theater—Lorenzo da Ponte—who wrote Mozart's libretto.

Once again Salieri and his cohorts tried to make trouble for Mozart. They influenced musicians and singers to demand impossible alterations in the music which, of course, Mozart refused to do. And once again the emperor intervened. During the rehearsals, the singers fell in love with Mozart's music. As one of them (Michael Kelly) later recalled: "The players on the stage and in the orchestra were electrified. Intoxicated with pleasure they cried again and again, and each time louder than the preceding one: 'Bravo! Bravo! *Maestro!* Long live the great Mozart.' . . . It seemed as if this storm of applause would never cease."

The Burgtheater was packed when *The Marriage of Figaro* was heard on May 1, 1786. The audience demanded so many repeats of arias that the opera took almost twice as long to perform as otherwise

The boy Mozart, with his father and his sister, performing in Paris in 1763. Five years later, at the age of twelve, he wrote his first two operas.

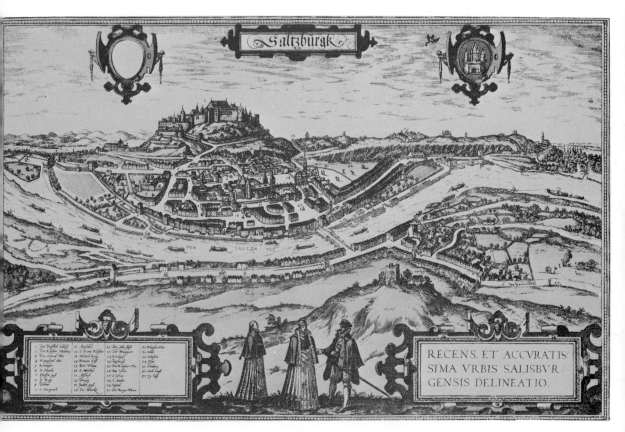

A view of Salzburg in the eighteenth century.

Figaro (Cesare Siepi) drills Cherubino (Teresa Berganza) for his future army career, while Susanna (Mirella Freni) looks on. A Metropolitan Opera production of Le Nozze di Figaro.

Don Giovanni (Cesare Siepi) in a Metropolitan Opera production.

Die

Zauberflöte.

Eine
Oper in drei Aufzügen,
neubearbeitet
von
C. A. Vulpius.

Die Musik ist von Mozart.

Aufgeführt auf dem Herzoglichen Hoftheater zu
Weimar zum erstenmal am
16. Januar 1794.

Leipzig, 1794.
bei Johann Samuel Heinsius.

Papageno.

The title page of Mozart's Die Zauberflöte, printed in Leipzig in 1794.

Tamino (George Shirley) in a scene from a Metropolitan Opera production of Die Zauberflöte, designed by Marc Chagall.

would have been necessary. From his royal box, the emperor kept continually shouting, "Bravo!"

Indeed, *The Marriage of Figaro* had all the appearance of becoming an even greater triumph than *The Abduction from the Seraglio*. But the wily Salieri planned otherwise. While Mozart's opera was attracting capacity audiences, Salieri hurriedly put into production a catchy little opera by a Spaniard, *Una Cosa rara,* which he well knew would capture Viennese hearts with its bright tunes and dances. Salieri proved right. By succumbing to the superficial appeals of *Una Cosa rara,* the Viennese turned sharply from *The Marriage of Figaro.* Mozart's opera had to close down after only nine performances and was forthwith forgotten by Vienna. But not elsewhere, as we shall soon see, and certainly not by posterity.

Da Ponte's libretto was of the kind you would expect in an *opera buffa*. Da Ponte first had to remove the attack against the aristocracy contained in the original French play by Beaumarchais from which his text was taken. The Austrian emperor had demanded this expurgation; otherwise he would not have commissioned the opera. Revised, Da Ponte's text became a complex tale of intrigues among the highborn and their servants: Count Almaviva; the Countess; the Countess's maid, Susanna; the Count's page, Cherubino; and, of course, Figaro. Figaro, the Count's swaggering valet, is betrothed to Susanna and is therefore justifiably concerned at the overtures the Count is making to her. Various secret meetings are arranged between the would-be lovers, which lapse into farce when Cherubino must disguise himself as Susanna, and Susanna and the Countess disguise themselves as each other, to trick and thereby shame the Count. But in the end, Figaro wins Susanna, and the Count and Countess are reconciled.

It is a far from average *opera-buffa* libretto, with touching grace, witty dialogue, and situations that move swiftly and naturally. But it is Mozart's music that makes this opera immortal. The music continually leaps and sighs, frowns and chuckles, mocks and romanticizes—delineating character with the most penetrating insight, allowing the orchestra to interpolate comments of its own on what it thinks of the characters and their goings-on. From beginning to end Mozart's miraculous lyricism traverses the emotional gamut from the light and frivolous to the heights of eloquence: the light and the gay in Figaro's mocking attempt to teach Cherubino how a soldier behaves in "Non più andrai"; eloquence in the Countess's despair at her husband's infidelity ("Porgi amor") and her nostalgic recollections of her one-time happiness with him ("Dove sono"). And with what profound psychological understanding of character does Mozart write when he produces music for two or more characters—each part reflecting the inmost thoughts and feelings of each of the characters.

But masterpiece or no, *The Marriage of Figaro* was dropped from the Burgtheater repertory. As for Mozart—financially he was worse off now than he had been when he had first come to Vienna. He derived a good deal of personal satisfaction from the response of the city of Prague, which went mad over *Figaro*. "Here," he wrote with unconcealed delight, "no one hums, sings or whistles anything but airs . . . of *Figaro*. No other opera draws . . . except *Figaro*." But even a successfully produced opera is not overly lucrative for its composer. Mozart returned to Vienna a happier man, but hardly a richer one.

But he had brought back with him from Prague a commission to write a new opera. When there was important work to be done, all else in Mozart's life was relegated to insignificance. Once again the libretto was the work of Da Ponte—*Don Giovanni,* based on the fabled escapades of the notorious libertine Don Juan, in seventeenth-century Seville. The Da Ponte libretto was such a blend of *opera buffa* and tragic opera that he invented a new term for it, *dramma giocoso* ("gay drama"). Gay, it is, from time to time—but the drama far outweighs the gaiety.

Don Giovanni pursues three women: Donna Anna, whose father, the Commendatore, is killed by Giovanni in a duel; Donna Elvira, whom Don Giovanni has discarded, leaving her embittered; and a peasant girl, Zerlina, betrothed to the peasant Masetto. Donna Anna is joined by her lover Don Ottavio and Donna Elvira in a plot to avenge the Commendatore's death. Giovanni continues being very much the roué, the world being his playground. Seeing a statue of the Commendatore, Giovanni mockingly invites it to supper. While Don Giovanni is enjoying a solitary feast in his palace the statue, come to life, arrives and orders Giovanni to repent his ways, a request he laughs off. Flames spring from the ground, seize Giovanni, and drag him to his doom while demons below describe the tortures awaiting him in Hell. Da Ponte and Mozart added a brief epilogue, a sextet in which all the remaining principal characters rejoice in Giovanni's tragic end.

With a nimbleness of touch characteristically his own, the composer passes from the levities of *opera buffa* to expressions of love, grief, anger, passion, and tragedy. When Giovanni's servant, Leporello, enumerates Giovanni's many conquests with women in the so-called Catalogue Song ("Madamina") or when Giovanni, disguised as his servant, serenades Donna Elvira's maidservant in "Deh, vieni alla finestra," we are in *opera-buffa* territory.

Not *opera buffa,* but typical Mozartean wit, do we encounter in the banquet scene just before Giovanni's confrontation with the statue of the Commendatore in the closing act. Here, a little orchestra performs for Giovanni a snatch of "Non più andrai" from Mozart's own *Marriage of Figaro,* while Leporello comments sardonically. The orchestra also strikes up some strains from *Una Cosa rara,* the little opera that had succeeded in sending *The Marriage of Figaro* off the boards in Vienna (a delicious bit of arrogance on the part of Mozart). This is typical tongue-in-cheek Mozartean humor—just as the minuet, in the ballroom scene, and the lovely duet of Zerlina and Giovanni, "Là ci darem la mano" show typical Mozartean grace and charm, and Don Ottavio's love song "Il mio tesoro," is typical Mozartean lyricism.

But it is as a tragedian, and as a portrayer of character through music, that Mozart reaches the heights, beginning with the ominous chords for trombones with which the overture opens. There is such over-powering drama in, say, Donna Anna's principal arias and in the banquet scene where Giovanni meets his final doom that Tchaikovsky was led to say that episodes like these rank "only with the best scenes of Shakespeare for compelling truth and depth of expression."

In Prague *Don Giovanni* was a triumph; in Vienna, where it was given in 1788, it was a failure. The Austrian emperor was one of the few sufficiently perceptive to appreciate what Mozart had accomplished in this opera. As a result, at long last, he was ready to give Mozart a job at court—Gluck's job, left vacant by that master's death, but with such a drastic cut in salary that Mozart was incapable of providing his family with even basic necessities. He was reduced to pleading for loans from friends, promising them "a suitable interest." As if things were not bad enough, Mozart's health was deteriorating: worry and continual frustrations and despair were taking their toll. Yet the tide of his creative production remained unstemmed, nor was the quality of his inspiration tarnished. On the contrary: creatively he was developing all the time, growing more and more inventive and original in unlocking in his music the secrets that the texts of his operas failed to reveal.

Mozart now had just three more years left to live. In that time, producing a veritable flood in all forms of music, he completed three more operas, two of which are outstanding. (The third, *La Clemenza di Tito* [1791] is not in the repertory today.) Both of the others are comedies—
written, mind you, when he was at a low point of his life and his spirits.

One is an *opera buffa, Così fan tutte (So Do They All)*, text again by
Da Ponte. The other is a German comic opera, *Die Zauberflöte (The*
Magic Flute). The first is an excursion into amatory complications,
most of it frivolous or with mock sentiment or romantic feelings. The
other has an involved plot filled with obscure symbolism. In each in-
stance, the text would surely have sent the opera into oblivion had not
the genius of Mozart touched it and transformed it to pure gold.

In *Così fan tutte,* as in so many *opere buffe,* there is a busybody who
sets the plot spinning; here it is Don Alfonso, in eighteenth-century Naples. He bets two soldiers, Ferrando and Guglielmo, that their sweet-
hearts would be unfaithful, given the opportunity. The two gentlemen
tell their respective girl friends, Dorabella and Fiordiligi, that they must
suddenly leave for the wars—a fabrication allowing them to disguise
themselves as Albanian noblemen and woo the sisters. They succeed so
well, with the help of the girls' maid, that a marriage contract is about
to be signed. The "Albanians" remove their disguises and once again
become Ferrando and Guglielmo. They take the girls severely to task
for their infidelity, then forgive them.

Così fan tutte was produced at the Burgtheater in 1790. In one way
this is perhaps Mozart's most remarkable opera. That a plot so mechani-
cally contrived, in which things continually happen to tax the credulity
of the audience, where heroines are made to appear like imbeciles and
so much of the humor is synthetic, could stir Mozart's creativity and
imagination to a boiling point is remarkable. The score, from its sparkling little overture to the extraordinary vocal sextet with which the
opera ends, never lags in inspiration. Between arias of the most affecting
beauty and emotional intensity and vocal ensembles (of which there is a
copious supply) written with incomparable mastery and subtlety, the
music is an endless reservoir of satire and sardonic humor. Even among
Mozart's comic operas it is stylistically in a class all by itself. That is
why the English musicologist Eric Blom maintained that "not by any
conceivable chance" could *Così fan tutte* "lend a single one of its numbers to any other work of his. The whole perfume and flavor of the
music is new and unique."

With *The Magic Flute* Mozart had an even poorer text to work with.
No matter! Mozart could have set a menu to music and have made it a
song for angels. The text was by Emanuel Schikaneder, a Viennese impresario who needed an opera for his theater, the Theater auf der Wieden.
The book he delivered to Mozart is a hodgepodge combining supernatural powers with Masonic and political symbolism, in a plot that is half

fairy tale and half love story. The universal message of brotherhood of man becomes the thread to tie all the diverse elements into a single package.

Tamino, a handsome prince, aided by Papageno, a birdcatcher, goes to save Pamina. She is the daughter of the Queen of the Night and held captive by Sarastro, supposedly an evil sorcerer. A magic flute is the instrument that will keep Tamino from harm. At the "sorcerer's" palace, Tamino discovers that Sarastro is actually the priest of a cult representing the highest ideals; and he is detaining Pamina to save her from her evil mother. Sarastro proposes to wed Pamina to Tamino if the prince successfully performs tests of courage. He performs them bravely, with the help of his flute, wins Pamina, and becomes a member of Sarastro's holy order. As for Papageno, for whom most of the comic situations are reserved, he does all the wrong things, in spite of which he, too, wins a lovely bride.

The songs Mozart wrote for Papageno are in the German folk-tune idiom of the *Singspiel,* for Papageno is a typical *Singspiel* character. Elsewhere, however, Mozart achieves pages of ecstatic beauty, dramatic power, and spirituality. Two arias by Sarastro ("O Isis und Osiris" and "In diesen heil'gen Hallen") are of such surpassing nobility that George Bernard Shaw, who was once a music critic, remarked this is the only music he knew that could have come from the lips of God.

The success of *The Magic Flute* on September 30, 1791, was overwhelming. Wonder of wonders—even Mozart's archenemy, Salieri, sang its praises! In the ensuing decade, the opera received 233 performances at the Theater auf der Wieden, making Schikaneder a wealthy man. The opera's popularity spread quickly outside Austria; sixty-five German towns had produced it by 1800. In the thirty or so years after that it had been successfully given in Moscow, Paris, London, Stockholm, Copenhagen, Milan, and New York.

The Magic Flute provides us one of many evidences of Mozart's uncommon capacity to separate the man in him from the musician. As a man he was in the depths of despair while writing his opera, completely depleted in strength, in a state of almost uninterrupted melancholia. He was dying, and he knew it. A Requiem that had been commissioned he was actually writing for himself, racing against time and death to complete it. He did not live to do so. Wracked though he was with pain, and with the long shadow of death hovering over him, his musical self remained healthy and sunny whenever he was required to write farcical music for the merrier episodes of his opera.

Mozart died less than three months after the premiere of *The Magic Flute*—on December 5, 1791. The day he was buried was recorded as rainy. Mourners were a pitiful handful. A miserable third-class funeral was all that his widow could afford. Mozart was buried in a pauper's grave in the churchyard of St. Mark's Cathedral with no cross or tombstone to identify the place; when his widow came to visit his grave some time after his death she could not find it.

Paradox of paradoxes! Lying there in an unidentified pauper's grave was the one who had left the world a musical heritage without equal; who was one of the two or three greatest composers opera has known, and who, as the father of German opera in *The Abduction from the Seraglio* and *The Magic Flute,* had fashioned not only two indestructible masterworks but a new chapter in music history as well.

6

German Romantic Opera

Ludwig van Beethoven, Karl Maria von Weber

Before Mozart, the two opposing forces in opera had been the French and the Italian. After Mozart, it was the Germans who were pitted against the Italians.

In some respects the aims of German opera were an extension of those of the French: concern for the play; emphasis on orchestration and harmony; preference for dramatic or emotional expression over ornamented arias. Beginning with Mozart, composers in Germany and Austria would go beyond the French in stressing the importance of text-setting, of symphonic writing, of extending the dramatic qualities of arias (which came to be called *scenas*). At the same time, a distinctly Germanic style of melodic writing developed—more ponderous than that of the French or the Italians, better suited to the guttural sounds and the inflections of the German language. Finally, the best of the German and Austrian composers became increasingly adept at achieving characterizations through musical sound.

With scattered exceptions after Mozart—a notable one being Wagner's *Die Meistersinger* (*The Mastersingers*)—the Germans and Austrians were far less interested in comedy than in melodramas and fantasies. In some of the latter, German composers used texts delivering a message or a moral, or symbolizing an ideal. Germans liked to intellectualize, to spiritualize—something the Italians avoided. Mozart had anticipated some of these German tendencies in *The Magic Flute.*

As for the Italians, of whom we shall speak in detail in ensuing chapters, they still doted on the human voice, displayed in glorious arias, often at the expense of dramatic values and of orchestral sound.

German opera blossomed fully in the early nineteenth century when romanticism swept across Europe. Romanticism replaced the discipline, objectivity, and subservience to rule that had characterized the classical era. Romanticism introduced freedom of method and style, subjective feelings, poetic expression. The first main exponent of the German romantic opera school was Karl Maria von Weber (1786–1826).

But before Weber had carried German romanticism into opera, German opera produced a work of the first importance—the only opera by one of music's supreme masters, Ludwig van Beethoven (1770–1827). *Fidelio* was written when Beethoven was thirty-five and had already produced a great many of the instrumental works for which we so honor him today. Beethoven had arrived at full maturity as a composer when in the early 1800s a newly appointed director of the Theater-an-der-Wien commissioned him to write music for an opera based on the German translation of a French text—Bouilly's *Léonore,* a play that had profound implications for Beethoven. He was the proud republican who believed passionately in human dignity, freedom, and the brotherhood of man, and who had utter contempt for tyranny and despotism in all forms. The moral, social, and political values reverberating in Bouilly's drama, therefore, struck a responsive chord with Beethoven.

In Beethoven's opera, the heroine is Leonore, whose husband, Florestan, is imprisoned unjustly by his political enemy Pizarro in eighteenth-century Seville. To save her husband, Leonore disguises herself as a young man named Fidelio and becomes the jailer's assistant. When Pizarro learns that the Prime Minister is coming to inspect the prison, he decides to do away with Florestan, a plot Leonore overhears. She volunteers to enter Florestan's dungeon to dig his grave. Just as Pizarro is about to stab Florestan, Leonore restrains him at the point of a pistol. The arrival of the Prime Minister frees Florestan and reunites him with his devoted, heroic wife.

Florestan as the victim of autocracy, Leonore as the symbol of freedom, and the overall theme of the play—the triumph of right over wrong—stirred Beethoven profoundly. To few of his works did he bring such dedication and high-minded purpose. Always he was rewriting *Fidelio,* revising and changing it, never satisfied that his music measured up to the nobility of the message he was trying to propound. One aria was rewritten eighteen times; one chorus, ten times. "This work has won me the martyr's crown," he once said. "Of all my children this is the one that cost me the worst birth pangs, the one that brought me the most sorrow; and for that reason it is the most dear to me."

Fidelio is a flawed masterwork. For one thing, Beethoven never wrote felicitously for the voice; for another, in writing for the stage he was no musical dramatist, the way Mozart had been before him, and Weber and Wagner were after him. Yet it is a masterwork. Several of his long arias, in which the symbols of the play are most pronounced, are supreme—particularly Leonore's fiery and passionate challenge to tyrants in "Abscheulicher! wo eilst du hin?"; he gives voice to one of the most inspiring choruses in all German opera, that of the prisoners when, emerging from their cells into the blinding sunlight of the courtyard, they sing "O welche Lust." When in this chorus they exclaim, "We *will* be free, we *will* find peace" they speak for the oppressed of the world. And in the final chorus in praise of Leonore, Beethoven sounds his own paean to liberty.

This opera also boasts one of Beethoven's symphonic masterworks, the majestic *Leonore Overture No. 3.* Dissatisfied with the overture he had originally written for the opera's premiere on November 20, 1805 (a performance that was a failure), Beethoven wrote a completely new one when his opera was revived in Vienna a year later. The overture he had used for the world premiere is now known as *Leonore Overture No. 2. Leonore Overture No. 1* (a simplified, condensed version of *No. 3*) came in 1807 for a production of *Fidelio* in Prague that never materialized. And the fourth overture, named *Fidelio,* was the one Beethoven completed in 1814 for another revival of his opera in Vienna. Often, when *Fidelio,* the opera, is performed today, the *Fidelio Overture* is played before Act I, and *Leonore Overture No. 3* between the two scenes in the second, and final, act.

The use of spoken dialogue and the style of two or three of the musical numbers in *Fidelio* are carryovers from the *Singspiel.* In spite of this, *Fidelio* carries German opera closer to its ultimate destiny. The large vocal numbers (or *scenas*), the depth and breadth of the symphonic writing, the emphasis on ethical and moral issues were influences that had an enormous effect on the German composers who followed Beethoven.

78   Beethoven, then, is the bridge between Mozart (high priest of classi-

cism in opera) and Karl Maria von Weber, Germany's first major romantic opera composer.

Fate had never dealt too kindly with Weber even from his birth,
which took place in Eutin, Germany, on November 18, 1786. The boy
was born with a diseased hip. For the first four years he could not walk,
and after that only with a ponderous limp. He always had a delicate
constitution. To compound misery with misfortune, the child Weber never
knew the stability of a permanent home or enjoyed the advantages of a
formal education. His father was the director of a traveling theatrical
company, and as such kept his family continually on the move. They
never stayed long enough in one place for Karl to attend school or make
friends.

But there was music—Weber's sole means of flight from sickness and
solitude. But even here pain outweighed pleasure, however much music
meant to him. Since he was so extraordinarily gifted, his father dreamed
of developing him into a Mozart-like prodigy who could be exploited for
financial gain. He kept the child at his music study hour after hour,
though Karl's sickly constitution was incapable of coping with such fa-
tigue. Weber's first teacher was his father, who gave him lessons on the
piano and in singing. After that, the boy had other teachers, one of
whom was Haydn's brother, Michael. But father Weber was doomed to be
disappointed. Karl Maria was no prodigy as a performer, and certainly
not one of Mozart's caliber. The father's dream of reaping a fortune
through his son evaporated into mist.

But as he grew up, Weber revealed an exceptional gift for composition. He published some piano pieces when he was twelve. A year later
he wrote an opera (never performed). By the time he was seventeen he
had written two more operas, both of which were produced between
1800 and 1803 and were admired.

After spending about two years in Vienna studying composition with
the renowned theorist Abbé Vogler, Weber became conductor of the
Breslau Opera in 1804. He proved so extravagant in spending money for
mounting operas lavishly that in less than two years he was dismissed.
He found work first with Duke Eugen of Württemberg, then living in Sile-
sia; after that at the palace of Duke Ludwig in Stuttgart. One of his
functions in Stuttgart was to serve as the duke's secretary. While in this
position, Weber unknowingly became involved in a scheme to sell government appointments. He was arrested, imprisoned for two weeks, then ordered to leave Stuttgart for good.

A page from the monograph score of Beethoven's Fidelio (act 1, finale).

Contemporary sketches of Ludwig van Beethoven, by Lyser.

The dungeon scene from Fidelio *with (left to right) Rocco (Giorgio Tozzi), Leonore (Leonie Rysanek), Florestan (Jon Vickers), and the Prime Minister (John Macurdy). A Metropolitan Opera production.*

A scene from Der Frieschütz *with Max (Sandor Konya), Aennchen (Edith Mathis), and Agathe (Pilar Lorengar). A Metropolitan Opera production.*

Karl Maria von Weber.

Weber's future was looking none too bright. His only salvation was that he kept on writing operas and getting them performed. A charming one-act German comic opera, *Abu Hassan,* found considerable favor in Munich in 1811.

After a three-year period as musical director of the Prague Opera, to which he was appointed in 1813, Weber was named head of the German Opera in Dresden in 1816, an appointment confirmed for life a year later. The post was one of the most important in Germany. Weber could now hold his head high and find the confidence (in spite of his physical disabilities) to propose marriage to a singer, Caroline Brandt. Their marriage took place in 1817, and it was a happy one, for Weber was a man of the utmost charm and good humor, with a warm and affectionate nature, and was a thoroughly enjoyable companion.

The German Opera in Dresden, as its name implies, devoted itself to the production of operas in the German language. This fired Weber with the ambition of writing a German-language opera of his own, thoroughly Germanic in style and spirit. Searching for a suitable text, he came upon a ghost story in a collection of German fairy tales and legends. He asked Friedrich Kind to adapt it into a libretto. It took Weber three years to write his music—so ambitious was his design, and such fastidious attention and painstaking labor did he apply to every detail of his score. When he was finished he could look at his manuscript with satisfaction. Nobody had to tell him that he had fully realized his ambition to produce a native German opera, the first operatic masterpiece of the romantic movement: *Der Freischütz* (*The Free-Shooter*).

With *Der Freischütz* Weber forthwith became the standard-bearer for all young German romantics, whether they were poets, dramatists, novelists, or musicians. These young men, releasing themselves once and for all from the limitations imposed upon them by classicism, sought the license to allow their imagination to roam about in the worlds of dreams, fantasies, superstitions, supernatural mysteries. These romantics wanted to evoke the German past, to affirm the German spirit. German backgrounds, landscapes, experiences became the source of their inspiration. For the younger musicians, the vibrations of the German folk song echoed in their melodies; the feet of elves and gnomes, fairies and forest spirits danced to the sprightly rhythms of their new music. In *Der Freischütz,* German legend, fantasy, landscapes, and folk music found their first important operatic medium.

No wonder, then, that Weber's opera was a success of gigantic proportions when produced in Berlin on June 18, 1821. After the final curtain nobody left the theater. As Weber himself reported: "Amid the deafening shouting, flowers and verses were flung from all directions. The success of *Der Freischütz* was immense, unparalleled." The morning after the premiere one of Germany's celebrated young romantics, E. T. A. Hoffmann, placed a wreath on Weber's brow—a symbol that Weber had become the leader of German romanticism.

In the opera, Max, a young huntsman, must win a shooting trial in order to marry Agathe, the girl he loves. Kaspar, another huntsman, who has sold his soul to Samiel, a demon, encourages Max to use seven magic bullets, which Kaspar forges for Max in the Wolf's Glen. During the hunt Max recklessly uses up six of his bullets. His last bullet he aims at a passing dove, but he strikes and stuns Agathe. Max now confesses to his Prince the source of his magic bullets. The Prince forgives him and promises that his marriage to Agathe will be allowed.

The supernatural to which the German romantics were so addicted played an important part in this plot based on German folklore. In writing music for a supernatural scene, Weber was in his element. The music of the Wolf's Glen scene is so dramatic and eerie that nothing quite like it had previously been realized. Glorification of German landscapes is also important in Weber's tone-painting, particularly in his tonal descriptions of the beauty and mystery of the forests.

But perhaps Weber's greatest strength lay in his gift for arias, ensemble numbers, and choruses whose identity and personality sprang naturally from German folk music. There can be no questioning the Germanic nature of Kaspar's drinking song ("Hier im ird'schen Jammertal"), of the huntsmen's chorus ("Was gleicht wohl auf Erden"), of Max's hymn to the forests ("Durch die Wälder"), and of the thanksgiving chorus of the people that closes the opera. The most celebrated aria, however, is the one Agathe sings in the second act as, looking out of her bedroom window, she contemplates the beauty of the night ("Leise, leise"). Weber quotes this aria in his overture, which is a symphonic masterpiece.

As in *Fidelio,* there is still a good deal of *Singspiel* in *Der Freischütz*. Spoken dialogue is used. Popular-sounding tunes are favored. But even more than *Fidelio,* Weber's opera was a precursor of later German opera practices. Weber originated the repetition of fragmentary melodic ideas; probably these were the inspiration for Wagner's later development of *leitmotivs,* or leading motives. Also to be heard again in Wagner's work is the frequent use of the orchestra to heighten atmosphere and suggest supernatural phenomena and symbolism. Weber's conscious effort to unite several different arts into a single texture was also a source from which sprang the Wagnerian concept of the unity of the arts.

Writing to Weber about *Der Freischütz,* Beethoven said: "I am glad, I am glad. For this is the way German opera must get the upper hand of Italian singsong."

Weber wrote two more operas in which the German principles of *Der Freischütz* were further developed. He created *Euryanthe* for Vienna, where it was produced in 1823. The libretto of this opera was so ridiculous that it swept the work into a virtually permanent neglect his music does not deserve. There is no point in summarizing the story, but there is point in commenting, however briefly, on some of the music. Its wonderful overture is virtually a tone poem in which again and again the faint voice of Wagner can be detected, though Wagner's greater works were still many years away. One or two of Weber's *scenas* are equally remarkable, for example the ecstatic hymn to Euryanthe's beauty, "Unter blühenden Mandelbäumen."

Oberon, commissioned by Covent Garden in London, where it was seen in 1826, was Weber's last work. Since it was written for England it had an English text, though based on a French romance. The composer was seriously ill with tuberculosis when he accepted this assignment. Sensing that death was not far off, he took the commission in order to leave some inheritance to his family. Once he had decided to do the opera, he studied English to acquaint himself with the libretto. When he left for London, his wife remarked sadly, "I have just heard his coffin lid shut!"

In spite of its English libretto, *Oberon* is the essence of German romanticism. We are here carried into the world of fairies and elves and those mysterious woodlands where they make their home. Fantasy is given free rein. The text is an involved story (all such German fantasies usually are). Its main characters are Oberon, king of Fairyland, and the fairy Titania with whom he is in love. They quarrel, and Oberon vows to leave Titania forever unless there can be found a pair of lovers capable of proving their faithfulness to one another. Such a couple are discovered in Sir Huon and Rezia, each of whom had seen each other in a vision. After numerous adventures that defy credibility, Sir Huon and Rezia are the ones to prove to Oberon that faithful lovers can be found, and he becomes reconciled with Titania.

Oberon is rarely performed today, sharing that fate with *Euryanthe* for the same reason—an impossible libretto. A shame! There is so much 87 good music in *Oberon!* There is music in which the fairyland world comes to life; in which sylvan scenes and airy spirits are perfectly realized with an exquisitely light touch and winged imagination. There is here, once again, a wonderful overture, evoking the land of fairies, elves, and forest spirits. There are two remarkable *scenas:* Rezia's "Ocean, Thou Mighty Monster" (almost of a Wagnerian grandeur) and Huon's song "From Boyhood Trained." The opera also boasts an exceptional vocal quartet in "Over the Dark Blue Waters." All these numbers, incidentally, are briefly quoted in the overture.

Weber himself wrote that *Oberon* was "the greatest triumph of my life. . . . To God alone belongs such glory." It was his greatest success, and it was his last one. After the premiere, his health disintegrated. He knew that never again would he see his country, home, or family. Early on the morning of June 5, 1826, he was found dead in bed. He was buried in England, but eighteen years later his body was transferred to Dresden, Germany. For this, his second burial, Wagner wrote special music and delivered the eulogy. Wagner could hardly have realized at that time that he himself was destined to carry on where Weber had left off. Wagner's great future was still before him, while Weber's work now belonged permanently to the past. Had Weber never lived, it is altogether possible that Wagner would never have dreamed his Gargantuan dreams, brought them to life, and thus fulfilled his own destiny.

7

The Flowering of
Bel Canto

Vincenzo Bellini, Gaetano Donizetti,

Gioacchino Rossini

In the early decades of the nineteenth century a royal triumvirate ruled the destinies of Italian opera. They were Bellini, Donizetti, and Rossini.

A key to the works of this distinguished trio of composers lies in the term *bel canto,* meaning "beautiful song" or "beautiful singing." But *bel canto* carries implications above and beyond the soaring, swelling melody of which all three composers were consummate masters. It also suggests the exploitation of the possibilities of the human voice as to perfection of tone and intonation, agility, elegance of phrasing, purity and beauty of sound, smoothness of successive tones (called *legato*), perfection of control—the most exacting technical virtuosity.

The one name that comes most often to mind when we speak of *bel canto* is Vincenzo Bellini (1801–35). This is because song was the sole weapon in his compositional arsenal. He was deficient in his harmonic writing; his orchestration leaves much to be desired. He did not even possess a particularly strong feeling for the stage. But what he did possess was a genius for song. He produced songs as naturally as a bird does. As Paul Henry Lang put it so well, "his whole soul bathed in the happiness of the flowing melody, warm, scented, caressing." The aria

OPERA was the be-all and the end-all of his greatest operas. Through *bel canto,* wooden characters become human, synthetic dramatic scenes acquire theatrical interest.

Born in Catania, Sicily, Bellini attended the Naples Conservatory, where his first opera was given. With *Il Pirata* (produced at La Scala in 1827) he first gained renown for his melodic powers. In the opera houses of our own day Bellini is most often represented by two operas, *La Sonnambula* (*The Sleepwalker*) and *Norma*. In both, his genius at *bel canto* finds few if any equals.

La Sonnambula was introduced at the Teatro Carcano in Milan on March 6, 1831. The heroine is Amina, whose sleepwalking habits complicate her love affair with Elvino. He suspects her of infidelity because, during her sleepwalking, she enters and is found in Count Rodolfo's bedroom. Amina's condition, when discovered by Elvino, sets matters right between them—but not before Amina temporarily loses her mind with grief over the man she has seemingly lost.

There are surely few finer examples of *bel canto* than "Ah! non credea mirarti" in which Amina, convinced Elvino has abandoned her, compares the dead love affair to withered flowers that she wants to revive with her tears.

Norma received its world premiere at La Scala nine months after *La Sonnambula* was first heard—on December 26, 1831. Norma is the high priestess of the Temple of Esus during the occupation of Gaul by the Romans in about 50 B.C. She is in love with the proconsul, Pollione, with whom she has had two children; but Pollione now is more interested in Adalgisa, virgin of the temple, who has desecrated her holy vows by reciprocating his love. When Norma discovers that Adalgisa is her rival for Pollione, she decides to commit suicide and begs Adalgisa to take care of her two children. In vain does Adalgisa plead with Norma not to go through with her threat; in fact Adalgisa promises to give up Pollione. But Norma cannot be swayed. After a battle of the Gauls and the Druids against the Romans, Norma threatens Pollione with a dagger. With death facing him, Pollione insists his love for Adalgisa is eternal. Reaffirming her own great love for Pollione, Norma goes to her death in a flaming pyre. Conscious-stricken, Pollione follows her into the fires.

Wagner said of *Norma* that "this opera among all the creations of Bellini is the one which, with the most profound reality, joins to the richest vein of melody the most intimate passion. . . . The music is noble and great, simple and grandiose in style."

Unquestionably the most famous single aria in the opera is "Casta diva," sung by Norma and the chorus as a prayer for peace.

Bellini's last opera was *I Puritani* (1835) which contains one of the most dramatic and eloquent "mad" scenes in Italian opera, that of the heroine, Elvira. It is called "Qui la voce." Bellini died in Puteaux, France, eight months after the premiere of this opera.

The ease and rapidity with which Gaetano Donizetti (1797–1848) wrote operas is proved by the fact that he completed sixty-seven of them. Most are not remembered even by knowledgable operagoers, but in recent years several have been revived most successfully because they are the source of some wonderful *bel canto*. Among these works are *Anna Bolena* (1830), *Lucrezia Borgia* (1833), *Roberto Devereux* (1837), *Linda di Chamounix* (1842), and *Maria di Rohan* (1843).

Unlike Bellini, Donizetti had more than one string to his creative lyre. Together with an uncommon gift for heavenly song, Donizetti had a keen dramatic strength, a strong feeling for declamation and musical characterization, and more than passing skill in harmony and orchestration. He was at home both in tragic and comic operas. In each of these two categories he has bequeathed masterworks: in tragic opera, *Lucia di Lammermoor* and *La Favorita;* in *opera buffa, L'Elisir d'amore* and *Don Pasquale;* in *opéra-comique, La fille du régiment.* In discussing Donizetti we shall, however, confine ourselves to his three best-loved and most-performed operas—and those in which he is at his greatest: *Lucia di Lammermoor, L'Elisir d'amore,* and *Don Pasquale.*

Donizetti, the son of an employee in a pawnshop, was born in Bergamo. After attending the conservatory in Bologna, he wrote three operas between 1816 and 1817, all in imitation of Rossini, who was in considerable vogue and of whom we will speak shortly. Donizetti's period of apprenticeship and his indebtedness to Rossini persisted in his next thirty operas. One of these, *Zoraide di Granata,* produced in Rome in 1822, so aroused the first-night audience that some of them lifted the composer on their shoulders and carried him to the Capitol to be crowned "king of opera." Twenty of the thirty apprentice operas were produced between 1822 and 1829; four of them came in the single year of 1828.

A new phase for Donizetti began in 1830 with *Anna Bolena,* in which he was able once and for all to free himself from Rossini. A Donizetti personality was beginning to emerge in his writing: his own style of *bel canto;* a mastery in writing for more than a single voice; his telling theatrical effects in his music.

Having now found himself creatively, Donizetti went on to prove that he was Rossini's successor in the art of writing *opera buffa.* In this genre he first proved his indisputable mastery with *L'Elisir d'amore* (*The Elixir of Love*), which took him only fourteen days to write. It was first given in Milan on May 12, 1832. The story is typical of *opera buffa.* Nemorino, a farmer, tries to win the love of the wealthy and beautiful Adina by the use of a love potion, or elixir, marketed by the charlatan Dr. Dulcamara. The love potion, of course, is a fake. Adina announces she is going to marry an army sergeant. But in the end Nemorino receives an inheritance that makes him highly desirable to the village girls, who begin flocking around him. This arouses Adina's interest and jealousy. She now decides she is in love with Nemorino who, in turn, is convinced that it was Dr. Dulcamara's potion that worked the trick.

As beautiful a tenor aria as you will find in any *opera buffa* is "Una furtiva lagrima," with which Nemorino soothes and placates the jealous Adina when she sees the girls swarm around him. This masterful example of *bel canto* was such a favorite with Enrico Caruso that he convinced the Metropolitan Opera to revive the opera so that he might sing the aria. But besides proving his royal gift at melody, Donizetti showed in *L'Elisir d'amore* how nimble his fingers were in fashioning swift comic passages, patter songs, vivacious ensemble numbers, and deft orchestral accompaniments.

Three and a half years after *L'Elisir d'amore* Donizetti proved his genius at tragic opera with *Lucia di Lammermoor,* based on a romance by Sir Walter Scott. The opera was introduced in Naples on September 26, 1835. This is a melodrama filled with treachery, deception, misunderstandings; its plot involves madness, death, suicide. The place is Scotland; the time, the seventeenth century.

Lucia of the house of Lammermoor is in love with Edgardo. Her brother, determined to have her marry the wealthy Arturo Bucklaw, will stop at nothing to break up his sister's romance with Edgardo. In this, fate becomes his ally, since Edgardo must leave for France. Lucia's brother intercepts Edgardo's letters to her and then convinces her that Edgardo has abandoned her permanently. Heartbroken, Lucia decides to marry Arturo. During the festivities attending the signing of a marriage contract, Edgardo makes a sudden reappearance. Seeing his beloved about to marry another man, he denounces Lucia and curses the house of Lammermoor. During the wedding festivities Lucia appears in her bridal gown in a trance. She has lost her sanity and slain her husband.

No sooner does Edgardo learn of this tragedy when he hears the terrible news that Lucia has collapsed and died. Now aware that Lucia has been faithful to him all the time, Edgardo stabs himself.

The first-night audience was so wildly enthusiastic that Donizetti (never too stable physically) was seized by fever and had to be put to bed. Nor did the success of *Lucia* end with its premiere. Within six years, it was heard and cheered in virtually every major music center, including New Orleans. It has remained one of the most popular of Italian operas, and with good reason. The vocal sextet, "Chi mi frena," is surely one of the most famous ensemble numbers in all opera. It is heard at the end of the second act, during the ceremony attending the signing of the marriage contract and the unexpected arrival of Edgardo. Each of the characters in the sextet gives voice to his or her own reaction to what is taking place, so that each of the six different melodies (weaving and interweaving through one another with the most remarkable dexterity) reflects a different emotion. Besides boasting this celebrated sextet, the score includes that brilliant coloratura piece that through the years has been cherished by the world's greatest sopranos, Lucia's "Mad Scene": "Ardon gl'incensi" followed by "Spargi d'amaro pianto."

The fame he achieved with *L'Elisir d'amore* and *Lucia di Lammermoor* brought Donizetti commissions to write new operas for the Opéra and the Opéra-Comique in Paris. He finally settled in the French capital in 1839, staying there virtually up to the time of his death. In that time came some notable operas: *La Fille du régiment,* an opéra-comique in 1840 that stirred the French with its martial airs and patriotic text, particularly the chauvinistic finale, "Salut à la France." In the same year of 1840 the Opéra produced the tragic opera *La Favorita,* where we find that wonderful aria "O mio Fernando," though in its own time this opera was far more popular for its stirring climactic scenes and ballets than for its lyricism. Following a brief visit to Vienna to assist in the production of *Linda di Chamounix* in 1842, Donizetti was back in Paris to write the *opera buffa, Don Pasquale,* and see it produced at the Théâtre-Italien on January 3, 1843.

Don Pasquale is one of the half dozen or so greatest *opere buffe* in history. It might even be considered the last of this species, since *opera buffa* went into comparative decline after the mid-1840s, with only spasmodic revival of the form in the twentieth century in works like Wolf-Ferrari's *Il Segreto di Susanna* and Gian Carlo Menotti's *Amelia Goes to the Ball.* Some consider *Don Pasquale* Donizetti's best opera, the best integrated, the one that maintains a lofty standard most consistently, the one with the most varied lyric invention, and the one most subtle in its humor and characterizations.

Don Pasquale, an elderly bachelor, objects to his nephew, Ernesto, marrying a lovely widow, Norina. As far as he himself is concerned, Don Pasquale has matrimony very much on his mind. His friend and physician, Dr. Malatesta, secretly in league with Ernesto, raves over the beauty and allure of Sofronia (the doctor's supposed sister, who doesn't actually exist). Disguised as Sofronia, Norina captures the heart of old Pasquale, who proposes marriage. A mock marriage follows. Sofronia now begins driving her husband out of his mind with her volatile moods, caprices, and irate tempers. Finding himself burdened with a shrew, Pasquale is overjoyed to discover that his marriage was not real. He forgives his doctor friend for having fooled him and turns Norina over to Ernesto all too happily.

Buffa music springs and leaps throughout the score in episodes like the one where Norina and the doctor conspire to fool Pasquale ("Vado, carro"), or the gay second-act finale that begins with Pasquale's anguished cry that he has been betrayed. But we must not forget that Donizetti was a master of *bel canto* even in *opera buffa*. The wonderful lyricism of Norina's aria "So anch'io la virtù magica" or Ernesto's serenade to Norina, "Com'è gentil," is vocal writing of a creator born with the gift of melody in his heart.

Donizetti wrote one more opera and completed two that had been unfinished; then his life's work was at an end. Most of his mature years he suffered from a cerebrospinal disease that, while it did not arrest his productivity, continually harassed him physically. After 1844 he was further victimized by melancholia and given to harrowing hallucinations. The tragic truth was that he was losing his mind. After suffering a stroke, he had to be confined to an asylum, from which he was released in 1847 to be placed under the care of his brother in his own native city, where he died a half year later, in 1848.

The most idolized of the three Italian opera composers discussed in this chapter—indeed, the most idolized of all Italian composers of his generation—was Gioacchino Rossini (1792–1868). He was also the one who was most gifted, inventive, and versatile. Not until Verdi appeared to dominate the Italian operatic scene was there a composer to match Rossini's fame and genius.

The paradox about Rossini is that while it is possible to speak of him in superlatives, it is also possible to find much in his art to depre-

cate. Rossini's inborn talent far outstripped both his integrity and his dis-
crimination. He wrote too much and he wrote too quickly. Lazy by nature, he was reluctant to make revisions when they were necessary, preferring to retain second-rate, sometimes shoddy material rather than go through the nuisance of concocting something better. He often took the shortcut. He borrowed melodies—sometimes from his own earlier works, sometimes even from the works of other composers. Plagiarism bothered him not at all; lifting a phrase, a line, or even a melody from another composer made the job of finishing an opera so much easier. An overture from one of his earlier operas often served for several later ones, be they tragic or comic. He accepted any text, however ridiculous it might be. He did not hesitate to resort to set formulas in meeting the needs of singers, to suit special situations, or in catering to his public.

One face of the coin, then, reveals a hack, almost a charlatan. Turn the coin around and you have the face of a genius. *Bel canto?* Rossini's melodies may not have the plangent loveliness or the sunshine of Bellini in his most inspired moments, nor do they possess the dramatic power of the best of Donizetti. But Rossini, when he was in his element, produced lyricism that was radiant and glorious, made all the more effective by his mastery in writing for the voice. There was a wonderful spontaneity and ease in his melodic writing.

Buffa? Rossini's pen dripped with laughter, mockery, sardonic humor, in the same glib way in which his tongue dropped quips and witty retorts.

Melodrama? Rossini could summon a power and a passion that led Meyerbeer, the early Verdi, and the early Wagner to imitate him. The realism with which Rossini translated stage action into music was an inspiration to Mascagni and Puccini.

Like all true geniuses, Rossini was an innovator. He was one of the first to eliminate dry recitatives—to have the orchestra accompany the voices throughout the opera instead of using the harpsichord or cembalo for some of the recitatives. From then on, because of Rossini, the demarcation line separating recitative and aria would be less rigid and formal, so naturally would recitative flow into aria.

Before Rossini, singers improvised florid passages in arias, often spontaneously (a privilege allowed them by the composer). Rossini began the practice of writing most of the ornamentation himself, in order to control how much the singers could embellish his music. Henceforth this became the standard procedure.

Rossini developed the resources of orchestration by introducing in-

Rosa Ponselle as Norma, a role she sang at the Metropolitan Opera from 1927 to 1932. Many critics believed this part was the dramatic soprano's finest vocal achievement, and one to be remembered in operatic history.

Il Barbiere di Siviglia, *act 2.* (*Left to right*) *Don Basilio* (*Giorgio Tozzi*), *Dr. Bartolo* (*Fernando Corena*), *Count Almaviva* (*Luigi Alva*), *Figaro* (*Mario Sereni*), *Rosina* (*Teresa Berganza*), *Berta* (*Shirley Love*). *A Metropolitan Opera production.*

Gioacchino Rossini.

Dr. Dulcamara (Fernando Corena) arrives by balloon in a Metropolitan Opera production of L'Elisir d'amore.

Lucia (Joan Sutherland) reappears in a trance among the wedding guests. A Metropolitan Opera production of Lucia di Lammermoor.

struments others before him had avoided and thereby introducing new colors and effects into his accompaniments. He was not afraid to employ unusual harmonic combinations to inject excitement or surprise. There were even times when he assigned greater importance to the orchestra than to the singers. One of his effective techniques in comic opera, for example, was to assign the main melody to the orchestra while the voice or voices were heard in a patterlike accompaniment. In his orchestral writing he made such frequent use of crescendo to heighten dramatic interest that the "Rossini crescendo" became part of his basic stock in trade. (It can be found in most of his famous overtures.) In short, as the English music critic Ernest Newman said of Rossini, "he broke away, bit by bit, from a good deal of the older formalism of structure." At the same time he developed a structure that would identify Italian opera for years to come.

He was born in Pesaro, Italy, on February 29, 1792. Since his father traveled around a good deal playing in small-town theater orchestras, the child Gioacchino was raised by his grandmother and an aunt until 1804, when his parents finally took root in Bologna. There, beginning in 1807, Rossini attended the conservatory. By then, he was already the composer of some chamber and vocal music, and an opera.

Rossini was unable to complete his course of study at the conservatory because his family's poverty made it necessary for him to earn a living. He found various jobs, including directing an orchestra and playing the harpsichord.

Chance led to the writing of the first of his operas to be produced. A Venetian company planned to present four one-act comic operas, each by a different composer. One of these composers failed to come through with the assignment. A friend of Rossini's prevailed on the opera director to turn the libretto over to the young, unknown composer, who accepted the assignment for a fee of $100. With the haste that would henceforth characterize his work, Rossini completed the score of his little opera, *La Cambiale di matrimonio,* in three days. Produced on November 3, 1810, in Venice, Rossini's opera proved so successful that it was given over a dozen performances.

Several more of Rossini's operas (tragic as well as comic) were heard during the next two years. But it was in the field of *opera buffa* that he made the strongest impression. Two were particularly well received: *La Scala di seta* (remembered today exclusively for its melodious overture) and *La Pietra del paragone.* The first was produced in Venice in 1812; the latter in Milan the same year. *La Pietra* was regarded so highly that

besides receiving fifty performances it earned for its composer an official
exemption from military service, which was then required of all young
Italians.

His success kept pace with his fertility. Between September 26, 1812 (the premiere of *La Pietra*), and February 20, 1816 (the world premiere of his masterpiece, *The Barber of Seville*), eight Rossini operas were introduced. The best were comedies. Two of these have in recent years, through revivals and recordings, revealed to us that during this period Rossini's *buffa* style was already fully developed. In spite of deplorable librettos (the reason why these operas have so rarely been given in the past), each can provide a present-day audience with auditory delight. They are *Il Signor Bruschino* (1813) and *L'Italiana in Algeri* (1813).

During this same year of 1813 Rossini also wrote *Tancredi,* a tragic opera that received a tumultuous response when introduced in Venice. We remember it for its overture and for one of its arias, "Di tanti palpiti," as wonderful an example of Rossini's genius in *bel canto* as we can encounter anywhere. This aria became such a hit in Venice that the impresario (fearing familiarity might breed contempt) resorted to legal action to prevent people from humming or singing it in the streets.

A contractual agreement between Rossini and a major European opera impresario (Barbaja), led the composer to finish twenty new operas between 1815 and 1823. By terms of his contract, the prolific Rossini was allowed to write operas for other impresarios, too. This is why it was not for Barbaja, but for an opera director in Rome, that Rossini created his most famous opera, an *opera buffa* that is so perfect a realization of this form that it remains the criterion of what *opera buffa* should be. I am, of course, referring to *Il Barbiere di Siviglia* (*The Barber of Seville*), introduced in Rome on February 20, 1816.

If the names of characters in this opera such as Figaro and Count Almaviva sound familiar, it is because they are also found in Mozart's *The Marriage of Figaro,* written thirty years earlier. The reason why the same characters appear in both Mozart's and Rossini's operas is because the librettos of both were derived from plays by Beaumarchais, dealing with the same characters. However, the action of *The Barber of Seville* precedes that of *The Marriage of Figaro.*

As in Mozart, the text moves briskly while employing familiar *opera buffa* devices. In seventeenth-century Seville, Count Almaviva is in love with Bartolo's rich ward, Rosina. Bartolo discourages Almaviva because he wants Rosina (and her wealth) for himself. Almaviva, therefore, is compelled to assume various disguises to reach Rosina: as a humble student named Lindoro; as a soldier; as a music teacher. In some of these intrigues, Figaro, a barber, is Almaviva's fellow conspirator. Almaviva, disguised as a music teacher, unfolds to Rosina during a lesson plans for their elopement. But the wily Bartolo is suspicious. Deciding to marry Rosina posthaste, he summons a notary to draw up the marriage contract. A bribe persuades the notary to substitute Almaviva's name for that of Bartolo on the contract. This deed accomplished, Almaviva and Rosina are finally married. Bartolo finds solace in the fact that the happy married couple allow him to retain Rosina's inheritance.

If it took Rossini only thirteen days to write the score for *The Barber of Seville* (certainly a speed record for the completion of such an unblemished masterwork) it is partly because he used a good deal of borrowed material. The overture (a symphonic classic) was previously heard in three other Rossini operas. Melodies for *The Barber of Seville* were also lifted from other Rossini operas, and some were taken straight out of Haydn and Gasparo Spontini. Rossini's practice of interpolating other people's music into his opera continued even after the first-night performance. A composer named Romani provided Rossini with an aria to replace a more difficult one Bartolo had sung in the first performance.

The borrowings, however, assume insignificance when considered against the shining pure gold of Rossini's creativity in the music he wrote directly for this opera: Almaviva's ecstatic serenade "Ecco ridente"; Figaro's patter song about the many functions he must perform above and beyond his duties as a barber, in "Largo al factotum"; Rosina's coloratura aria as she reads a letter from her beloved, "Una voce poco fà." Whether using borrowed or original material, the opera never sags either in its inspiration or in the buoyancy of its spirit. No wonder, then, that Beethoven said of this opera, "It will be played as long as opera exists."

A combination of unhappy circumstances and accidents resulted in a fiasco for Rossini's *Barber* on opening night. Some in the audience had come to make trouble. These were admirers of Paisiello who resented Rossini using the same text that their favorite composer had previously set to music and that had become such a classic by 1816. They completely ignored the fact that Rossini had asked Paisiello for permission to write another *Barber* (something he was not required to do, since in those days it was general practice for many different composers to set the same text); that Paisiello had given his consent most graciously; and that on his opening night Rossini had used the title of *Almaviva* so that

his own *opera buffa* might not possibly be confused with Paisiello's.

Paisiello's followers created a disturbance throughout the evening. To compound disaster upon malice, a series of stage accidents made a shambles of the performance. At one point one of the characters accidentally fell through a trapdoor; at another point a cat (not called for in the text) strolled leisurely across the stage; at a third place, a string of Almaviva's guitar snapped. Laughter and derision, then, from the unbiased segment of the audience, were added to the vociferous shouts of disapproval from the biased. "Never had the theater walls been shaken by such a tumult," reported a critic of London's *Musical World*. "It was not cries and hissings alone but real howlings. . . . When at the end of the performance the house reverberated with boos, Rossini lost his composure. He rushed out of the opera-house and locked himself in his house."

But the second-night presentation told a far different story. Paisiello's men were no longer around, convinced as they were that Rossini's opera was now surely destined for limbo. This performance went smoothly. Several important changes made the opera even more attractive than it had been originally, including the addition of the serenade "Ecco ridente" and the substitution of Romani's aria for one by Rossini. Rossini, expecting another disaster, did not come to the theater, though he had been scheduled to conduct. When a mighty ovation sounded following the final curtain, a messenger was dispatched to Rossini's home to drag him to the opera house. He came wearing a cotton cap, slippers, and swanskin trousers—the informal dress he favored for lounging. The audience went into a furore when he mounted the stage. Then they followed his carriage to his home, shouting: "Long live Rossini! Long live the great *Maestro!*"

From then on *The Barber of Seville* had easy going. First throughout Italy, then in the rest of the music world, it was performed to packed houses and was the recipient of the most ecstatic enthusiasm. It is still one of the best-loved Italian *opere buffe* ever written, whether the part of Rosina is sung by a mezzo soprano (as Rossini had originally intended) or by a soprano (as has been most frequently the custom since 1826).

The Barber of Seville made Rossini the most famous composer of Italy. He enhanced this reputation during the next half dozen years with such comic-opera delights as *La Cenerentola* (*Cinderella*) and *La Gazza ladra* in 1817, and a serious opera, *Mosè in Egitto* in 1818. Though his operas spread far and wide, Rossini himself remained rooted to Italy until 1822, when he crossed the border for the first time to make a triumphant visit to Vienna. Meanwhile, in March of 1822 he married a distinguished Spanish singer, Isabella Colbran, who appeared in the starring role of a serious Rossini opera, *Semiramide,* introduced in Venice on February 3, 1823.

Following his first trip outside Italy, Rossini went to London by way of Paris in 1823. He was personally received by the British king and earned a fortune giving concerts for the nobility. Then in 1824 he returned to the city that would henceforth be his permanent residence: Paris. There, for two years, he managed the Théâtre-Italien, where Italian operas were produced. In 1826, King Charles X appointed him "first composer of the king." At the same time, the king contracted him to write five new operas for Paris during the ensuing decade.

The only opera Rossini completed under this arrangement became his greatest serious opera—and, as it happened, the last opera he ever wrote. It was *Guillaume Tell* (*William Tell*), which for many years held second place to *The Barber of Seville* as Rossini's most frequently performed opera. *William Tell* is a work of outstanding importance, but it was not recognized as such when the Paris Opéra offered the world premiere on August 3, 1829.

It would be difficult to say which is more familiar to more people: the story on which this opera is based; or the overture which has become such a fixture in symphonic literature, and is possibly the most popular opera overture ever written.

The hero, William Tell, steps out of the pages of Swiss legend. He was a fourteenth-century leader of a revolt by Swiss patriots against the Austrian oppressors then ruling Switzerland. In the opera, Arnold, a young friend of William Tell, is in love with Mathilde, the sister of Gessler, the tyrannical ruler, and this makes him at first reluctant to fight for his country's freedom. But when his father is imprisoned and slain by Gessler, Arnold knows he must join the patriots. During a Swiss festival, William Tell has to shoot an apple off the head of his son at Gessler's orders. Tell complies with a perfect aim that spares his son's life. But, bitterly, Tell informs Gessler that had his son been killed, Tell had reserved a second arrow for Gessler himself. This leads Gessler to imprison William Tell, too. William Tell escapes and kills Gessler with an arrow, while the Swiss patriots overcome the Austrians. Switzerland is emancipated. Arnold and Mathilde can begin to plan a future life together in peace.

This is Rossini's most ambitious opera from the point of view of its use of elaborate settings, pageants, folk dances, dramatic incidents. It is also his longest opera. As he originally wrote it, it took six hours to per-

form but, after the premiere, Rossini cut it down to normal length. The
opera rings truer than earlier serious music of Rossini in the way in
which the music carries over the sentiments, nobility, and high tensions
of the play. There is in this opera far greater emotional impact and sin-
cerity in the eloquent arias and duets then even in some of the more glorious *bel canto* pages of earlier Rossini operas: in the prayer "Sois im-
mobile," in which William Tell begs his son to remain still as Tell aims
his arrow at the apple; in Arnold's recollection of his happy boyhood in
"Asile héréditaire"; in Mathilde's poignant song, when she thinks of her
beloved, "Sombre forêt."

The folk dances have an authentic Swiss character (the "Passo a sei,"
for example, performed by the shepherds, in the first act). And then, of
course, there is the wonderful four-part overture, which Rossini wrote
exclusively for this opera rather than borrowing something he had written earlier—an overture thoroughly attuned to the varying moods and
episodes of the drama. None of his other overtures have the expansive-
ness of structure and richness and variety of melodic material that this
one does.

In *William Tell* (which in later years earned the accolades of Berlioz,
Mendelssohn, Verdi, and Wagner, among others) Rossini proved he was
still Europe's leading opera composer. He was now only thirty-seven
years old. Having achieved altogether new dimensions in his operatic
thinking and writing, Rossini seemed destined to produce even greater
operas, comic as well as serious. And yet, although he lived another
thirty-nine years, he never wrote another opera. Never before, as his
biographer Francis Toye pointed out, has there been "any other artist
who thus deliberately, in the very prime of life, renounced that form of
artistic production which has made him famous throughout the civilized
world."

Why Rossini came to so sudden and permanent a halt in the writing
of operas (a halt that some writers have called "the great renunciation")
has never been satisfactorily explained. True, Rossini was rich and could
now well afford to indulge himself in idleness, in the pursuit of good
times, in the satisfaction of his voracious appetite for gourmet foods and
fine wines, and in entertaining his friends and admirers in a royal manner. But he had been rich before *William Tell,* and easily could have
pampered himself without undertaking the writing of a six-hour opera
that opened up new vistas.

It may well be that once he had written *William Tell* he was convinced he could no longer turn back to the familiar formulas of earlier

years that had made writing operas so easy and effortless. It is possible that *William Tell* had so taxed his inner resources that he could no longer summon the energies to undertake operas of equal scope. Besides, he did not have the health for hard, sustained work in the 1830s, suffering as he did from a painful disease of the bladder and acute neurasthenia, a nervous condition. We know that the first time he rode in a railway train, in 1836, his nerves were so on edge that he fell into a dead faint; that the death of one of his friends brought on in him a violent, prolonged illness; that frequently, seemingly without provocation, he would become so distraught that he had to be bedridden.

When he did compose (for he could not totally abandon writing music) he completed some choral music and piano pieces. But the thought of returning to opera apparently never entered his mind, even after a marked improvement in his health took place.

In his later years, his salon became famous in Paris. Leading cultural and social luminaries came regularly to eat his wonderful food, drink his rare wines, exchange ideas, indulge in stimulating conversations—but most of all to enjoy Rossini's quick wit, which was often as sharp as a razor edge. One nobleman visiting Rossini reminded the composer he had met him at a dinner at which a delicious macaroni pie had been served. "The macaroni pie, I remember well," Rossini, the gourmet, replied quickly. "You, I don't." A visiting composer once brought him two compositions for his criticism. Rossini listened patiently to the first. Without waiting to hear the other, he remarked, "I like the second better." In his last years, completing a Mass, he affixed the following mocking comment at the end of the work: "Good God! Here is my poor Mass. Thou knowest that I was born to write comic operas and that my patrimony consists in a little heart and less science. Be, therefore, compassionate and leave me enter Paradise."

He was as superstitious as he was self-indulgent and witty. Perhaps he had every right to be, as fate proved. When in November 1868 Rossini died in Paris from complications following a heart attack, he breathed his last on Friday the thirteenth.

Treasures of French Opera

Giacomo Meyerbeer, Charles Gounod,

Georges Bizet

In adopting for *William Tell* a grander manner than he had previously favored for tragic operas, Rossini was swimming with the tide. French opera lovers, as we already have remarked, enjoyed spectacles, pageants, ballets, and scenes charged with the drama of clashing mobs or armies. As time went by, French composers catered to their audiences by introducing ever bigger scenes, more lavishly mounted ballets, and more highly charged drama. One of these composers was Gasparo Spontini (1774–1851), an Italian-born musician who in 1803 had come to Paris, where he achieved fame for the spectacular visual effects and grand finales of such operas as *La vestale* (1807) and *Olympie* (1819). Another opera that had the grand manner was *Masaniello, ou La Muette de Portici* (1828), the work of a Frenchman, Daniel François Auber (1782–1871). Rossini probably would not have written *William Tell* in the style he chose had he not been impressed and influenced by Spontini and Auber.

Spontini and Auber and *William Tell*, however, represented only the beginnings of a new trend in French opera: "grand opera." The composer who is really the founding father of this movement was himself not a Frenchman by birth. He was Giacomo Meyerbeer (1791–1864), who was born in Germany, trained in Italy, but eventually became a Frenchman.

With Meyerbeer, "grand opera" came to mean many things, of which extravagance in scenic mounting and ballets, the use of processions and pageants, and dramatic climaxes involving huge crowds were just a part. Grand opera also stressed melodramas—sometimes on medieval or other historical subjects, sometimes on religious or political themes. The treatment was passionate, sometimes violent. The composer's goal was to raise audience response to a high pitch of excitement. The music used the fullest resources of voices (particularly combined in ensembles and choruses) and orchestra (with an increased palette of instrumental colors).

In developing French grand opera, Meyerbeer became the dominant figure in French stage music during his lifetime. His name originally was Jakob Liebmann Beer. He was born in Berlin on September 5, 1791. The son of a banker, he grew up in wealthy and cultured surroundings. A grandfather had left him a huge legacy, which ensured his wealth for the rest of his life. Adding the name of his benefactor (Meyer) to his own was a condition of the legacy, and so he called himself Meyerbeer. Jakob was changed to Giacomo when, in Italy, Meyerbeer became involved with Italian opera.

Meyerbeer made his first public appearance, as pianist, when he was seven, only three years after he had begun studying. His talent made such an impression on Muzio Clementi that Clementi emerged from retirement in 1802 to become the boy's teacher. (Clementi was one of the most renowned pianists and piano teachers of his day, the author of *Gradus ad Parnassum,* a book of exercises familiar to most young pianists.) After that Meyerbeer studied theory with various teachers including Abbé Vogler, who had previously been Weber's teacher. Vogler took the boy Meyerbeer into his house in Darmstadt and treated him like a son for two years.

By 1813, Meyerbeer had written several works, including two operas that had been produced respectively in Munich and Stuttgart. Both were failures. For a while Meyerbeer seriously thought of giving up composition for good to devote himself exclusively to the piano. With this in mind he went to Vienna, where he studied intensively for ten months. But on the advice of the powerful Salieri, he went to Italy to study opera. In Venice Meyerbeer was so enchanted with Rossini's operas that he was seized by the ambition to become an opera composer. He now changed his first name to Giacomo and began writing Italian opera.

Karl Maria von Weber had directed two of Meyerbeer's German operas in Dresden. But as in other places and in other times, a sharp division separated the Italian and German attitudes toward opera. By 1823, when Meyerbeer saw Weber again, Weber condemned the composer's having settled in the camp of the enemy—the Italians. (Weber, of course, had been the spokesman for German romantic opera since the production of his *Der Freischütz.*) The movement Weber represented did not appeal to Meyerbeer. Nevertheless a good deal of Weber's criticism made a deep impression on him. In spite of his strong Italian leanings, Meyerbeer soon began combining his love for Italian lyricism with the German concern for orchestration and harmony. Meyerbeer first revealed this tendency in *Il Crociato in Egitto,* produced in Venice in 1824.

For a number of years after that Meyerbeer wrote no more operas. He was reevaluating what he had accomplished, deciding what direction to take. In 1826 he came to Paris, where his theorizing was affected by still another influence, that of the French—French drama, French culture, French history. When finally Meyerbeer went back to writing operas, he was a far different composer than he had been before coming to France. His style now mingled Italian, German, and French tendencies in a manner uniquely his: the blending of Italian melody and dramatic French declamations with sophisticated German harmonies and orchestration. Meyerbeer was now determined to outdo his French predecessors in interpolating into his operas the kind of materials the French favored. In this he had the cooperation of one of France's most prolific dramatists: Eugène Scribe, whose texts deployed the complete panoply of stragecraft and exploited fully the surges and sweeps of high drama.

Their first opera was *Robert le diable,* the work with which French grand opera first comes to full glory. The French responded to it with an outburst of the enthusiasm they had previously reserved for their beloved Rossini, when it was given at the Opéra on November 21, 1831. Indeed, *Robert le diable* became one of the most successful operas of the period, earning several millions of dollars in profit within the next quarter of a century.

In *Robert le diable,* Meyerbeer and Scribe gave the French a truly spectacular opera. Dead nuns become revived to perform a voluptuous dance. Demons join in a chilling chorus, and Sicilian knights fill the stage with their colorful uniforms and their resounding voices. There is much that at times is electrifying and at other times arresting as the story of Robert, a thirteenth-century Norman duke in Palermo, unfolds. His mother is mortal, but his father is a devil disguised as a man. In love with Isabella, Robert enlists the diabolical powers of his father to abduct her. He is dissuaded from going through with this sordid plan by the poignant pleading of Isabella. Filled with remorse, Robert disowns his father, who is seized by the underworld spirits.

Meyerbeer's music is vividly descriptive—grotesque and diabolical when the text requires and in other scenes eloquently lyrical in true *bel canto* tradition, as in Isabella's love song to Robert, "Robert, toi que j'aime."

Meyerbeer's next opera was grander still: *Les Huguenots,* again with a libretto by Scribe, given at the Opéra on February 29, 1836. Here Meyerbeer set a religious subject, the bitter struggle between the Catholics and the Protestant Huguenots in sixteenth-century France. Militant Protestantism is musically symbolized through the consistent recurrence in the opera of the famous Lutheran chorale "Ein' feste Burg." From this time on, religious subjects would appeal to many French composers.

Raoul de Nangis, a Huguenot nobleman, is heard in the first act singing one of the opera's most beautiful romances, "Plus blanche que la blanche hermine." He is describing how that very day he has saved a lady's life without discovering who she is. She turns out to be Valentine, daughter of the Catholic Count de Saint Bris, and betrothed to Count de Nevers. It is not long before Raoul and Valentine fall in love. This meets with the favor of Count de Nevers, who feels that the marriage of these two might end the schism between the Catholics and the Huguenots. When Raoul learns that Valentine had been betrothed to the Count he at first becomes bitter. His insults to Valentine are sparks inflaming the Catholics against the Huguenots and arouse Valentine's father to challenge Raoul to a duel, which is immediately stopped by the Queen.

Raoul eventually repents his behavior toward the woman he loves and comes to her boudoir to beg for forgiveness. There he overhears a plot of the Catholics to massacre the Huguenots. After Raoul and Valentine go through a private marriage ceremony at church, they find that the massacre has begun. In the ensuing disaster, both Raoul and Valentine are killed.

Les Huguenots is a consistently blood-tingling melodrama and spectacle. "The effervescence of the emotions excited by this masterpiece makes one wish to be a great man in order to place one's glory and genius at Meyerbeer's feet." Thus said the famous French composer Hec-

tor Berlioz. In later years Verdi was influenced by *Les Huguenots* in writing parts of *Aida,* and Wagner maintained that *Les Huguenots* (especially the fourth act) represented one of the peaks in opera.

Indeed, there is much in this opera to arouse emotions and satisfy the senses even today: particularly the Page's powerful salute to the noblemen in "Nobles seigneurs"; in the blessing of the Catholics by three monks in the "Benediction of the Swords"; in the realistic music for the clash between the Catholics and the Huguenots and in the massacre scene. And highly tense dramatic and rousing choruses alternate with melodies that touch the heart: the already-mentioned "Plus blanche que la blanche hermine"; the Page's first-act cavatina, "Une dame noble et sage"; a poignant description of the Touraine countryside in France in "O beau pays de la Touraine"; and Valentine's poignant lament when she feels she has lost Raoul's love, "Parmi les pleurs."

Another religious subject, based on an actual event from Dutch history, absorbed Meyerbeer and Scribe when they wrote *Le Prophète,* performed at the Opéra on April 16, 1849. This story was told with the pomp and ceremony that were the strong suits of both the librettist and the composer. One orchestral excerpt is a favorite at "pop" or "semiclassical" concerts: "The Coronation March." The grandeur with which the coronation scene of John of Leyden is staged is matched by Meyerbeer's stately march music.

This is just one of several scenes to arouse an audience's enthusiasm. Another is a ballet that includes a stunning skating scene; a third is the attack on the Münster Cathedral; a fourth, the finale, in which the stage is consumed by fire.

As a change of pace, Meyerbeer wrote two light operas after *Le Prophète,* one of which is *Dinorah* (1859), remembered mainly for the coloratura aria, "Ombre légère," ("The Shadow Song").

Meyerbeer returned to grand opera with what has proved to be both his best work and his last one. He spent a quarter of a century writing it. Even after the opera went into rehearsal he continued to alter the score, so sure was he that he was producing his life's masterwork. He was still working over parts of the opera when he died.

That opera is *L'Africaine* (*The African Maid*), with libretto by Scribe. This is the most human of Meyerbeer's major works; spectacle and display play a subsidiary role to emotion and characterization. "Its score," says the historian Donald Jay Grout, "remains an example of the composer's mature style, purged of many earlier excesses, rich in melodic beauties, and containing some interesting harmonic refinements." *111*

　For this drama, Scribe reached into Portuguese history, the main character being the great explorer Vasco da Gama. Returning from an expedition, he describes to the king's councilors the island of Madagascar, which he had discovered. He has brought back with him two natives, Selika and Nelusko. Da Gama entreats the councilors for a ship and supplies so that he can return to the island and claim it for Portugal. When he is turned down, the explorer denounces them so vehemently that he is imprisoned. There he is tenderly cared for by Selika, which arouses the jealousy of Nelusko, who loves her. Inez, daughter of Don Diego, is in love with da Gama, even as is Selika. Inez arranges for his release from prison and provides him with a ship. After a shipwreck, da Gama, Selika, and Nelusko reach Madagascar, where in time they are joined by Inez. With queenly grace (for she turns out to be the queen of Madagascar) Selika surrenders Vasco to Inez and provides them with transportation back to Portugal. Once the pair has departed, Selika poisons herself, and her faithful lover, Nelusko, dies with her.

There are not many pages in Meyerbeer to compare with "O Paradis" for radiant lyricism. This is da Gama's tribute to the glorious beauty of Madagascar. A picturesque Indian march contributes stage glamour. Throughout the opera, Meyerbeer succeeded in introducing an exoticism that vividly recreates the colorful background of Madagascar, as well as helping to etch with authentic colors the native characters of Selika and Nelusko.

Death seized Meyerbeer suddenly on May 2, 1864, while he was still fussing over the details of his score (even though the opera was already in rehearsal). *L'Africaine* was produced posthumously on April 28, 1865. It would have given the composer no little satisfaction to see the way in which his masterwork was received. The French public knew they were in the presence of operatic greatness, and they responded accordingly.

Meyerbeer proved a most influential force in opera. The ceremonials, processions, and grand scenes to which he was so addicted we find in even Italian operas after 1840, including some by the great Verdi. Cecil Gray, an English music historian, went so far as to maintain that *Aida* is "musically little more than a grandiose pendant or sequel to *L'Africaine*" though he might have added that the same is true of the texts. Even in Germany, Meyerbeer's influence was felt.

Of course, Meyerbeer's impact was felt most strongly of all in France: as early, in fact, as 1835 when Jacques Halévy (1779–1862) completed his best opera, *La Juive* (*The Jewess*). In this opera Eléazar, in fifteenth-century Constance, sacrifices the life of Rachel, a girl he has raised as his own daughter (though she turns out to be the long-lost offspring of a cardinal) rather than have her convert from Judaism to Christianity. From this opera we get that tender tenor aria "Rachel, quand du Seigneur," Eléazar's lament that he must sacrifice Rachel.

Another opera of Hebraic interest in which more than once the touch of Meyerbeer is detected is *Samson et Dalila (Samson and Delilah)* (1877) by Camille Saint-Saëns (1835–1921). It is based on the biblical story about the strong-armed leader of the Hebrews, Samson, whose love for Delilah, the Philistine, leads to his capture and destruction. "Mon coeur s'ouvre à ta voix" (familiar in its English translation, "My Heart at Thy Sweet Voice") is the opera's best-known aria—Delilah's seductive song to Samson.

Between Meyerbeer's time and the end of the nineteenth century, several forms other than grand opera came into favor in France. One particularly important is *opéra lyrique* ("lyric opera"). Without completely abandoning Meyerbeer's tendencies to feature spectacle and ballet, composers of lyric opera emphasized a gentle lyricism whose sweetness avoided the saccharine. Deep feelings, whether romantic or tragic, were expressed with dignity and restraint. The musical writing was marked by refinement and grace rather than overstatement.

Probably the most celebrated opera to come from France belongs in this category: *Faust* by Charles Gounod (1818–93). It is its composer's masterwork. The only other of his operas alive in the repertory is *Roméo et Juliette (Romeo and Juliet)* (1867), based on Shakespeare's tragedy, from which has come Romeo's song comparing Juliet's beauty to the sun "Ah! lève-toi, soleil" and the waltz Juliet sings about her desire to taste life's sweetness, "Je veux vivre dans ce rêve."

Faust preceded *Romeo and Juliet* by eight years, having been introduced in Paris on March 19, 1859. Its text is based on Goethe's poetic-philosophic drama of the same name, but greatly rewritten to emphasize theatricalism and romance rather than philosophic concepts. In the opera, as in Goethe's drama, Faust makes a deal with the devil, Méphistophélès, to exchange his soul for a return of his youth. As a young man again, Faust meets and makes love to Marguérite. After the passage of time, Marguérite becomes convinced she has been abandoned by her lover. She kills their child, for which crime she is imprisoned. Faust penetrates her cell to help her escape. Though she is joyous at seeing Faust again, she insists she must suffer for the terrible sin she

The Paris Opéra (the Académie de Musique) in a photograph of the 1890's. Under construction from 1861 to 1875, the building was designed by Charles Garnier to surpass in size and luxury any theater then in use throughout the world.

Edouard de Reszke as Méphistophélès in Faust.

Marguérite (Mirella Freni), Faust (Gianni Raimondi), and Méphistophélès (Giorgio Tozzi) in a Metropolitan Opera production.

Georges Bizet in September, 1860, in a drawing by Gaston Planté, made during Bizet's trip home from Italy.

Célestine Galli-Marié created the role of Carmen in the opera's premiere at the Opéra-Comique in Paris on March 3, 1875.

Minnie Hauk, an American singing actress, was Brussels', London's and New York's first Carmen (all in 1878). Her interpretation was noted for its sensual and defiant qualities.

Emma Calvé, a French soprano, first sang Carmen in France in 1892 and in America in 1893, where her performance created "an indescribable sensation." She was considered to be the peerless Carmen, whose vivid interpretation reflected all the varied dramatic aspects of the character.

Mary Garden, born in Scotland, sang Carmen in New York and Chicago. Her interpretation of this role, and of many others, was noted for its conviction and personal insight.

Geraldine Farrar, a graceful lyric actress, was a favorite of New York audiences. Her Carmen was a beguiling and sophisticated one. She sang the role for the first time in New York on November 19, 1914, with Enrico Caruso as Don José and Arturo Toscanini conducting.

Maria Jeritza, "the Viennese thunderbolt," became a great favorite in Vienna early in her career. A spirited and vivacious singer, she sang Carmen in New York in the 1920s, in a vigorous and eye-catching portrayal of the role.

committed. After praying for salvation, she dies. A chorus of angels announces that she has found redemption.

The presence of the Meyerbeer grand-opera style is found in *Faust* in many places: in the famous "Soldiers Chorus" ("Gloire immortelle"); in the celebration of the villagers at a fair where we hear the waltz "Ainsi que la brise légère"; in the orgiastic ballet witnessed by Faust and Méphistophélès in the last act, a scene that is today often deleted. But in aria after aria Gounod proves he is not a mere echo of Meyerbeer but a creative force in his own right by producing melodies filled with human values and emotional responses. These are among the most popular: Marguérite's song at the spinning wheel, "Il était un roi de Thulé," followed by her "Jewel Song" ("Ah! je ris de me voir"); Marguérite's brother Valentin's expression of concern that he must leave his sister behind unprotected as he departs for war, "Avant de quitter ces lieux"; Marguérite's outpouring of ecstasy at seeing Faust come to her cell, "Sa main, sa douce main" and her later prayer for salvation, "Anges purs, anges radieux."

When first produced, *Faust* was an *opéra-comique* rather than a lyric opera, since spoken dialogue and not recitatives were used. This is the distinction that sets the two genres apart. In this form, with spoken dialogue, the opera proved only a modest success. But after recitatives replaced the dialogue, *Faust* proved a triumph (this was in 1869). *Faust* continued from then on to gain world acceptance. So dear was this opera to the British Queen Victoria that just before her death she pleaded to have some of its scenes performed for her. And by 1883 *Faust* had become so famous that it was the opera chosen to open the first season of the Metropolitan Opera in New York.

Another glory of French lyric opera started out as *opéra-comique: Carmen* by Georges Bizet (1838–75). When Bizet first wrote his score he, too, used spoken dialogue, and this is the way *Carmen* was heard at the Opéra-Comique in Paris on March 3, 1875. (It is still played that way at that opera house.) But elsewhere, dialogue was replaced by recitatives prepared not by the composer himself but by Ernest Guiraud. There is still another way in which *Carmen,* as we now hear it, differs from the way it was introduced. Today a number of ballet sequences are interpolated (using background music from other Bizet compositions). As an *opéra-comique* in 1875 *Carmen* had no ballets.

The libretto comes from a literary classic, a story by Prosper Mérimée, whose heroine, Carmen, is a seductive employee in a cigarette factory in nineteenth-century Seville. She flirts with Don José, a soldier, and completely enraptures him to the point where he deserts his service to follow her first to her haunt, a disreputable tavern, and then to a mountain pass where gypsy smugglers have made their hideout. But Carmen soon tires of Don José and becomes interested in the great toreador Escamillo. On the day of a bullfight in Seville, Carmen arrives with Escamillo, the latter welcomed as a hero. After Escamillo enters the bullring, Don José is seen. He is dishevelled and distraught. In vain he pleads with Carmen to return to him. When she refuses he stabs her fatally with a dagger. Emerging from his bullfight, Escamillo finds Don José weeping over Carmen's dead body.

There was much in *Carmen* to disturb audiences in 1875. The vivid portrayal of a character as immoral as Carmen caused shock. Never before had an opera presented girls onstage smoking cigarettes. Some listeners objected to the music, thinking it was too Wagnerian, because Bizet assigned such importance to the orchestra and on random occasions used a leading-motive technique. Nevertheless, *Carmen* was by no means the total failure that some of Bizet's early biographers suggested. As a matter of fact, some critics hailed it, a publisher paid a handsome price for the publication rights, and the opera company kept it in its repertory the following season.

Of course, before long, *Carmen* seized and held the enthusiasm of the entire opera world; few operas have become such abiding favorites with audiences everywhere. And with good reason. It is a veritable cornucopia of melodic riches. Its two most frequently heard arias are Carmen's song about the fickleness of love, the "Habanera" ("L'amour est un oiseau rebelle") and Escamillo's "Toreador Song" describing the excitement of a bullfighter's life ("Votre toast"). It is an interesting point that in the "Habanera" Bizet used a melody by Sebastián Yradier in the mistaken belief that it was a Spanish folk song. Carmen's "Seguidilla" inviting Don José to meet her in a disreputable tavern ("Près des remparts de Séville"), Don José's "Flower Song" ("La fleur que tu m'avais jetée") and Carmen's "Card Song" ("En vain pour éviter") are also numbers of great beauty. Besides its wealth of melody, the opera is equally notable for its choral and orchestral episodes, most of which capture the atmosphere of Spain with Spanish-type or gypsy-type rhythms, melodies, and luminous orchestration.

There are many other French lyric operas that have deservedly achieved world recognition. *Mignon* (1866) by Ambroise Thomas

(1811–96) is based on a classic by Goethe, *Wilhelm Meister*. Arias deserving special attention include Mignon's recollection of a distant land where she had spent her childhood ("Connais-tu le pays?") and Philine's coloratura polonaise, "Je suis Titania."

Lakmé (1883) by Léo Delibes (1836–91) is appealing for its exotic setting—India—and will always be remembered for its brilliant coloratura aria, Lakmé's "Bell Song."

Then there are *Manon* (1884) and *Thaïs* (1894) by Jules Massenet (1842–1912). Not many French composers had Massenet's talent for tender lyricism and touching sentiment, and these are the qualities that have made the two operas so famous. The excerpts most likely to be heard from Manon include "Adieu, notre petite table," "Ah! fuyez, douce image," and a gavotte, "Obéissons quand leur voix appelle." A highly effective innovation in *Manon* is the use of spoken dialogue (not recitative) over an orchestral accompaniment. In *Thaïs* it is an instrumental rather than a vocal excerpt that has popularized the opera even to many who have never seen it produced: the "Meditation" for solo violin and orchestra, heard between scenes of the second act, and repeated toward the close of the opera. Thaïs is a beautiful courtesan who repents her ways and finds redemption in religion, through the efforts of a monk who falls in love with her after her salvation. The "Meditation" is a tonal description of Thaïs' redemption.

The literal translation of the term *"opéra-comique"* is "comic opera." But when we talked of various famous works in this category we noticed that most examples of *opéra-comique* are very serious indeed, in fact sometimes tragic; that the basic difference between *opéra-comique* and "grand" or "lyric" opera is that *opéra-comique* uses spoken dialogue instead of recitatives.

France, however, was not without comic opera, a medium known as *"opéra bouffe."* (Theaters in Paris presenting light stage entertainment were known as *"bouffes."*) This form is unpretentious, indulges in levity and frivolity, and is slanted for popular acceptance; it bears a closer relationship to Austrian operettas and American musical comedies than it does to Italian *opera buffa*.

The foremost composer of *opéra bouffe* was Jacques Offenbach (1819–80). He brought to this medium such a flair for fresh, lilting tunes, for comedy, satire, and parody, that he elevated *opéra bouffe* to artistic status—so much so that some of his most famous works are performed by major opera houses. His masterwork is *Orphée aux enfers*

(*Orpheus in the Underworld*) (1858), a sacrilegious take-off on the Olympian gods that took Paris by storm. The overture is a classic in the repertory of light music. Two other important Offenbach *opéras bouffes* are *La Belle Hélène* (1864) and *La Périchole* (1868), the last of which has enjoyed many highly successful presentations at the Metropolitan Opera in an English translation. La Périchole's "Letter Song" ("O mon cher amant") is perhaps one of Offenbach's most glorious melodies.

Offenbach always harbored a secret ambition to write a serious opera. He did so just before his death, ending his career with a lyric opera of first importance. It is *Les Contes d'Hoffmann* (*The Tales of Hoffmann*), presented by the Opéra-Comique in Paris on February 10, 1881. The libretto comes from several fantastic stories by E. T. A. Hoffmann. Each of the three acts describes one of the hero's love affairs. The first is with a doll, Olympia, who looks human; the second is with a Venetian courtesan, Giulietta; the third is with Antonia, who dies of tuberculosis. Each love affair is controlled by the machinations of an evil genius, who takes the form of different characters in the different acts.

Offenbach had intended his heroines and his evil geniuses to be sung by a single soprano and baritone respectively. But most often the tendency has been to use three different singers for the heroines, and four different singers for the evil geniuses. Within the past few decades, however, Offenbach's wish has occasionally been followed. Lawrence Tibbett, Martial Singher, and George London are among those who have sung the parts of all four evil geniuses, while Anna Moffo, Joan Sutherland, and Beverly Sills have sung the three heroines.

One number above all others emerged from this opera to become famous in all types of transcriptions. It is the second-act "Barcarolle," sung by Giulietta and Hoffmann's companion, Nicklausse. This is an eloquent hymn to the beauty of a Venetian night and to the magic of love ("Belle nuit, ô nuit d'amour").

9

Italian Genius

Giuseppe Verdi

In the second half of the nineteenth century, two composers ruled over the world of opera like monarchs. One was Giuseppe Verdi (1813–1901) in Italy, the other, Richard Wagner in Germany. Each was the greatest opera composer his country produced. Each represented the culmination of techniques, styles, and approaches that for years had characterized the opera-writing of their respective lands. And almost as if it were some act of predestination, each was born in 1813.

With Verdi and Wagner commanding the reverence and adulation of their respective imitators and admirers, the long-existing clash between Italian and German traditions in opera came to a climax.

Verdi was a composer of "operas"—that is to say, he continued in the direction his Italian predecessors had traveled. Wagner was the creator of a new operatic form, which he baptized "musical drama." Verdi brought the Italian past to its ultimate fulfillment. Wagner was the revolutionary who overturned past practices to become the voice of the future.

Of the two, Wagner was the more egotistic, the more sophisticated, and the greater intellectual. Verdi was a simpler and humbler man, never forgetting he was descended from peasants. Verdi's father was an innkeeper, and his mother was the daughter of an innkeeper. The elder Verdis were married in 1805. They had two children. One of them, a girl, was mentally defective. The other, Giuseppe, born in Le Roncole in the duchy of Parma on October 10, 1813, was a musical genius.

When his parents acquired a spinet it instantly became Giuseppe's favorite toy. His face shone when first he struck a C-major chord. The next day, unable to repeat the chord, he went into such a tantrum that he smashed the spinet with a hammer.

Music study began in early childhood with the local organist. After a few lessons little Verdi was able occasionally to substitute for his teacher at church services. Upon the death of his teacher, Verdi took over the church position completely. To fulfill this duty, he had to walk three miles to and from Le Roncole (since, at ten, he had been sent to Busseto to live there with a cobbler so that he might attend its school). One Christmas morning, before dawn, on his way from Busseto to Le Roncole, Verdi fell into a ditch and would have drowned had not he been rescued by a passing peasant.

A well-to-do merchant in Busseto, Antonio Barezzi (a passionate music lover, an amateur flute player, and founder and president of the local philharmonic orchestra) arranged for the boy Verdi to study with Busseto's most gifted musician, Ferdinando Provesi, for four years. During this period Verdi engaged in many and varied musical activities in both Le Roncole and Busseto. He also did considerable composing: many marches for brass band, various orchestral pieces, half a dozen concertos, and some church music. A few of his orchestral works were played at church and public concerts.

By the time he was eighteen, the tie binding Verdi and Barezzi was so close that the merchant took him into his own household as a son. Verdi fell in love with Barezzi's daughter, Margherita. Barezzi looked favorably on this match, but before permitting the lovers to consider marriage, he wisely insisted that Verdi complete his music study at the Milan Conservatory. In 1832, Verdi applied for admission there and was turned down, first because he was four years older than regulations required, and second, because his piano playing left much to be desired.

With Barezzi providing the funds, Verdi remained in Milan for three years studying counterpoint privately with Vincenzo Lavigna, who also encouraged him to attend opera performances and study opera scores. The teacher described his pupil as "discreet, studious and intelligent," prophesying that Verdi would some day "prove a great honor to me and our country."

His musical training completed by July of 1835, Verdi returned to Busseto where, six months later, he was appointed municipal music director. His duties included teaching music in school and conducting the philharmonic orchestra. His livelihood assured, Verdi married Margherita Barezzi on May 4, 1836.

It took Verdi three years to write his first opera, *Oberto,* its premiere taking place in Milan (where the Verdis were now living) at La Scala, on November 17, 1839. A fair success (it was dropped from the repertory after fourteen performances), it did succeed in attracting the interest of the publisher Ricordi, who commissioned Verdi to write an *opera buffa.* That *opera buffa* proved a fiasco when given at La Scala in 1840—possibly because during its writing Verdi suffered the disaster of the death of his young wife and his two children. It took Verdi half a century to try his hand a second time at comic opera.

It was with his third opera, *Nabucco,* that Verdi's career in opera can be said to have really begun. "Nabucco" is Italian for Nebuchadnezzar, the Babylonian king, one of the most powerful monarchs of the ancient world. The locales of ancient Babylonia and Jerusalem made possible the kind of magnificent stage settings, costumings, spectacles, and ballets that Verdi had so come to admire in Meyerbeer. And there was much in the involved plot to arouse audience passion, with one melodramatic development following another in rapid succession: war, insanity, revenge, suicide, intrigue, and the eleventh-hour escape from death of the king's daughter. No wonder, then, that the Italians went wild over *Nabucco* when it was heard at La Scala on March 9, 1842. Donizetti left the auditorium in a daze, muttering to himself, "Beautiful, beautiful." The critic Felice Romani wrote that the opera had "an emotional quality all its own that profoundly affects spectators." Verdi found himself an idol of the Milanese opera public overnight. Sauces, ties, hats were named after him.

Nabucco represents major progress over Bellini, Donizetti, and Rossini in the writing of tragic opera. The sweetness and elegance of *bel canto* here gives way to arias of vigor and dramatic power. Some of the choruses attain a sublimity altogether new to Italian opera—particularly the "Hebrews' Chorus" ("Va, pensiero"), the Hebrews' lament at the news that they are to be massacred.

The decade that followed brought eleven Verdi operas, the most significant being *I Lombardi* (1843), *Ernani* (1844), and *Macbeth* (1847).

Ernani was Verdi's first opera to be performed in New York and Lon-

don. In *Macbeth,* Verdi emerges as an unrivaled Italian opera dramatist. Again and again he introduced musical subtleties that caught the
changing nuances in the Shakespearean drama and the varying moods of
the characters.

The first of Verdi's three creative periods (which had begun so inaus-
piciously with *Oberto*) ended impressively with *Luisa Miller* in 1849. It
is through the operas of his second period—from *Rigoletto* through
Aida—that Verdi became the most famous Italian composer of all time.
Despite the magnificence of the two operas of his third period, and the
fact that they are the greatest operas of his entire career, it is the most
popular operas of his second period that are now most often performed,
are most frequently recorded, and with which the composer is most
often identified.

Most of the librettos Verdi used during this fertile second period
were of a kind to sharpen his instinctive dramatic instincts. *Rigoletto,*
based on a drama by Victor Hugo, was the first of these. The title character is a deformed jester to the Duke of Mantua in the sixteenth century. Rigoletto has been a protective father to Gilda, his daughter. When
he learns that Gilda loves the Duke, a notorious rake, Rigoletto decides
to do away with his employer by hiring a paid assassin to kill him. The
assassin, in turn, is induced to save the Duke's life, kill somebody else,
and pass the victim off to Rigoletto as the Duke. Gilda, who has over-
heard the plot, knocks on the door and is stabbed. Her body is dumped
into a sack and delivered to Rigoletto. When Rigoletto suddenly hears the
Duke singing a mocking song of love from a distance, he tears open the
sack and discovers the grim truth.

The aria Rigoletto hears the Duke sing is as beloved a tenor aria as
is encountered in Italian opera—"La donna è mobile," describing the
fickleness of women. Verdi knew how good this melody was. He was convinced that its lyricism was so contagious it would infect whoever heard
it. Afraid the tune might become famous throughout Venice before the
opera could have its premiere there (on March 11, 1851), he refused to
turn over its music to the singer until the day of the dress rehearsal.

Verdi's incandescent lyricism is what makes *Rigoletto* so popular.
The duke's cynical commentary about women in "Questa o quella," Gilda's joyous outpouring of her feelings of love in the coloratura aria
"Caro nome" are just two of many examples of melodies as brilliant as
the Italian sun and as lovely as Italian landscapes. But besides its wonderful arias, *Rigoletto* possesses one of the two greatest ensemble num-

bers Verdi wrote. It is the quartet "Bella figlia dell' amore." Here the Duke and one of his girl friends exchange flirtatious overtures while Gilda reveals her jealousy and Rigoletto his rage.

Verdi once again revealed his remarkable gifts in writing both arias and ensemble numbers in an opera with possibly one of the worst librettos he ever set to music. This is *Il Trovatore* (*The Troubadour*). There are so many subsidiary plots enmeshed in the main one that it requires mental agility to unravel the puzzle. Even when the puzzle is solved, it is difficult to accept seriously some of the improbable developments that take place. Reduced to its basics, its story is as follows. Count di Luna and Manrico are rivals for the love of Leonora. Manrico believes he is the son of the gypsy, Azucena. When the Count imprisons Azucena, Manrico summons his men to battle the Count's forces. Manrico is captured and incarcerated with his "mother." Heartbroken at these developments, Leonora poisons herself. As Manrico is being executed, Azucena reveals to the Count that Manrico is the Count's long-lost brother.

It speaks volumes for Verdi's genius that he was able to translate dramatic absurdities into inspired music. There are so many wonderful excerpts in this opera that what one wit said of *Hamlet* also applies to *Il Trovatore:* "It is full of quotations." In this opera we encounter the second of Verdi's great ensemble numbers, the "Miserere" ("Ah! che la morte"), a song of doom by Leonora, Manrico, and a chorus of prisoners. One of Verdi's most familiar choral pieces is the "Anvil Chorus" ("Vedi! le fosche notturne spoglie") sung by the gypsies while swinging their hammers on anvils. Another is the soldiers' chorus, "Squilli, echeggi la tromba guerriera." A favorite duet is "Ai nostri monti." The finest arias run the gamut of emotion, with "Stride la vampa," "Il balen del suo sorriso," "D'amor sull' ali rosee," and "Tacea la notte placida" as four particular gems.

It is then not difficult to understand why the opera proved so sensational at its premiere in Rome on January 19, 1853. The *Gazzetta musicale* reported: "The music transported us to heaven." So popular did the opera become in a short time that three companies presented it simultaneously in Venice alone. The rest of the world also responded with enthusiasm, which has since never diminished.

Hardly was the ink dry on the manuscript of *Il Trovatore* when Verdi completed another opera that circled the globe and has remained one of his strongest box-office attractions. It is *La Traviata* (*The Lost One*); its world premiere was in Venice on March 6, 1853.

The libretto was based on a sentimental romance by Alexandre

Dumas, *La Dame aux camélias*. Violetta, a courtesan, and her lover, Alfredo Germont, go to live in Violetta's country place near Paris. Alfredo's father comes to convince Violetta that, for the sake of his family's future, she must give her lover up. Her love leads her to make this great sacrifice. She abandons Alfredo and returns to her former disreputable ways. Convinced that Violetta has deserted him because she prefers wealthy men and the gay life, Alfredo grows so bitter that, at a gambling house where he proves unusually lucky, he throws his winnings contemptuously at Violetta. Only when Violetta lies dying of tuberculosis does Alfredo learn the truth about her sacrifice. He rushes to her side, promising to take her back with him to Paris. Violetta dies in Alfredo's arms.

Simplicity and tenderness are the main qualities found in the music. The most famous aria, "Ah, fors è lui," and the immediately following "Sempre libera," however, both have an interest above and beyond their melodic beauty. They tell us in their music more about the courtesan Violetta (before she falls in love with Alfredo), about her philosophy on what constitutes a good life, than do the words. In the same act, "Un dì felice," a duet of Alfredo and Violetta, brilliantly contrasts Alfredo's tenderness with Violetta's cynicism—once again giving us a better understanding of the respective characters. Three other musical numbers are popular for their emotion and lyricism: "Di Provenza il mar," in which Alfredo's father reminds his son of his boyhood happiness in their native province; Violetta's farewell, "Addio del passato," and Alfredo and Violetta's dream of their future happiness, "Parigi, o cara."

For many years some legends about the premiere of *La Traviata* have been accepted as truth by even eminent musicologists: that at the first performance the opera was produced in costumes and scenery contemporary with the period in which it was given, and that the first performance was a fiasco for this reason and also because many in the audience thought the text too immoral. But recent research in Venice has uncovered facts that should henceforth be acknowledged. The premiere was praised by the critics and hailed by the audience; it was so well liked that it was given ten performances within a brief period (and not withdrawn after the second presentation, as had been believed). The gentle charm, the sweet sadness and sentiment, the touching drama of the opera were as irresistible in 1853 as they are today.

The eighteen years separating *La Traviata* from *Aida* found Verdi completing other distinguished operas. These included *I Vespri siciliani* (*The Sicilian Vespers*) (1855), *Simon Boccanegra* (1857), *Un Ballo in maschera* (*A Masked Ball*) (1859), *La Forza del destino* (*The Force of*

Destiny) (1862), and *Don Carlos* (1867). Each is in the permanent opera repertory. Each is rich with Verdi's expressive lyricism and vivified by his gift for theatricalism. But good as these operas are—and however many treasures of melodies they bring—their luster is dimmed by the splendor of *Aida*. For *Aida* is grand opera in which Meyerbeer-like pageantry is blended with Verdi's pronounced dramatic feeling, subtle understanding of character, an emotion that never descends to sentimentality, and a seemingly never-ending flow of Italian melody that helps to develop the story line rather than impede it.

Verdi wrote *Aida* for a new auditorium in Cairo, Egypt—the building of which was part of a monumental celebration for the opening of the Suez Canal in 1869. However, *Aida* was not produced until 1871. Verdi did not agree to write the opera until 1870, and then the extravagant scenery and the lavish costumes all ordered from Paris were delayed in being finished and transported to Egypt because of the Franco-Prussian War.

The khedive who had commissioned the opera for Cairo did everything to make the opening performance the last word in opulence. Solid gold and silver ornaments were worn by the principal characters. The singer portraying the Egyptian king was bedecked in jewels. The settings were authentic reproductions of Egyptian scenes and architecture. The staging was regal: in the magnificent "Triumphal March" of the second act three hundred people, as well as horses and elephants, crowded the stage.

Actually this premiere was more of a carnival than an artistic presentation. Verdi (who had refused to come to Egypt because he was afraid of sea travel and detested pretentious festivities) was in a rage. He said that the Egyptian performance was "no longer art but a trade, a pleasure party, a hunt."

But the performance of *Aida* given with considerable more dignity and restraint at La Scala on February 8, 1872, under the composer's personal supervision, was far more in character with the opera as Verdi had conceived it. It was still a stunning spectacle—with its profusion of exotic and ritual ballets, ceremonies, and grandiose victory celebration. But the human equation was not allowed to be smothered by ponderously overstaged scenes. *Aida,* while remaining a glorious sight for the eye, also proved to be vibrant, human musical theater.

The setting is Egypt in the time of the pharaohs. Aida, daughter of the king of Ethiopia, is now a slave in Egypt. She and Amneris, daughter of the Egyptian king, are rivals for the love of Radames, captain of

La Scala Theater in Milan.

Giuseppe Verdi conducting a performance of Aida.

An engraving of a scene from the first performance of La Traviata *in London on May 24, 1856. Violetta was sung by Marietta Piccolomini.*

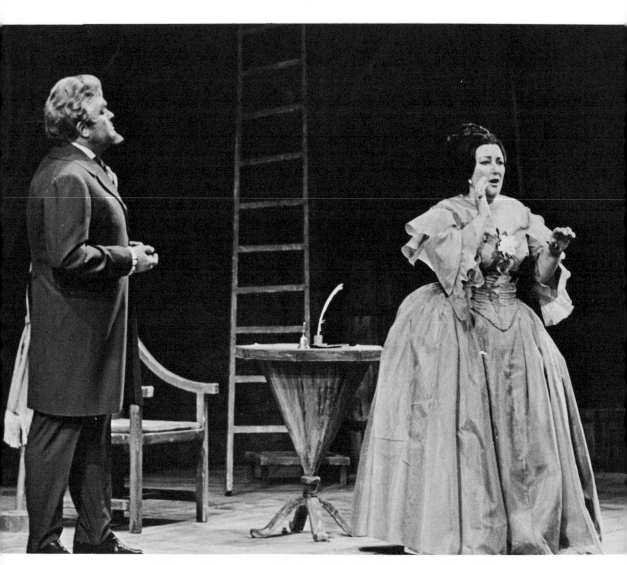

Violetta (Montserrat Caballe) with Alfredo's father, Giorgio Germont (Cornell MacNeil), in a Metropolitan Opera production of La Traviata.

Aida (Leontyne Price) with her father, the Ethiopian king Amonasro (Mario Sereni), in a Metropolitan Opera production.

Nannetta (Judith Raskin) and Fenton (Luigi Alva) in a Metropolitan Opera production of Falstaff.

the Egyptian guards. Radames favors Aida, just as Aida prays for Radames' victory when he heads an army to attack her country, Ethiopia. Radames returns victorious, an occasion that inspires a monumental ceremony. The captives he brings back are freed, with the exception of Aida's father, the Ethiopian king. The latter successfully prevails on Aida to get from Radames a secret military plan whereby the Ethiopian army can successfully attack Egypt. Denounced as a traitor, Radames is condemned to die by being buried alive in a sealed tomb. When the tomb is closed, Radames discovers Aida is in there, too—come to die with him.

Early in the opera we hear one of Verdi's most resplendent tenor arias, "Celeste Aida," with which Radames rhapsodizes over his beloved's beauty. Other distinguished numbers are either highly lyrical or dramatically stirring. In the former category we find Aida's expression of nostalgia for her native land in "O patria mia," and the farewell duet to the world of Radames and Aida in the closing scene, "O terra, addio." In the latter belong Aida's prayer for an Egyptian victory, "Ritorna vincitor." Unforgettably stirring also is the music of the "Triumphal March" and the ballet music during the ceremonies honoring Radames for his victory.

By the time he had written *Aida,* Verdi was the most highly venerated and wealthiest Italian opera composer of his time. Neither fame nor fortune could change the peasant in him. He used to say that if he had not been a composer he would have liked to be a farmer. Actually, he did become a farmer. In 1848 he acquired a parcel of land at Sant' Agata, near Busseto, which he developed into a richly productive farm. Here he spent his summers almost to the end of his life. During the winter he occupied a beautifully appointed house in Genoa. He was happiest, however, when in summer he could wear his rough peasant clothes at Sant' Agata, his crushed hat over his weatherbeaten bearded face, his sturdy peasant boots.

At Sant' Agata he could return to the kind of elementary living in which he was most at ease. He always seemed uncomfortable in an urban existence, where the social life was so active and where he had to appear in elegant clothes. At Sant' Agata he would rise at five in the morning and watch the dawn creep up as he roamed over his fields. In the afternoons he rode on horseback inspecting his lands, his produce, and his animals, and paying personal calls on his tenant farmers.

He shared his life with his beloved wife, the former Giuseppina Strepponi, whom he married on August 29, 1859. She had been a famous prima donna who had created the leading female role in Verdi's *Nabucco.* But she gave up her own career to devote herself completely to her husband.

To all Italians, Verdi was not only their greatest composer but also a political hero. For many years much of Italy suffered under the rule of Austria, a rule that patriotic Italians tried to overthrow. A good many of the librettos Verdi set to music used the uprising of people against tyranny as a theme—the reason why Verdi, so often in his career, had to come to grips with censors. To Italian patriots, Verdi became a symbol of Italian liberation. When it was finally achieved, and Italy's first parliament was formed by Cavour, Verdi was elected a deputy. This was in 1863. But though he was a patriot through and through, Verdi was not cut out for a political career; he soon resigned from his post as deputy. A decade later, the king of Italy (in further recognition of Verdi's loyalty to and love of his country) conferred on him the honorary post of senator.

During the sixteen years following *Aida,* Verdi wrote no operas. He sometimes spoke of writing music for Shakespeare's *King Lear,* but it was just talk. When he did write music at this time it was for the concert stage. His most important such work was the majestic *Requiem* (for solo voices, chorus, and orchestra), a masterpiece written in 1874 in memory of Italy's eminent novelist, Alessandro Manzoni.

One of the main reasons why Verdi avoided writing operas was because he had come to appreciate Wagner's genius and to understand the significance of Wagner's revolution in opera. Verdi began feeling that his own kind of opera had been made old-fashioned by the new methods and aesthetics conceived, and so magnificently fulfilled, by his great German contemporary. Verdi was too deeply steeped in Italian operatic traditions to imitate Wagner. At the same time he could not suppress the fear that whatever else he would write for the stage would only repeat what he had already done.

But he was wrong. He was still capable of giant achievements—indeed, achievements greater than any he had previously realized—though it took him many years to make the effort. What rekindled the dying embers of Verdi's operatic creativity and set it into conflagration was one of the finest librettos ever conceived. It was by Arrigo Boito (1842–1918) and was based on Shakespeare's drama *Othello.*

Boito was a brilliant Italian critic and composer as well as a librettist, the creator of both the text and the music of a remarkable opera, *Mefistofele* (1868), derived from Goethe's *Faust.* Boito urged Verdi to come out of his operatic retirement to write the score for his text, *Otello*. Verdi was reluctant. But the power and imagination of Boito's libretto was a force that, in the end, Verdi could not resist. Verdi worked long and hard during 1884 and 1885. Then his opera was finished. "I breathe again," Verdi exclaimed with relief. Boito's comment was, "The great drama has become a reality."

The fact that the giant Verdi had written his first new opera in fifteen years gave the premiere of *Otello* at La Scala, on February 5, 1887, international significance. The response of the distinguished first-night audience was phenomenal. There were twenty curtain calls. When Verdi finally appeared on the stage thunder erupted in the auditorium. Later that night, hundreds of his admirers gathered under his window to shout, "Viva, Verdi!"

One can readily understand the reason for such enthusiasm. In *Otello* Verdi, writing in a style new for him, had risen to higher altitudes of greatness than those achieved in his rich second period. Influenced by Wagner, Verdi's writing for voice and orchestra acquired new dimensions, tapped new dramatic resources. Once again affected by Wagner, Verdi dispensed with recitatives, arias, and ensemble numbers as such to produce an uninterrupted and unified musical texture—parts dramatic, parts passionate, parts highly lyrical, parts tender, but all combined into an integrated whole. Never before had Verdi's feeling for the theater, for his characters, and for making music and words one been so keen. There are innumerable wonderful pages in this score, but among the best known are "Credo in un Dio crudel" by Iago, and two numbers by Desdemona, "Salce, salce" (better known as the "Willow Song"), and "Ave Maria."

The tragic plot is familiar. Inflamed by his conniving and jealous lieutenant, Iago, Othello (the newly appointed black governor of Cyprus) becomes convinced that his lovely white wife, Desdemona, has been unfaithful to him. In vengeance Othello murders her; then, made aware he has been a victim of treachery, he commits suicide.

However amazing it was that, after so long an absence from the stage, Verdi should disclose altogether new facets in his writing of operas, what he accomplished in his next opera, *Falstaff,* is more remarkable still. This was the master's last work for the stage—and what an incredible farewell it proved to be! Once again an extraordinary libretto by Boito based on Shakespeare (this time from *The Merry Wives of Windsor* and parts of *Henry IV*) proved the irresistible stimulus for Verdi to return to his workbench. This time, however, Verdi was required to pro- *141* duce music for a comedy, his first such attempt since his fiasco half a century earlier. What power of will, what courage did it take for Verdi (approaching his eightieth birthday) to try his hand a second time in a style in which he had once failed so miserably! But as Boito told him, "There is only one way of ending your career better than with *Otello,* and that is to end it with *Falstaff.*"

Once again, as with *Otello,* the merry tale of Falstaff is so well known that only a cursory summary is needed. Falstaff is a fat, lecherous man who considers himself very much of a Don Juan. The setting is Windsor, England, in the fifteenth century. Falstaff tries to make amatory overtures to two married women. He becomes the butt of ridicule at their hands and later on the pathetic victim of a prank perpetrated on him by these two ladies and other conspirators. In Windsor Park they terrify him by assuming disguises as supernatural beings.

Falstaff is one of the greatest comedies in opera. That the dark, grim drama of *Otello* could be followed by music as sparkling, effervescent, witty, and light-handed as that which Verdi conceived for this masterpiece is one of his most memorable accomplishments. But as the English writer R. A. Streatfeild noted, there is much more in *Falstaff* than just wit and a gay heart, more than perfection of workmanship, more even than entrancing lyricism within an integrated, inextricably unified score. For example, Streatfeild points out that "in the last act, Verdi strikes a deeper note. He has caught the very charm and mystery of the sleeping forest with exquisite art. There is an unearthly beauty about this scene, which is new to students of Verdi. In fairy music, too, he reveals yet another side of his genius. Nothing so delicate nor so rich in imaginative beauty has been written since the days of Weber." Among the more memorable episodes in this opera are "È sogno?"; the serenade "Dal labbro il canto estasiato," and Falstaff's "Quand'ero paggio."

To describe the premiere of *Falstaff* at La Scala on February 9, 1893, as a triumph equal to that of *Otello* would be overstating the case. Many in the audience, including some of the critics, found it difficult to reconcile Verdi with comedy. It took familiarity with *Falstaff* for the opera world to recognize the wonders of this Verdi opera.

With the death of his wife in 1897, Verdi lost both the will to live and to create. (He did, however, manage to complete *Four Sacred Pieces,* which are choral works.) He refused to visit his beloved Sant' Agata any more. Instead he "vegetated" (the word is his own) in rooms at the Grand Hotel in Milan. A paralytic stroke in 1901 was the beginning of his end. Mercifully Verdi did not suffer long. Six days later, on January 27, he died at dawn.

A whole country mourned. Schools were closed. Eulogies were delivered in the Senate. Over a quarter of a million of his admirers lined the streets to bid him farewell when, a month after his death, his body was moved from its first grave to its final resting place—on the grounds of the Musicians' Home that he had founded and supported. Many wept openly as the procession moved slowly through Milan accompanied by the strains of the famous "Hebrews' Chorus" from *Nabucco,* conducted by Toscanini.

"Tutto nel mondo è burla"—all the world's a stage, and all its people merely players. This is the vocal fugue sung by the ensemble to end *Falstaff.* Verdi's musical world had been the Italian operatic stage. On that stage he was the principal character, without an equal or even a challenging rival.

Melodious Realism

Giacomo Puccini

Between the time Verdi wrote *Otello* and *Falstaff,* a significant new movement had arisen to change the character of Italian opera. It is known as *verismo,* or "naturalism." This movement was partial to stories with commonplace characters, settings, and situations with which audiences could identify themselves. Librettists in this new style devised passionate, violent plots built up in a realistic manner. In line with realism, composers working in the *verismo* style avoided florid vocal writing completely, favoring melodies with a strong melodramatic character and orchestral and choral episodes that established moods. This does not mean that composers of *verismo* operas abandoned songful, heartfelt lyricism. Far from it!

The father of *verismo* was Pietro Mascagni (1863–1945). The opera with which the movement came into existence was *Cavalleria rusticana* (*Rustic Chivalry*). After winning first prize in a competition, it was heard in Rome on May 17, 1890. Its immediate success was of giant proportions. There were forty curtain calls. After the performance opera lovers stormed Mascagni's house and so crowded the street outside its entrance that the composer had to sneak inside through a window. Because of *Cavalleria rusticana,* the king of Italy made its composer Knight of the Crown of Italy, and an Italian town made him an honorary citizen. Medals bearing his face were sold in shops. Melodies from the opera were sung and played throughout Rome.

Nor were the opera's success and Mascagni's fame confined exclusively to the Holy City. Before a year had passed, *Cavalleria rusticana* was acclaimed all over Italy; within three years it was heard in virtually every major opera house in the world. Never again was Mascagni destined to write an opera that even remotely approached such popularity; and it remains the chief opera by which he is remembered today.

In a Sicilian village in the nineteenth century, Santuzza, a village girl, is in love with Turiddu who, in turn, is more interested in Lola, the seductive wife of a teamster. Lola's husband, Alfio, and Turiddu are embroiled in a duel in which Turiddu is a fatal victim, much to Santuzza's grief.

This tragedy transpires on Easter day, the religious spirit of which is evoked in the ever-popular atmospheric orchestral intermezzo between the two scenes of the opera's single act. Some of the lyrical gems include Turiddu's offstage tribute to his beloved, "O Lola," heard just before the ending of the opening orchestral prelude and Santuzza's confession to Turiddu's mother of her deep love for and betrayal by Turiddu in "Voi lo sapete." These and other arias are integral to the development of the plot in a manner henceforth identifying *verismo* operas.

The instantaneous success of *Cavalleria rusticana* led other Italians to join the *verismo* bandwagon. There was Ruggero Leoncavallo (1858–1919), composer of *Pagliacci (Strolling Players),* introduced in Milan on May 21, 1892. In a prologue and two acts, *Pagliacci* is a play within a play. After the orchestral prelude, a hunchbacked clown, Tonio, comes in front of the drawn curtain to explain that the play about to be witnessed is about real people in a true-to-life incident. This is the celebrated prologue, "Si può?"

Tonio then asks that the curtain be lifted. We are in a Calabrian town, to which a troupe of strolling players, headed by Canio, has come. In this group is Tonio, who is in love with Canio's wife, Nedda, while Nedda is interested in the peasant Silvio. When Tonio finally reveals his true feelings to Nedda she responds with cruelty. Tonio gets his revenge by conniving to have Canio witness a secret meeting between Nedda and Silvio. Heartbroken at discovering that his wife has deceived him, Canio breaks down in a sobbing aria, "Vesti la giubba," the high point of the opera and one of the best-known tenor arias ever written.

In the second act, the troupe performs a play whose story is curiously like the action that has actually been taking place among the company of players. During the performance, Canio forgets he is performing a role. He first bitterly denounces Nedda for her infidelity, then stabs her. Silvio, in the audience, leaps to the stage to help Nedda only to become another fatal victim of Canio's weapon. Canio turns to the audience and comments tragically that "the comedy is ended."

Because *Cavalleria rusticana* and *Pagliacci* together fill out an evening's entertainment—and because they are both in the *verismo* style—it is customary to present them on the same program. The first time this happened was at the Metropolitan Opera in 1893, creating a tradition since followed by that company and other major opera houses.

Verdi's successor as Italy's most famous opera composer—Giacomo Puccini (1858–1924)—was strongly influenced by *verismo* in the passionate stories he set to highly realistic music. Yet he was able to achieve his own identity, one far different from that of either Mascagni or Leoncavallo. Puccini had elegance, a haunting tenderness, a bittersweetness of melody, an uncommon talent for portraying female characters, together with a continual bent for innovation and experiment that put his greatest operas in a class by themselves.

Descended from a long line of professional musicians, Puccini was born in Lucca on December 22, 1858. He received musical training early. Upon the death of his father, the organist and choirmaster of the Lucca cathedral, the town authorities designated the boy, who was only five, to succeed his father when he became of sufficient age. His music study took place at the Pacini Institute, a period in which Puccini wrote some church music performed in Lucca.

He aspired to follow in the footsteps of his father and grandfather by becoming a church musician. But one day he heard Verdi's *Aida,* performed in Pisa—the first experience Puccini had with opera. He had to walk the thirteen-mile distance between Lucca and Pisa to hear the work, which affected him profoundly. A new world sprang to life before his ears and eyes. By the time he got home he knew he would become an opera composer, like the great Verdi.

A subsidy from Margherita, the queen of Italy, made it possible for Puccini to continue his music study at the Milan Conservatory between 1880 and 1883. One of his teachers there was Amilcare Ponchielli (1834–86), who in 1876 had become famous for his opera *La Gio-*

conda, a work still popular, and from which comes the familiar "Dance of the Hours."

Ponchielli was responsible for Puccini writing his first opera soon after he had graduated from the conservatory in 1883. At Ponchielli's urging, Puccini wrote a one-act opera, *Le Villi,* for a competition. He did not get the prize, but his opera was performed by a secondary opera house in Milan on May 31, 1884. La Scala produced it the following season, and the publisher Ricordi not only issued the score but also commissioned Puccini to write a new opera. This second opera, *Edgar*— given at La Scala in 1889—was a debacle. This so discouraged Puccini that he contemplated going to South America to join his brother there and give up music for business. One hold Milan had on him, however, was the lovely Elvira Gemignani, who in 1886 had given him a son, Antonio, and who had become his life's mate.

He did not give up writing operas, once he decided to remain in Milan. He went to work on a text whose heroine was Manon Lescaut in the romance by Abbé Prévost that Massenet had already used for an opera (*Manon*) that had won world recognition. Puccini, the novice, was challenging a champion—and he recognized the danger involved. But the character of Manon Lescaut (the first of Puccini's unforgettable female portraits) fascinated him, as did her tragic love affair with the young Des Grieux. This was material that suited his musical style perfectly. Puccini felt his creative powers awakened.

Puccini's gamble in competing with Massenet paid off. Puccini's *Manon Lescaut* was produced in Turin on February 1, 1893. The affecting tenderness, the poignancy, the grace that would characterize Puccini's musical writing in later operas were already in evidence— especially in arias like "Ah, Manon, mi tradisce," in which young Des Grieux accuses his beloved of having betrayed him, and Manon's yearning to return to the humble abode where she had known such happiness with Des Grieux. The first-night audience was as ecstatic over the opera as the critics. The reviewer for the Milan *Corriere della sera* said: *"Manon Lescaut* is the work of genius conscious of his own power, master of his art, and perfecter of it. *Manon* can be ranked with classical operas." Already, Puccini was beginning to have a following. More than that he was becoming recognized as the one most worthy to wear the robes of Verdi.

He wore those robes well, as he proved with his next opera, *La Bohème,* a story about Bohemian artists in Paris. Puccini knew that

Leoncavallo was also working on an opera based on this very same subject, but this did not discourage him. "There will be two *Bohèmes*," he quietly told Leoncavallo when the latter met him at a café to dissuade Puccini from competing with him.

Puccini's opera was the one heard first—in Turin on February 1, 1896. On that evening it looked as if Leoncavallo would probably emerge the victor in his competition with Puccini, since Puccini's opera was not well received. It was too simple in its material, had too much *verismo* in its naturalism, was too much concerned with love, compassion, humanity, and pathos rather than with big climactic scenes to satisfy the Turinese public. But later the same year, in Palermo, *La Bohème* received a much better reaction as the human values of the opera became more fully evident, and the gentle sadness of Puccini's wonderful score moved many in the audience to tears. By the end of the nineteenth century, *La Bohème* had become a favorite in Europe and America. Poor Leoncavallo! His own *La Bohème* was heard in Venice on May 6, 1897. It was a good opera and was recognized as such. But it was not long before it was thrown into total obscurity by the luminous incandescence of Puccini's masterwork—something for which Leoncavallo never forgave Puccini.

Puccini's opera does not begin with an overture but with just a few introductory measures in the orchestra (a general practice with him, just as it had been—with a few important exceptions—with Verdi). We are in an attic in the artists' quarter of Paris in 1830 with Rodolfo, a poet, and his artistic, or Bohemian, friends. Across the hall lives Mimi, who is wasting away with consumption. Rodolfo and Mimi fall in love. In spite of frequent hunger and cold, the Bohemians manage to enjoy life—especially when one of them comes upon enough funds to buy food, drink, and fuel for all. In time, after misunderstandings and quarrels, Rodolfo and Mimi decide to part permanently. But at one of the improvised celebrations in Rodolfo's attic, one day, Mimi arrives. She is deathly sick. Rodolfo puts her to bed and sends out for medicine. The lovers are reconciled—but too late, for Mimi dies.

No Italian opera composer half a century earlier would have dared to present so faithful a picture of life among artists in Paris in which the characters come so vibrantly to life, where the main interest is centered on their personal involvements and problems, frustrations and sorrows, and little joys. This is true *verismo,* just as it is true Puccini. In his most famous arias Puccini is gentle, melancholy, sensitive: in Rodolfo's autobiographical narrative to Mimi, "Che gelida manina"; in Mimi's aria

Santuzza (Grace Bumbry) sings to Mamma Lucia (Carlotta Ordassy) of her love for Turiddu. A Metropolitan Opera production of Cavalleria rusticana.

Giacomo Puccini.

*Butterfly (Gabriella Tucci) with her son and the American consul,
Sharpless (Clifford Harvuot). A Metropolitan Opera production.*

At the world premiere of La Fanciulla del West *at the Metropolitan Opera on December 10, 1910, the role of Johnson was sung by Enrico Caruso (center). Pasquale Amato (right) created the role of Jack Rance. The conductor was Arturo Toscanini.*

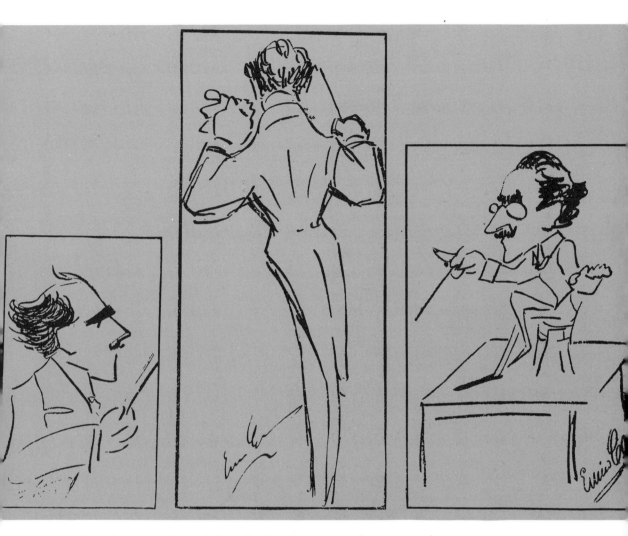

*Sketches of Maestro Toscanini conducting an opera performance and
(right) a rehearsal, drawn by the tenor Enrico Caruso.*

that follows in which she yearns for the warmth of springtime in "Mi chiamano Mimi"; in the love duet of Mimi and Rodolfo, "O soave fanciulla." And Puccini can also be as full of life's joy as are the Bohemians when they celebrate Christmas Eve at a café in the Latin Quarter—as in Musetta's coquettish waltz, "Quando m'en vo' soletta."

Puccini maintained his position as Verdi's successor with two masterpieces: *Tosca,* given in Rome on January 14, 1900; then *Madama Butterfly,* produced at La Scala on February 17, 1904.

Tosca came out of a blood-and-thunder French drama by Sardou, which lent itself to the virile, passionate music favored by the *verismo* movement. Three dynamic chords that precede the rise of the first-act curtain are heard throughout the opera to identify its villain, Baron Scarpia. In Rome, in 1800, Scarpia, chief of police, seeks to win the love of Tosca, a beautiful opera singer. His principal obstacle is the painter Cavaradossi, who loves and is loved by Tosca. Cavaradossi's ecstasy over Tosca's beauty, expressed in "Recondita armonia," is the first of several melodic gems.

Scarpia connives to have Cavaradossi arrested and condemned to death. He also arranges for Tosca to be present to hear Cavaradossi's cries of anguish as he is being tortured in an adjoining chamber. In her great aria "Vissi d'arte," Tosca becomes bitter at the way fate has been cruel to her, she who has always been true to art, love, and prayer. Tosca makes a bargain with Scarpia, to give herself to him if in turn he releases Cavaradossi. Scarpia makes a pretense of ordering Cavaradossi's release. Convinced her lover is safe, Tosca fatally stabs Scarpia. But Cavaradossi is still in his cell awaiting execution. There he bids Tosca good-bye in "E lucevan le stelle." When Cavaradossi is the victim of a firing squad, Tosca goes to her death by jumping off a high wall.

It seemed to have been Puccini's fate to have his greatest operas dismissed lightly or rejected at first hearing, only to have them bask in the sunshine of world adulation later. This had happened to *La Bohème,* and it happened again to *Tosca.* In stressing violence, particularly in the vividly pictorial music accompanying Cavaradossi's torture, Puccini was giving his audience an unpalatable diet—unpalatable, that is, when first tasted. But *Tosca,* like *La Bohème,* proved an acquired taste. In less than five years the shock of Puccini's realistic musical writing seemed cushioned, and the powerful drama found admirers everywhere.

Madama Butterfly was also a failure when first produced. One can understand why. The esoteric setting in Japan, something not usual in opera; Puccini's interest in naturalism that induced him to quote "The

Star-Spangled Banner" to identify Americans, and, in portraying the Japanese, to spice his writing with the Oriental five-tone scale and exotic harmonies; the introduction of American characters and a Japanese heroine in an Italian opera; ending his opera with discordant outcries in the orchestra to accentuate the tragedy that had befallen the heroine—all this was just too foreign, too startlingly new to suit the tastes of audiences unaccustomed to such heresy in opera. Almost as soon as the curtain rose, sounds of disapproval were heard in the theater, until pandemonium developed. From his seat in the box, Puccini screamed at the audience: "Louder, you beasts! Shriek at me. Yell! But you will see who is right. This is the best opera I have written." The following morning a Milan newspaper had this blazing headline: "The Fiasco of Maestro Puccini."

After the premiere, at the advice of Toscanini, Puccini made some revisions that made his opera somewhat more traditional. Where the opera had previously been in two acts it was now divided into three. The role of the hero was developed to enable him to sing a new aria. Puccini also included some other fresh musical material in his identifiable lyric style.

With these changes, *Madama Butterfly* was given in Brescia on May 28, 1904. The changes seemed to have made the difference (or perhaps the audience by now had come expecting the opera's exotic setting and characters and original musical treatment). The enchanting work cast its spell. Its success elsewhere in Italy followed immediately. Thus like a phoenix rising from the ashes of defeat, *Madama Butterfly,* repeating the history of *La Bohème* and *Tosca,* soared to victory. The composer had been vindicated, a particularly sweet development for Puccini since he had written this opera at a time when he had been an invalid for many months—the result of an automobile accident in 1903 in which he was almost killed but escaped with a fractured right tibia.

Who does not know the pathetic tale of *Madama Butterfly,* a tale made famous before Puccini wrote his opera through an American drama by David Belasco that had been a great hit both on Broadway and in London? Madama Butterfly is Cio-Cio-San—in nineteenth-century Nagasaki—who has a love affair with the American naval lieutenant Pinkerton, whom she expects to marry. They have a child. But after going away, Pinkerton returns, bringing with him an American wife. Cio-Cio-San, after bidding permanent farewell to her son, whom she has agreed to give to Pinkerton, goes behind a screen and plunges a dagger into her heart.

155

And who is not familiar with its wonderful melodies, particularly "Un bel dì," in which Cio-Cio-San expresses her confidence that her lover will return to her? The duets "Amore o grillo" and "Viene la sera," Pinkerton's aria "Addio, fiorito asil," and Cio-Cio-San's farewell to her son, "Tu, Tu, piccolo iddio!" are hardly less eloquent.

Puccini, grown famous and wealthy through the success of his operas, was a man of the world—sophisticated, handsome, well poised. Always dressed in the latest fashion, his dapper hat tipped over a strikingly attractive face, his mustache neatly trimmed, he was somebody to notice and admire, even if you did not know he was the most celebrated Italian opera composer since Verdi. He had the air of a nobleman, and he lived like one, at a Florentine villa at the edge of a lake, at Torre del Lago, which he shared with his common-law wife, Elvira, and their son. He was a gourmet whose table was famous. He loved beautiful women and high-powered cars, which he drove at breakneck speed. He smoked incessantly.

He had everything a man might desire—genius, money, luxury, a handsome appearance, worldwide adulation, the love of friends. Yet he was more often melancholy and despondent than happy. One of the reasons for his almost chronic melancholia may have been that he greatly underestimated what he had accomplished and what he was capable of doing in opera. "The only music I can or will make is that of small things," he once said. On another occasion, in discussing Wagner, he remarked that "beside him we are all mandolin players."

The world continued to do him homage. In 1906, he was invited by the Metropolitan Opera to come to America for the first time to help supervise a production of *Madama Butterfly* (a premiere for that company). When his ship docked, he learned that *Manon Lescaut* was being given at the Metropolitan. He headed straight for the auditorium, arriving after his opera had begun. At the end of the first act the audience discovered that Puccini was among them. The ovation that burst out awed Puccini. As for the *Madama Butterfly* premiere at the Metropolitan Opera on February 11, 1907—this, too, was given a regal reception, particularly after the final curtain.

Infatuated with America, and deeply moved by the way Americans were honoring him, Puccini decided to write an opera with an American setting—a token of gratitude. For this purpose he again chose a play by David Belasco: a love story involving the female owner of a saloon and an escaped bandit in California during the days of the gold rush. She contrives to save his life when he is captured by the law and sentenced to hang; then they get married. *La Fanciulla del West* (*The Girl of the Golden West*), as Puccini called his new opera, was given a magnificent world premiere at the Metropolitan Opera, which had commissioned it, on December 10, 1910.

Some of the world's greatest performers participated: Caruso and Emmy Destinn, with Toscanini in the conductor's pit. The cream of New York society was present for what was one of the most brilliant and most talked-about premieres in the early history of the Metropolitan Opera. Thus the new Puccini opera got a wonderful send-off. But the opera never quite succeeded in capturing the love of even rabid Puccini fans. Puccini was not at his best writing an opera about the old American West, and not in his element introducing into his score syncopated rhythms to give it an American air. His opera, for all his efforts to flavor it with American condiments, remained an Italian dish—but one disguised as an American delicacy.

The critics did not have to tell Puccini that his opera was one of his lesser efforts. Stung by his setback, Puccini wrote no more operas for the next seven years. When he broke this silence, he still failed to return to the heights of *La Bohème, Tosca,* and *Madama Butterfly. La Rondine,* mounted in Monte Carlo on March 27, 1917, was Puccini in a light mood—a sort of compromise between opera and operetta. Except for one or two arias, this is not the work of a master.

A commission from the Metropolitan Opera then led to the writing of three one-act operas, collectively known as *Il Trittico (The Triptych).* It was heard on a single evening in New York on December 14, 1918. Each opera has a strikingly different personality. *Il Tabarro (The Cloak)* is a somber drama in which the lover of a faithless wife is murdered by her husband. *Suor Angelica (Sister Angelica)* combines tragedy with religion. In a seventeenth-century convent a nun, after failing to expiate an old sin, commits suicide. The most popular of this trio of little operas is a comedy, *Gianni Schicchi,* in which a wily lawyer in thirteenth-century Florence devises an elaborate plot to gain the inheritance of a recently deceased wealthy man. *Gianni Schicchi* has the spirit of *opera buffa.* "Addio Firenze" is Schicchi's tribute to Florence in a spirit of mockery, while in "O mio babbino caro" Puccini satirizes his own sentimental type of aria.

Puccini wrote only one more opera, and that one was left unfinished by his death—*Turandot,* in many respects his most original, experimental, and adventurous work. Influenced by some of the new techniques being used by composers in the early twentieth century, Puccini used discords, unorthodox scales and modulations, and even the then avant-garde technique of using two tonalities simultaneously. The libretto is set in China in legendary times. Turandot is a beautiful princess who offers to marry any man able to answer three questions; if he fails to do so he must give up his life. Prince Calaf, who is loved by a slave girl, Liù, is ready to meet this challenge, much to Liù's distress. But Calaf answers the three questions. After some other complications arise and are overcome, a genuine love interest binds Turandot and Calaf. Liù, having lost the man she loves, commits suicide.

Together with a modern style and occasional excursions into Orientalism, Puccini filled his opera with the kind of gentle, sensitive melodies for which he had become so beloved. The best-known arias are "Non piangere, Liù" (Prince Calaf's consolatory words to Liù when she reveals how she fears for his life) and "Nessun dorma," in which Prince Calaf, conscious how troubled Turandot is, wishes he could soothe her with a kiss.

Puccini was working on the third act of *Turandot* in 1924 when he was stricken by cancer of the throat. Following an operation in Brussels, he died of a heart attack on November 29, 1924. His body was returned to Milan, and two years later transferred to a mausoleum at Torre del Lago.

The world premiere of *Turandot* took place at La Scala on April 25, 1926. Before he died, Puccini had said to Toscanini (then the musical director of La Scala) that if *Turandot* was not completed, it should be performed in its unfinished state. This is exactly how the opera was performed on opening night, although the score had actually been completed by another composer. At the first performance, in the middle of the third act, the opera stopped short. The curtain remained raised. The performers stood frozen in the positions they had previously assumed. Turning around to the audience, Toscanini said, while tears streamed down his cheeks: "Here, here, the master laid down his pen."

However, when we hear Turandot now it is not as an unfinished opera. The work of completing it was done by Franco Alfano (1876–1954), himself a well-esteemed opera composer. He revealed unusual empathy with Puccini in assuming the master's style. Listening to the complete *Turandot,* we find it truly difficult to say where Puccini stops and Alfano begins. The seams in the sewn-together fabric do not show. Could he have known, Puccini would have been happy to know that, thanks to Alfano, his career had ended with a completed master-work.

II

Germanic Greatness

Richard Wagner

Even in their last operas, Verdi and Puccini had poured new wine into old bottles, the bottles that their predecessors had created for them. Richard Wagner (1813–83) also started out that way. In his earlier works we can readily recognize the influence of Weber and Meyerbeer. Then slowly Wagner began coming to the realization that if opera were to achieve its destiny as a vibrant, compelling art form, it had to change its character completely. Once Wagner saw the vision of what opera's future should be, he could no longer affiliate himself with the past. He had to chart his own course. In doing so, he discovered for opera a new world.

Wagner, therefore, represents for opera not evolution, as Verdi and Puccini did, but revolution. With Wagner comes the overthrow of the old order and the construction of a new one. With the later Wagner master-works a totally new concept, a new set of aesthetics, and new techniques come into being. Opera, with Wagner, becomes musical drama.

There is much in Wagner the man with which we can find fault. Indeed, the famous American composer and critic Deems Taylor once wrote a personal portrait of Wagner entitled "The Monster." Wagner was supremely selfish and ruthless. He held existing standards of morality, ethics, and codes of behavior in contempt and led his life according to his own questionable standards. He lied and cheated without a twinge of conscience. He was as incapable of generosity as he was of gratitude. He made love to the wives of his friends who helped support him and who promoted his music passionately. He was a hedonist whose own pleasures, desires, and needs were all that counted with him. In reaching for them he was oblivious to the hurts he inflicted even upon those near to him. People were there for him to exploit.

He lived exclusively for himself, convinced that the world owed him a debt it could never repay because he was a genius. He considered himself one of the greatest dramatists, poets, and musicians the world had known. He demanded a similar evaluation of himself from those who would be his friends; all others were enemies. Completely self-centered and self-adulating, he had only a single topic that interested him—his art.

He had all these disagreeable qualities and a carload of others. But as Deems Taylor comments in his portrait in *Of Men and Music,* "it doesn't matter in the least." Taylor adds, ". . . because this undersized, sickly, disagreeable, fascinating little man was right all the time. The joke was on us. He *was* one of the world's great dramatists; he *was* a great thinker; he *was* one of the most stupendous musical geniuses that, up to now, the world has ever seen. The world did owe him a living. . . . When you listen to what he wrote, the debts and heartaches that people had to endure from him don't seem much of a price."

We can and we must accept tolerantly Wagner's shortcomings as a human being, formidable though they are, not only because of what he accomplished—masterworks that caused a total upheaval in operatic history—but because where his art was concerned his integrity was of the highest. Regardless of how he behaved as a man, as an artist he never sold himself cheaply. In this area he could not cheat, be dishonest, avaricious, or motivated by monetary gains or personal considerations.

"Listening to his music," concludes Taylor, "one does not forgive him for what he may or may not have been. It is not a matter of forgiveness. It is a matter of being dumb with wonder that his poor brain and body didn't burst with the torment of the demon of creative energy, that lived inside him, struggling, clawing, scratching to be released; tearing, shrieking at him to write the music that was in him. The miracle is that what he did in the little space of seventy years could have been done at all, even by a great genius. Is it any wonder that he had no time to be a

man?"

Wilhelm Richard Wagner was born in Leipzig, Germany, on May 22, 1813. It is now thought likely that he was the illegitimate son of Ludwig Geyer, an actor, and Johanna, wife of Karl Friedrich Wagner. Karl Friedrich died when Richard was six months old. Geyer and the widow Wagner were married nine months later, and it was they who raised Richard. At elementary school, the boy revealed a keen interest in literature, history, Greek, and mythology. The lessons he took on the violin and piano, away from school, revealed no talent in the direction of music. As time passed, the boy's irresponsibility and indolence proved stronger than his native intelligence. He was expelled from the Thomasschule for failing to concentrate on his studies. The short period he spent at the university was devoted far more to drinking and gambling than to textbooks.

He had to find himself. And he finally did so through music. Discovery of the wonders of music first came to him when he heard Weber's *Der Freischütz* and Beethoven's *Fidelio* and Seventh Symphony. Wagner was so moved by this music that, without any training in composition, he completed a string quartet, a piano sonata, and a concert overture, the last of which was performed in Leipzig in 1830.

Only now did Wagner receive a formal musical education, which consisted solely of six months of training in composition with Theodor Weinlig. With this his formal music study came to an end. From then on he acquired all his musical knowledge by poring over textbooks and treatises, and by analyzing the Beethoven symphonies. When we take into account his later marvelous (possibly incomparable) technique, such rudimentary and haphazard musical schooling is beyond belief.

In 1832 Wagner wrote the libretto and some musical sketches for his intended first opera, *Die Hochzeit,* which he never finished. He also composed a symphony, which was performed both in Leipzig and Prague. Wagner's first completed opera, *Die Feen,* was written while he was employed as chorus master of the Würzburg Opera in 1834. It failed to interest any opera house and remained unheard until five years after Wagner's death. Here, as in all his later operas, Wagner was his own librettist.

His second opera, *Das Liebesverbot,* based on Shakespeare's *Measure for Measure,* became his first dramatic work to be produced. It proved such a fiasco when it was introduced by the Magdeburg Opera (where Wagner was then employed as conductor) in 1836 that the opera company, never very solvent in the first place, went into bankruptcy.

For about one year Wagner was the conductor of the Königsberg

Opera. During this time he married Minna Planer, an actress, on November 24, 1836. After leaving Königsberg, Wagner served for two years as music director of the Riga Opera. His lifelong weakness for borrowing money indiscriminately and spending it recklessly proved his ruination. Fired by the company for failure to pay his debts, he was faced with a prison sentence. He fled with his wife from Riga and had to be smuggled aboard a ship sailing from Prussia to London because his passport had been confiscated. Five weeks after arriving in London, the Wagners crossed the Channel into France. They arrived in Paris with letters of introduction to several powerful musicians, including Meyerbeer.

In Paris Wagner encountered nothing but disappointments, frustrations, and personal humiliation. His letters of introduction failed to open a single door leading to a job. To keep from starving, Wagner had to do hackwork. Once again he began piling up debts. This time, in 1840, he was unable to escape a brief prison sentence.

His creativity, however, could not be smothered by his heartbreaking setbacks. He completed a concert overture that is still performed—*Eine Faust Ouvertüre* (*A Faust Overture*)—and the libretto and music for a new opera, *Rienzi*. All this was achieved in 1840. He also finished outlining the libretto for still another opera, *Der fliegende Holländer* (*The Flying Dutchman*). *Rienzi* was turned down by the Paris Opéra, which, however, was willing to buy his outline for *The Flying Dutchman* for a French composer. Wagner had no alternative but to accept the poor bargain. He needed the money desperately, not only for food and shelter but also for renting a piano so that he could work on his own musical setting of *The Flying Dutchman*.

Writing his new opera seemed to intoxicate him. "Everything went easily, fluently," he later recalled. "I actually shouted for joy, as I felt through my whole being that I was still an artist." Before Wagner completed his music, the Paris Opéra produced *The Flying Dutchman* with a score by Pierre-Louis Dietsch. It was a failure.

Suddenly a radical change of fortune took place for Wagner. *Rienzi* was magnificently produced by the Dresden Opera on October 20, 1842, with Wagner supervising the production. This was an opera on the grand scale of Meyerbeer, and very much in Meyerbeer's style. The libretto, based on a novel by Bulwer-Lytton, provided numerous opportunities for spectacle in the telling of a people's insurrection, led by Rienzi, in Rome in the fourteenth century. The drama ends with the burning of the Capitol, in which Rienzi meets his death. The excitement of the play is well carried over in Wagner's music, of which the overture is representative. *Rienzi* proved such a triumph that it entered the permanent repertory of the Dresden Opera. Through its performances there, and elsewhere in Europe, it helped to make Wagner's name and work respected for the first time.

The Dresden Opera now also produced *The Flying Dutchman,* on January 2, 1843. It was hardly the success that *Rienzi* had been, though it was a much finer work. The idea for writing this opera first came to Wagner while he and his wife were aboard ship fleeing from Riga. During a storm, with the ship being lashed by winds and thundering waves, Wagner suddenly recalled a story by Heinrich Heine based on an old German legend. It told of a Dutch sea captain who was forced to sail the seven seas until he could find redemption through the love of a worthy, faithful woman.

Wagner saw himself as the Dutch captain. He, too, seemed destined to wander aimlessly searching for the haven of success. He, too, sought redemption through the true love of a devoted woman. (By this time Wagner and his wife were frequently at odds with one another.)

Once Wagner identified himself with the Dutch sea captain, the strange tale haunted him until he sketched out a story for an opera libretto. In it, the Dutch sea captain is doomed to sail aboard *The Flying Dutchman.* Once every seven years he can come to shore to seek out a woman to redeem him. He finds her, at last, in eighteenth-century Norway, in Senta, who, though she is betrothed to Erik, falls in love with the Dutchman, whom she had first seen in a dream. She has conceived the hope of becoming the instrument for his redemption. Hearing Erik pleading with Senta, the Dutchman believes that she has forsaken him. He sails off on his ship for another seven-year voyage. From atop a cliff, Senta cries out to him that she loves him. She then jumps into the sea, a sacrifice that brings about the Dutchman's salvation.

In *Rienzi* Wagner has followed Meyerbeer's path, in *The Flying Dutchman,* Weber's. Thoroughly German-romantic, in the manner first established by Weber, is Wagner's overture for *The Flying Dutchman,* which quotes three of the principal melodies of the opera, in each of which we hear reverberations of German folk songs: the sailors' chorus, "Ho-jo-he!" the sailor's song with chorus, "Mit Gewitter und Sturm," and Senta's ballad about her hope to redeem the Dutchman, "Traft ihr das Schiff." Recognizably Germanic too (though not heard in the overture) is the spinning song of Senta and her friends, "Summ' und brumm."

In the rest of the opera, Wagner carries on the German national traditions of Weber, in music that is consistently dramatic or atmospheric or pictorial. Even in his selection of his text Wagner was following in Weber's footsteps by dipping into German folklore, a practice he would henceforth follow.

In 1843 Wagner was appointed musical director of the Dresden Opera. During the six years he held this post he brought to it the same high purpose and intransigent conscience that he did to composing. It was through his efforts that the Dresden Opera became one of the world's greatest opera companies.

While performing his exacting duties at the Dresden Opera he completed *Tannhäuser,* introduced there—though none too successfully— on October 19, 1845. Once again the libretto was taken from a German medieval legend, and once more the hero tries to achieve redemption through the true love of a woman.

Tannhäuser is a minstrel knight in the thirteenth century who has been enjoying carnal pleasures with Venus in the Venusberg. Finally weary of his sensual life there, he returns to his fellow-knights at the castle of the Wartburg where he is also reunited with his one-time beloved, Elisabeth. During a song contest among the knights Tannhäuser causes such shock and dismay with his description of the passionate love he had known with Venus that he is ordered to leave the Wartburg and seek absolution from the Pope in Rome. Tannhäuser joins a band of pilgrims bound for Rome, while Elisabeth waits for his return. When he reappears, he is weary and haggard. He reveals to Wolfram, a fellow knight, that absolution could never come to him unless leaves sprout forth on the Pope's staff. His misery is magnified with the death of Elisabeth. Only then does he receive the news that the Pope's staff has miraculously sprouted leaves and that he has been absolved of his sins.

More than in his earlier operas, Wagner here uses the overture to summarize the action of the drama. This overture opens with the "Pilgrim's Chorus," which recurs throughout the opera. It is followed by a quotation of the bacchanale music from the opening Venusberg scene, and by Tannhäuser's ecstatic song of praise to Venus during the song contest of the knights.

Preceding the third act is an orchestral prelude to which Wagner gave the title of "Tannhäuser's Pilgrimage." This is somber music speaking of Tannhäuser's penitence and suffering and depicting Elisabeth's sympathetic response.

Of the many vocal passages that should be singled out because of their popularity are the following: the march music with chorus when the knights enter the great hall of the Wartburg ("Freudig begrüssen"), a hall to which Elisabeth had previously paid eloquent tribute in "Dich, teure Halle"; Elisabeth's prayer to the Holy Virgin for Tannhäuser's absolution, "Allmächt'ge Jungfrau"; and Wolfram's ode to the evening star, "O du mein holder Abendstern."

Wagner had traveled far in *Tannhäuser* toward what would become his ultimate artistic mission in opera. Already we can begin to detect hints of later methods. One is the use of the "leading motive" (*Leitmotiv*). This is a musical theme identifying a character, situation, object, mood, or idea, which recurs throughout the opera whenever the character, situation, object, mood, or idea is suggested in the text. In *Tannhäuser* leading motives are used sparingly—but they are there. Another later Wagnerian device found to a limited extent in *Tannhäuser* is the use of extended narrative, more melodic and expressive than recitative, though less lyrical than an aria. Such narratives give a character the opportunity to describe at length either his personal history or an experience. Tannhäuser's recital of his pilgrimage to Rome in "Inbrunst im Herzen" is one of these.

When *Tannhäuser* was first given, many in the audience were shocked by the sensuality of Wagner's text and music while others objected to the way in which the story glorified Catholicism. When the opera was introduced to Paris in 1861, it created a scandal for quite a different reason. For this performance Wagner wrote the bacchanale music for the opening of the first act, to cater to the love of the French for ballet. Since the rich and the powerful in Paris invariably arrived late at the opera house, they insisted that Wagner transfer the bacchanale to a later part of the opera, which he stubbornly refused to do. The anger of the social elite reached such a pitch that at each of the first three performances it instigated an explosive demonstration. Further performances of *Tannhäuser* in Paris had to be canceled.

Redemption through love. . . . This theme continued to fascinate Wagner as he progressed to his next opera, *Lohengrin. Lohengrin* forms the transition from Wagner's early operas, through *Tannhäuser,* to his later music dramas. The narrative writing is now used so expansively that the recitative is completely dispensed with; in *Lohengrin* we begin to get that continuous flow of music that would soon be Wagner's goal. Greater use of the leading-motive technique is found in *Lohengrin* than in *Tannhäuser;* the orchestra is used more symphonically; the importance of individual arias is minimized for the sake of a more unified musical texture. Perhaps nowhere is a new Wagner more in evidence than in the opening orchestral prelude. (Like Gluck before him, Wagner replaces the overture with a prelude to set the mood and establish the atmosphere for the opera.) The prelude to *Lohengrin* has a spiritual exaltation and radiance which we meet again in Wagner's last music drama, *Parsifal*.

The story of *Lohengrin* takes place in Antwerp in the tenth century. Elsa, a noblewoman of Brabant, is falsely accused of having killed her brother. She tells of how, in a dream ("Einsam in trüben Tagen"), she has seen a knight come forth as her protector. When a knight does arrive in a boat pulled by a swan, he refuses to identify himself or reveal whence he came. He extracts from Elsa the promise that she will never try to uncover his identity. The knight engages Elsa's accuser, Telramund, in battle, defeats him, then magnanimously refuses to kill him. Disgraced, Telramund and his wife, Ortrud, seek vengeance.

Now a magnificent procession leads Elsa and the knight to the cathedral where they are to be married. As Elsa mounts the steps, Ortrud and Telramund arouse her suspicions about the knight, maintaining he is a magician with supernatural powers. But the marriage proceeds, accompanied by the music of one of the most famous wedding marches ever written ("Treulich geführt"). Elsa's doubts about the knight begin to gnaw within her until she breaks her promise and asks him his name. Finally, in his narrative "In fernem Land," the knight reveals that he is Lohengrin, the son of Parsifal and a knight of the Holy Grail. His mission is to fight evil and injustice. Now that he has made his identity known he must leave Elsa and Brabant forever.

His swan-drawn boat comes to take him away. We now learn that the swan is Elsa's brother, who had been transformed through Ortrud's evil powers. Lohengrin tears the chain from around the swan's neck, destroys the evil spell, and restores Elsa's brother to his human form. Then Lohengrin departs, much to the distress of all the people of Brabant, and of Elsa, who falls dead.

Wagner completed the writing of *Lohengrin* in 1848. Its premiere had to wait two years, and had to take place in Weimar rather than Dresden, because by 1848 Wagner had become a political exile. In the revolutions that swept across Europe at the time, Wagner had become an active member of a radical group. When the revolution in Germany collapsed, the instigators were arrested. Wagner evaded prison by fleeing with his wife from Dresden, hiding for a while at the home of Franz Liszt in Weimar, and then in May of 1849 finding a new place to live—the city of Zürich

in Switzerland, where he remained a dozen years.

Franz Liszt was the musical director in Weimar, and Liszt decided to present *Lohengrin* in that city under his own responsibility—an act of rare courage and idealism when Wagner was in disgrace in Germany. That premiere took place on August 28, 1850. The opera was not too well liked at first, but within a decade it became the most widely performed and appreciated of all of Wagner's operas.

The dozen or so years that Wagner lived in Zürich were decisive both for the artist and the man. As an artist, Wagner now began to formalize his new ideas about opera, creating the first stirring of that revolution which ultimately transformed opera into music drama. Opera, he maintained, should be the synthesis of many arts, each serving the others as an equal partner, with music sharing the spotlight with (but never usurping it from) drama, poetry, acting, and staging. Nothing superfluous to the overall artistic concept can be included; all elements must be integral to it. Henceforth, therefore, Wagner dispensed with ballet, except in *The Mastersingers* and *Parsifal,* and rarely used a chorus.

The music should be a continuous flow, some parts more lyrical or dramatic than others, other parts extended narratives, but never broken up into recitatives, arias, ensemble numbers, and so forth. To achieve this fluidity Wagner did something then completely revolutionary in harmonic writing: he introduced so many chromaticisms (sharps and flats), that a basic tonality was often dispensed with. The music could thus move easily from one key to another even though discords were thereby frequently created.

The orchestra was to assume a role as important as—sometimes more important than—the voice. Its size was greatly expanded to full symphonic proportions and included some instruments never before found in an opera orchestra. One of these was of Wagner's own invention: the Wagnerian tuba, a compromise between the horn and the trombone, whose color was darker than either instrument and whose quality had greater virility.

The musical fabric of an opera was to be made up of dozens of leading motives, sometimes combined in complex polyphonic pattern, sometimes heard in succession. Through these leading motives the action on the stage would unfold in the music as vividly and as pictorially as in the text. The articulateness of music was expanded through the development of the techniques of singing and orchestral performance far beyond anything yet conceived.

In addition to this, Wagner worked out new schemes for staging; described in detail the structure of an ideal opera house; and clarified numerous other concepts that he felt would make for ideal opera performances.

To put theory into practice, Wagner began mapping out a mighty drama based on material from Teutonic myth and legend, particularly the story of the Nibelungs, an evil race possessing a hoard of magic gold. When he finished his first libretto, which he named *Siegfried's Death,* he realized he needed another music drama to precede it, explaining some of the plot developments in his libretto. As it turned out, each time he finished a libretto, he felt the need for another to go before and clarify the plot details. As finally conceived, this mighty work became four dramas, written in reverse order to that intended for their performance.

The first in order of performance is *Das Rheingold* (*The Rhinegold*), serving as a prelude to the next three texts. The other three are *Die Walküre* (*The Valkyrie*), *Siegfried,* and *Götterdämmerung* (*Twilight of the Gods*). By 1852 all four texts were finished, and a year later they were published. To the whole giant project (one without parallel in music, if not in all art) Wagner gave the collective title of *Der Ring des Nibelungen* (*The Ring of the Nibelungs*).

While all this elaborate thinking, planning, theorizing, and writing of librettos was going on, Wagner's personal life was becoming enmeshed in complications. Marital difficulties with Minna (for which both partners seem to share the blame) had reached the point of combustion. Minna could not understand why Wagner, who had already become so successful by writing in a more traditional format, should embark on an artistic project requiring so many years for completion. She thought no opera house would produce the operas because the demands made by this giant project on performers and stagecraft could not be met, and that writing it would reduce her husband and herself to permanent penury. Disagreement with him on any subject—and particularly about his art—was something Wagner could never tolerate. And so, husband and wife kept quarreling continually until their marriage erupted into open warfare. This stormy relationship before long depleted Minna's physical and mental resources.

Minna had an even more serious complaint against her husband than his work and artistic dreams. He was openly, unashamedly unfaithful to her. In 1850 he made love to the wife of one of his benefactors and almost convinced her to desert her husband. Then, after coming to Zürich, he fell in love and carried on a passionate relationship with Mathilde Wesendonk, wife of an affluent merchant who recognized Wagner's genius. Otto Wesendonk financed several Wagner concerts in Zürich, all proceeds going to the composer. In 1857, he provided the Wagners with a villa on the Wesendonk grounds in Zürich for a most modest rental. Wagner rewarded this generosity by trying to steal Mathilde permanently away from her husband. He failed. After a stormy session with his patron, Wagner was forced to leave his comfortable villa and head for Paris.

While the beneficiary of Wesendonk's generosity, Wagner proved highly productive artistically. By 1854 he had finished the music for *The Rhinegold* and by 1856 for *The Valkyrie*. Between 1857 and 1858 he wrote a cycle of songs to poems by Mathilde Wesendonk, the best known of which is "Träume" ("Dreams"), which Wagner played under Mathilde's window on her birthday. And, temporarily interrupting his Herculean labors on *The Ring of the Nibelungs* before proceeding with the final two dramas, he worked on a totally different music drama, *Tristan und Isolde* (*Tristan and Isolde*), a story involving an all-consuming love.

In 1861, he went to Vienna, where *Tristan and Isolde* was scheduled for its premiere. So difficult did this music appear to singers and orchestra players that they regarded it as impossible to perform. Wagner, of course, was completely unwilling to make a single change. *Tristan and Isolde* had to be given as he had conceived it, or not at all. After fifty-seven grueling rehearsals, the opera house finally decided to abandon *Tristan and Isolde*.

This, to be sure, was a crushing disappointment to Wagner, but hardly one to choke his creativity. By 1862, the second of two governmental amnesties finally permitted Wagner to reenter and travel in all parts of Germany. With the last of the two *Ring* scores still to be composed, Wagner went on to work on still another music drama, this time a comedy, the first such he had ever tried writing. Once he began to work out his ideas on *Die Meistersinger* (*The Mastersingers*), he was a new man. "I felt," he said, "once more the master of my Fate." It took Wagner five years—between 1862 and 1867—to write this opera.

In 1862, the now somewhat mentally disturbed Minna and Wagner were divorced. About a year later he fell in love again, this time with a woman who would share the rest of his life: Cosima von Bülow, daughter of Franz Liszt and wife of a distinguished pianist and conductor who was one of Wagner's most ardent admirers.

Hans von Bülow and his wife, Cosima, came to Munich in September of 1864 for von Bülow to fill the post of pianist to the king. Wagner followed them to that city a month or so later, taking residence in a royal house provided him by Ludwig II, recently become king of Bavaria. The king was a passionate Wagnerite. He became Wagner's most munificent patron, supporting him handsomely, enabling him to enjoy those luxuries which were as important to Wagner's well-being as food and drink. The king offered him something far more important, too. He would spare no expense in producing every music drama Wagner wrote and would personally see to it that they were presented according to Wagner's most exacting and fastidious requirements. And so, on June 10, 1865, there took place at the Munich Court Opera the world premiere of *Tristan and Isolde,* followed on June 21, 1868, by the first presentation anywhere of *The Mastersingers*. Hans von Bülow conducted both music dramas.

Since the two already-completed parts of the *Ring* cycle were not introduced until 1869 and 1870 respectively, *Tristan and Isolde* became the first of Wagner's music dramas to be heard. Here there was no compromise with the principles that were guiding Wagner in the writing of the *Ring*. The structure was as expansive as any one of the *Ring* dramas, the techniques for voice and for orchestra no less complex, and the idiom no less advanced and daring in its harmonic and tonal procedures. Here, as in the *Ring,* we find realized the concept of a synthesis of the arts; here Wagner successfully carried through his aim to produce "continuous melody"; here an elaborate use of leading motives and chromaticism is made. But there is an important difference between *Tristan* and the dramas in the *Ring*. In the *Ring,* Wagner's characters are legendary gods and goddesses; in *Tristan* they are human beings caught in the trap of a love affair they cannot escape, destroyed by a passion they cannot suppress.

Isolde is an Irish princess of legendary times who is brought to Cornwall by King Mark's faithful nephew, Tristan, a knight, so that she may marry the king. Tristan and Isolde had fallen in love but could not declare it. Now, aboard ship to Cornwall, through a love potion prepared by Isolde's servant, Brangäne, they are moved to admit their love for each other. After they reach Cornwall, and Isolde marries the king, she and Tristan are unable to deny their emotions, and manage to meet secretly. An ecstatic love idyll takes place in the garden of the palace. The love duet now heard ("O sink' hernieder") and the passionate phrases in the orchestra make the scene—known as the "Liebesnacht" ("Love-Night")—unquestionably one of the most sensuous love episodes in all opera. Tristan and Isolde are discovered in the garden by King Mark, one of whose men attacks Tristan and wounds him seriously.

Tristan is brought to a castle in Brittany by his faithful henchman. Isolde follows them there just before Tristan dies. Isolde's farewell to Tristan is the "Liebestod" ("Love-Death") music ("Mild und leise"), after which she sinks down on Tristan's body and expires. (At symphony concerts it is a frequent practice to couple the first-act prelude with an orchestral version of the "Love-Death" music.)

When we consider how completely different *Tristan and Isolde* is from any opera written before it, and when we realize that Munich was swarming with Wagner's enemies out to sabotage the premiere, the success of the opera at its first presentation is truly extraordinary.

Wagner, then, was beginning to build a base of followers who believed in his new operatic ideas and ideals. But as has already been implied, his enemies were also numerous; they were out to destroy him. Some of them felt that Wagner was exerting too strong an influence on the king; some resented the formidable costs involved in backing Wagner and his dramas: still others could not comprehend Wagner's kind of opera and reacted contemptuously to his pretentious methods and aims. And there were a good many people in Munich who were shocked by the way Wagner was conducting his personal life, with indiscretions he took no trouble to conceal.

Wagner's personal life in Munich involved Cosima von Bülow. With a total disregard of public opinion they carried on as tempestuous a love affair as Tristan did with Isolde (Hans von Bülow being placed in the role of King Mark in this true-to-life romance). In 1865 a daughter was born to Cosima von Bülow and Wagner whom they named Isolde. Hans von Bülow accepted this sorry situation as stoically as he could; up to the time of his final separation and divorce from Cosima he kept up the fiction that Isolde (and after that a second daughter, born in 1866) were his own children. It speaks volumes of von Bülow's honor as a musician that he refused to allow his personal bitterness against Wagner ever to influence in any way his high esteem of Wagner's art, which he continued to promote with full dedication.

In time, so potent did Wagner's enemies become that they were finally able to compel the king to send Wagner, Cosima, and their children out of the city. Wagner and Cosima found a new home in Triebschen, near Lake Lucerne in Switzerland, where they stayed six years, until 1871. The break between Cosima and her husband, Hans, was now irreparable. "If it had been anyone but Wagner," von Bülow said sadly, "I would have killed him." Cosima's father, Franz Liszt, horrified by his daughter's actions, refused for many years to have any personal contact with *171* either her or Wagner. But as with von Bülow, his anger and hostility in no way affected his lofty admiration of Wagner the genius.

On June 6, 1869, Cosima gave birth to a third child—a son, Siegfried. A year later, when Cosima's divorce from Hans von Bülow was at last finalized, Wagner and Cosima were married. In Cosima, Wagner had finally found the love, devotion, and dedication of a woman whose life's sole aim was to serve his every whim, mood, or need—an aim that Wagner fully approved.

Even with Wagner away from Munich, and even with Wagner's enemies using their influence at court, King Ludwig still stood ready to use his power and wealth to bring about the premiere of *The Mastersingers* in Munich. This took place at the Court Opera on June 21, 1868, with Wagner allowed to be present at the performance.

Die Meistersinger von Nürnberg (The Mastersingers of Nuremberg) —to give the work its full title—begins with a majestic overture that includes musical material from the opera. As in *Tannhäuser,* a song contest is the pivot on which the plot spins. The "mastersingers" were actual guilds of poet-musicians that flourished in Germany from the thirteenth to the sixteenth centuries. Of these Hans Sachs had been a distinguished member. These mastersingers created songs to set rules, usually on biblical subjects. Contests for such song writing were held regularly. In Wagner's music drama, the guild is one in Nuremberg, Germany, in the sixteenth century. Walther von Stolzing, a knight, loves Eva, whose hand in marriage may be won by the singer who captures the prize in a mastersingers' song contest. In a preliminary contest Walther makes a mess of his song writing since he has refused to adhere to the rigid guild rules governing composition.

This causes keen disappointment to Hans Sachs, a cobbler-philosopher, since he recognizes Walther's inherent original talent. In a dream, Walther hears a melody, which he later describes to Hans Sachs and which Sachs convinces him to present at the main song contest. With this so-called "Prize Song," during a festive ceremony, Walther wins both the contest and Eva's hand and becomes an official member of the guild. Walther's rival for the prize and for Eva is a ridiculous fellow called Beckmesser who has no trouble making a fool of himself at the contest.

It is not difficult to recognize in this story an attempt by Wagner to be autobiographical. Walther is Wagner, who achieves greatness and originality at the price of breaking established rules. Beckmesser, the villain, is a caricature of the powerful Viennese music critic, Eduard Hanslick, who was a tireless, virulent opponent of Wagner. Walther's success in the contest represents Wagner's own artistic victory over the opposing forces of reaction and stupidity.

It is a far different kind of Wagnerian music that we hear in *The Mastersingers* from that of *Tristan and Isolde* and the *Ring* cycle. Though this was Wagner's first try at writing comedy in music drama, he proved he could be broadly humorous as well as stingingly satirical, qualities found in none of the other Wagner music dramas. Wagner, for the first and last time, selected lovable characters like Walther, Eva, and particularly Hans Sachs, and presented them with encompassing sympathy and humanity. A warm heart pulses throughout this masterpiece, especially when Hans Sachs is on stage—one of the rare instances when Wagner succeeds in completely divorcing his own personality from that of a character he is portraying. "Almost everywhere else," says the historian H. C. Colles, "Wagner's heroes are tainted with his own egotism. What they will is right, and they conquer by their self-assertion. Hans Sachs conquers by his humility, he does not champion his own work but another's."

If *The Mastersingers* is Wagner's best-loved work, it is because in it there is something for everybody. To those who have a romantic streak, the opera brings the beautiful love of Walther and Eva, and the secret, frustrated love of Hans Sachs for Eva. Those who enjoy wonderful melodies can delight in Walther's "Prize Song" ("Morgenlich leuchtend"). Those who enjoy good ensemble numbers will encounter a gem in the quintet "Selig, wie die Sonne," in which various characters, including Hans Sachs and Eva, react to Walther's description of the melody that came to him in a dream.

Those who are partial to ballet can enjoy "The Dance of the Apprentices." Those who dote on picture-book settings can relish the colorful streets and houses of old Nuremberg, and the customs and costumes of the sixteenth century. Those who derive comfort from the fact that good people are rewarded can enjoy the happy ending for Walther and Eva, Hans Sachs's joy in Walther's victory, and the humiliation suffered by the villain, Beckmesser.

All of the above attractions might suggest that *The Mastersingers* is in the mold of old-fashioned opera. To a certain degree it is, in the importance it places on fully developed melodies, ensemble numbers, processions, and grandly conceived scenes. But every element of the old-school opera is so beautifully integrated into a single artistic concept that the musical-drama ideal has not been betrayed.

Through the generosity of King Ludwig II, and his unwavering belief in Wagner, the first two dramas of the *Ring* cycle were also first produced at the Court Opera in Munich—*The Rhinegold* on September 22, 1869, and *The Valkyrie* on June 26, 1870. Wagner regarded both performances as beneath his standards. Having already completed his third *Ring* drama, *Siegfried,* in 1869, and being deep at work on the final one, *Twilight of the Gods,* by 1870, Wagner knew with finality that if his entire *Ring* cycle were to be performed the way he had envisioned it, this would have to take place in a theater of his own, built according to his own specifications, and where his word would be the final law.

The idea of a Wagner festival theater seemed like the impossible dream of an egomaniac. What other opera composer had ever dared to hope for a theater devoted exclusively to his own works? In the fulfillment of his artistic destiny, no dream was impossible to Wagner; and with his enormous belief in his own music, he was convinced the world would be only too eager to create a shrine to an art as deserving as his.

And he proved to be right. The town of Bayreuth, in Bavaria, provided him with a tract of land. Wagner societies began sprouting up in America and Europe to raise funds for the building of a theater on that site. Wagner himself was indefatigable in conducting concerts to help raise money. King Ludwig II gave him a sizable loan.

On Wagner's birthday, in 1872, the cornerstone of the new theater was laid; for the occasion Wagner conducted Beethoven's Ninth Symphony. On April 28, 1874, Wagner and his family moved into a house built expressly for them in Bayreuth, the Villa Wahnfried, where Wagner lived the rest of his life, and which his widow, children, and grandchildren would occupy after him. And on August 13, 1876, the first Wagner festival was inaugurated at Bayreuth with *The Rhinegold,* in what was the initial presentation anywhere of the complete *Ring* cycle. *Siegfried* (on August 16) and *Twilight of the Gods* (on August 17) were world premieres.

The festival aroused world interest. Visitors poured into and overflowed the little town of Bayreuth. Some of Europe's greatest musicians attended, among them Tchaikovsky, Grieg, Saint-Saëns, Gounod, and Liszt. The major newspapers of Europe, and one American paper, sent special correspondents to cover this unprecedented artistic event. By the time *The Rhinegold* was given, late arrivals found it impossible to find a hotel room or ticket (both priced exorbitantly). All kinds of Wagner trinkets were sold in the shops. No talk was heard except on the subject of Wagner and his dramas.

The new auditorium (a short walking distance from the center of the

town) was built along altogether new principles. Every seat in the house
Germanic
 commanded a view of the stage. Behind the stage was the most advanced
Greatness
 stagecraft machinery and equipment to be found in any theater in the world. Orchestra and conductor were concealed under the stage out of view so that the audience might not be distracted from the stage action. New laws were laid down for the audiences. Nobody would be admitted once the orchestral prelude had begun. No applause would be allowed until the final curtain.

All these were just the trimmings to the main attraction: the production of the most gigantic operatic project ever conceived; a project consuming four evenings, with each of the evenings (*The Rhinegold* excepted) requiring about four hours for the performance.

Some mocked or severely criticized Wagner's grandiose aims and unorthodox practices. They felt that the *Ring* cycle was crushed under the ponderous weight of its overpretentiousness. Many thought parts of the dramas were a colossal bore, particularly when the long and numerous narratives related past events again and again in each succeeding work. But there were many others who, while failing to comprehend fully the immensity of Wagner's accomplishment, were conscious that major history was unfolding before their eyes. One such was Tchaikovsky, who wrote: "What happened in Bayreuth will be remembered by our grandchildren and our great grandchildren."

It would be easy for them to remember. Bayreuth established itself as a permanent summer festival town exclusively for Wagner's music dramas, following the master's strictest demands. It still is an attraction that sends opera lovers streaming into Bayreuth to overtax the capacities of hotels, restaurants, and auditorium.

Mythology rather than legend provided Wagner with the material for the *Ring*. *The Rhinegold* is the prelude to the other three dramas. As it begins the Rhinemaidens are guarding a hoard of magic gold beneath the river Rhine. If a ring can be shaped from it this gold would give its owner power to conquer the world. Alberich, a dwarf, steals the gold from the maidens. The scene shifts to a mountaintop looking toward the new stately abode of the gods, Valhalla, ruled by Wotan and his wife, Fricka. Valhalla has been built for him by the giants Fafner and Fasolt, who demand as payment the gold Alberich has stolen.

Wotan descends to the Nibelheim cavern where Alberich and his brother, Mime, make their home. Alberich has forged the ring and with its power is gathering a hoard of gold. Mime has made a helmet, the Tarnhelm, which when worn can transform the wearer into any shape he
175

Richard Wagner at his villa in Triebschen in 1869.

A contemporary cartoon of Wagner.

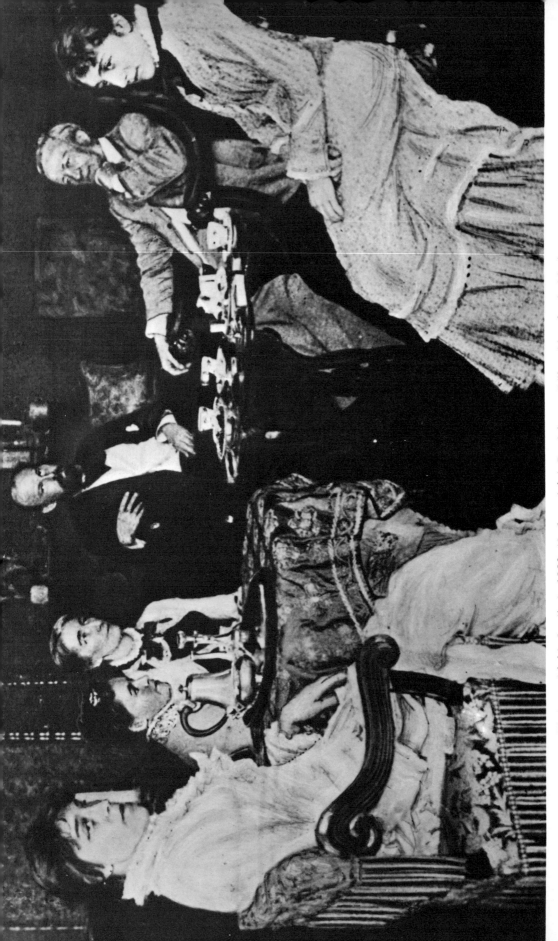

Wagner with his family in 1882. (Left to right) Daniela von Bülow (daughter), Marie von Gross, Cosima Wagner (wife), Paul von Jukowskij, Richard Wagner, Blandine von Bülow (daughter).

Two outstanding Wagnerian singers: Kirsten Flagstad as Brünnhilde, Lauritz Melchior as Siegfried.

Beckmesser (Karl Doench) sings for Hans Sachs (Otto Weiner) in the serenade scene from a Metropolitan Opera production of Die Meistersinger.

Siegmund (Jon Vickers) in a Metropolitan Opera production of Die Walküre.

Wotan (Thomas Stewart) in a Metropolitan Opera production of Die Walküre.

wishes. Through supreme cunning, Wotan gains the ring, the gold, and the Tarnhelm, which he is then compelled to turn over to the giants as the price for their building Valhalla. Alberich, though, has cursed the ring when it was taken from him. Immediately the two giants engage in a struggle to gain possession of the two magic prizes. One of them, Fasolt, is killed. The gods, headed by Wotan, enter Valhalla to the stately and majestic music Wagner devised for the closing scene, "The Entrance of the Gods into Valhalla."

The *Ring* begins its main story with the second work, *The Valkyrie*. Siegmund, a member of the Walsung tribe, finds refuge during a storm in the home of Hunding and Hunding's wife, Sieglinde. Sieglinde is actually the long-lost twin sister of Siegmund, both of them being the children of Wotan. Before they realize this, however, they fall in love. To Siegmund, Sieglinde reveals that a stranger (actually Wotan) had plunged a sword into a tree in the house; only a warrior-hero can remove it. After Siegmund and Sieglinde reveal to each other the depths of their love (Siegmund in "Winterstürme wichen dem Wonnemond," and Sieglinde in "Du bist der Lenz"), Siegmund removes the sword from the tree, calling it Nothung. Siegmund and Sieglinde then flee from the house.

In a rousing battle cry, "Ho-jo-to-ho," Brünnhilde, Wotan's daughter, agrees to assist Siegmund at her father's request. Wotan's wife insists, however, that Siegmund must be punished for having violated the sanctity of Hunding's home and stolen his wife. Wotan is forced to agree, and now tells Brünnhilde to do battle for Hunding. Brünnhilde, defying her father's commands, tries to help Siegmund when Hunding catches up with him and engages him in battle. But Wotan intervenes. Siegmund's magic sword is split in the battle with Hunding; Siegmund is killed. When Brünnhilde finds a hiding place for Sieglinde, Wotan decides to punish her.

The third act opens with a thrilling descriptive episode for orchestra, "The Ride of the Valkyrie." (The Valkyrie are maidens like Brünnhilde who lead dead heroes into Valhalla.) Brünnhilde, in spite of her father's orders, guards Sieglinde, whom she foretells will give birth to a son destined to become a hero. Brünnhilde also leaves with Sieglinde the broken parts of Siegmund's sword.

Wotan is in a rage over Brünnhilde's defiance. From the depths of her heart, Brünnhilde begs for forgiveness ("War es so schmählich"), but Wotan is forced to mete out punishment. Brünnhilde is to be banished from Valhalla forever. Paternal love, however, leads him to give his disgraced daughter protection. She will be put into a profound slumber and *183* will be surrounded by a ring of flames through which only a hero can penetrate; such a hero will then become her husband. Wotan's farewell to his daughter ("Leb' wohl") is perhaps the most poignant scene in the entire cycle. After that he gently places her on a rock, puts her to sleep, and summons Loge, god of fire, to circle flames around her.

The hero born to Sieglinde is Siegfried. As a grown man he is the central character of the third drama, which bears his name. He has been raised by Mime, the dwarf, who is trying in vain to mend the broken sword, Nothung. Mime knows that in the hands of young Siegfried it can become an invincible weapon. Wotan, disguised as the Wanderer, appears in Mime's cave to tell him that only a man without fear can make the sword whole. Siegfried is fearless, and it is he who forges the broken blade into one piece again.

In a forest, the giant Fafner, through the powers of the Tarnhelm, has transformed himself into a dragon. He is jealously guarding the ring fashioned from the gold of the Rhine. Alberich is eager to gain possession of the ring, and so is Wotan. But Fafner refuses to surrender it.

Siegfried comes to the forest, urged by Mime to kill the dragon with his sword. The beauty of the woods enchants him (as Wagner's "Waldweben" or "Forest Murmurs" describes so idyllically in the music). Then Siegfried slays Fafner. By chance he licks a drop of Fafner's blood off his finger, which gives him the power to understand the language of birds. A bird tells him about the Tarnhelm and the ring he had left behind in Fafner's cave. Siegfried retrieves the coveted prizes. When Mime comes to claim them, Siegfried destroys him with one blow of his sword.

The bird now tells Siegfried about Brünnhilde, lying asleep behind a curtain of flames. With a joyous cry, Siegfried follows the bird's directions, awakens Brünnhilde with a kiss, and in turn is welcomed with rapture by the awakened Brünnhilde. The opera ends with an ecstatic duet, "Heil dir, Sonne!"

In the prologue to the last drama, *Twilight of the Gods,* Siegfried prepares to set forth for adventure with Brünnhilde's blessing. Before leaving he presents her with the ring as a token of his undying love. As the scene changes, Siegfried's Rhine Journey is vividly described in an orchestral episode, "Siegfrieds Rheinfahrt." The first act then takes place in the hall of the Gibichungs, home of Gunther, his sister, Gutrune, and his half brother, Hagen, son of Alberich. Hagen has learned that Siegfried is about to arrive at the hall. He unfolds a plan to give the hero a potion that will make him forget Brünnhilde and fall in love with Gutrune. Hagen also wants Gunther to marry Brünnhilde.

His plan works. Having drunk the potion given him on his arrival, Siegfried forgets Brünnhilde, falls in love with Gutrune, and is ready to help Gunther with Brünnhilde. Through the magic of the Tarnhelm, Siegfried changes himself into Gunther's likeness, returns to Brünnhilde, snatches the ring from her finger and brings her to the hall of the Gibichungs. There, reassuming his own form, Siegfried claims Gutrune as bride, much to the horror of Brünnhilde. Determined to avenge herself, Brünnhilde discloses to Hagen and Gunther that Siegfried is vulnerable to fatal attack in only one part of his body: his back. Hagen and Gunther, plotting to destroy Siegfried and thus gain the ring, arrange a hunting party.

A new potion restores memory to Siegfried. He suddenly remembers Brünnhilde. Hagen pierces Siegfried's back with his spear. Dying, Siegfried bids his beloved wife a poignant farewell in "Brünnhilde, heilige Braut!" and then expires. His body is brought back to the hall of the Gibichungs to the exalted strains of "Siegfried's Death Music." At the hall, Hagen and Gunther battle fiercely for Siegfried's ring. Gunther is killed. In the powerful music of the "Immolation Scene" ("Starke Scheite schichtet mir dort") Brünnhilde orders a funeral pyre to be built, into which she rides to her death astride her horse. The dying flames give way as the Rhine waters rise. The Rhinemaidens seize Hagen and drag him into the river. From the Rhine the hand of one of the Rhinemaidens is seen holding the cursed ring that has brought about so much death and destruction. In the heavens can be seen the glow of Valhalla in flames. It is the twilight of the gods and the beginning of the time of human love.

By underlining the moral that the greed for gold is capable of destroying the world, Wagner was expounding a theme close to the heart of a social revolutionary. But even individual characters, episodes, and scenes are used symbolically to project Wagner's thoughts on religion, economics, politics, human behavior. Wotan, Alberich, and Mime represent lust for power. Siegfried is the "Superman," described in Nietzsche's philosophy as the man capable of conquering the world. To appreciate the *Ring,* however, it is hardly necessary to penetrate behind the facade of the dramas themselves to uncover the propaganda.

Nor is it very important to be able to identify the dozens of leading motives that Wagner uses with such extraordinary skill and imagination and complexity as the threads of his musical fabric. All we need do is to succumb to the magic of Wagner's music when the many emotional or dramatic episodes in his texts sweep his inspiration heavenward. When a climactic moment arrives, we find Wagner the musician speaking with a grandeur that has few equals. He never fails to rise to or go beyond the demands made upon him by his own text. Some of the best scenes come at the end of each of the four dramas where Wagner's music achieves an incomparable nobility, tenderness, eloquence, or titanic power.

He was unrivaled in finding the proper music for every possible image, emotion, concept, or idea. We get such realistic translations into tones of a scene or mood that we hardly need to listen to the words or watch the stage action to know what Wagner is describing. Articulateness such as this is matched by Wagner's supreme technical powers.

After the *Ring,* one more music drama absorbed Wagner. With it his life work comes to an end. His last drama was *Parsifal,* a striking contrast in subject matter and treatment from anything he had previously attempted. Its central theme is redemption through the Holy Grail, the legendary chalice from which Christ drank at the Last Supper; it was reputed to contain some of the blood he had shed at the Crucifixion.

The idea of writing *Parsifal* first came to Wagner from reading a poem based on a German medieval legend. The theme haunted him for years. Then by 1877 he had completed his libretto, and by 1882 his entire score was down on paper. Because of the intensely religious subject matter he was treating, Wagner called this work not a "music drama" but a "stage-consecrating festival drama"—in short, a kind of sacred service to be listened to with reverence. He let it be known that *Parsifal* was not to be performed anywhere but in Bayreuth. (His wishes, however, were not followed. After his death, and with the expiration of the copyright, *Parsifal* was produced outside of Bayreuth for the first time at the Metropolitan Opera in 1903 against the violent opposition of the Wagner family; it was not long before other opera houses followed suit.)

Not with sensual love is Wagner concerned in *Parsifal,* nor with the lust of gods and men for power and gold, but with high spiritual values. Though no devout Christian, Wagner became imbued with a mysticism and a religiosity in writing his festival drama. Compassion, suffering, and renunciation became the instruments through which the characters in *Parsifal* achieve salvation. The religious story was merely the frame to encase this concept.

The spirituality of this drama is immediately set forth in the first-act prelude, in which Wagner not only quotes some of the leading motives he would use in the ensuing acts, but also borrows a famous old German liturgical melody known as the "Dresden Amen." The curtain rises on a forest near Monsalvat, in the Spanish Pyrenees, during the Middle Ages.

Amfortas, keeper of the Holy Grail, suffers from a wound inflicted by
the magician Klingsor with a holy spear that once had pierced the flesh
of Christ. Amfortas can be saved only by someone pure in heart and
soul, an "innocent fool" who can gain possession of Klingsor's holy
spear and touch the wound with it.

Parsifal soon appears; he is the prophesied "pure" fool. Gurnemanz,
knight of the Grail, conducts Parsifal to the Hall of the Holy Grail
where the knights have gathered. The Last Supper is described. Lying on
a couch, Amfortas lifts the holy chalice, which suddenly becomes aglow.
When the knights leave, Parsifal shows that he has not comprehended
what has taken place, a fact that so infuriates Gurnemanz that he drives
Parsifal away.

As Parsifal approaches Klingsor's cattle, Klingsor calls upon Kundry, an enchantress, to seduce Parsifal and thus remove one whom he
recognizes as a menace to his powers. She enlists the help of flower
maidens who, in a magic garden, perform a dance for Parsifal ("The
Flower-Maidens Scene"). When Parsifal proves immune to their entice-
ments, Kundry herself tries to win him with tenderness, manifestations of
love, and pity. Suddenly Parsifal remembers Amfortas' suffering and the
scene he had witnessed in the Hall of the Grail. Their meaning now becomes clear to him. Parsifal rudely thrusts Kundry aside. He now knows
that it is he who must cure Amfortas and redeem the Grail. Kundry calls
to Klingsor for help, and he hurls his magic spear at Parsifal. It remains
suspended in midair. Parsifal seizes it and uses it to make the sign of the
cross, which causes Klingsor's castle to crumble to ruin and Klingsor
himself to be forever doomed.

Years have gone by. Parsifal, wandering in search of the Grail, has
come to a meadow near Monsalvat. Gurnemanz, now an old man, has
become a hermit. Amfortas is still a victim of intense physical suffering.
When Parsifal asks to be led to the Hall of the Grail, he is anointed
with oil, is baptized with spring water, and has his feet dried by Kundry
with her hair. Suddenly the country becomes radiant. This is Good Friday. The scene is transfigured with a holy light presenting a picture of
exaltation and peace magically caught by Wagner in the music of his
"Good Friday Spell." Then to the sound of tolling bells, Gurnemanz,
Kundry, and Parsifal ascend to the great Hall, where Amfortas is
brought to the throne in an impressive ceremony. Parsifal comes forward and touches and heals Amfortas' wound with the holy spear. Parsifal now brings forth the Holy Grail, which burns with an incandescent
light. As Parsifal kneels in prayer a dove flies over his head. Parsifal lifts

the Holy Grail as Amfortas and Gurnemanz bow reverently. Kundry, dying penitent, achieves absolution and salvation.

Though *Parsifal* is filled with numerous long and frequently dull narratives, though its action is so static at times that little happens to excite interest, and though the characters lack dimension, some musicologists regard it as the summit of Wagner's ideal of creating an integrated super-art. They believe it to be a source from which springs some of his most inspired music. The profound religious feeling caught in and generated by *Parsifal* makes this drama particularly appropriate for presentation during the Easter season, a fact recognized by the Metropolitan Opera, which from time to time has offered the work as a Good Friday production.

Spent emotionally in writing *Parsifal,* Wagner could still summon a supreme effort during rehearsals to see that the drama was properly produced, and that the spirit of holiness he aimed for was respected. *Parsifal* was first given at Bayreuth on July 26, 1882. It was so successful it was given sixteen performances.

The titanic energies Wagner had expended drained his health. His heart was beginning to give way. A sorely needed vacation brought him to Venice with his family, and with his father-in-law, Liszt, with whom he had finally become reconciled. (Cosima, however, remained intransigent in her refusal to forgive her father, up to the time of his death.) In Venice, Wagner was stricken by a fatal heart attack. He died on February 13, 1883. His body was carried back to Bayreuth, where he was buried to the strains of "Siegfried's Death Music." He was interred in the garden of his villa, Wahnfried, where to this day pilgrims come to pay him silent tribute.

No composer before him had been subjected to the kind of poisonous attacks and hatred suffered by Wagner. What he had accomplished was so new and revolutionary that reactionaries in music looked upon him as a destructive force. They severely criticized him for his megalomania; his giant-sized musical structures; his insistence on making music interpret nonmusical ideas and philosophies; his sensuous, passionate style that at times became almost orgiastic; his complete break with past operatic procedures, and his indulgence in unorthodox harmonic, tonal, and instrumental practices.

Typical of what his enemies said of him is this statement made by a Leipzig historian in 1871: "The diabolical din of this pig-headed man, stuffed with brass and sawdust, inflated in an insanely destructive self-aggrandizement by Mephistopheles' mephitic and most venomous hellish miasma into Beelzebub's Court, Composer and General Director of Hell's Music—Wagner!" Other critics wrote that "Wagner is the anti-Christ of art," and that "the immense predominance of dissonance over consonance puts a strain on the nerves which becomes often painful and cannot be endured . . . without causing utter prostation."

Wagner was abused and detested—but he was also worshiped by progressive musicians capable of taking a true measure of his genius. To these Wagnerphiles, his influence had the force of a hurricane. The Wagnerian storm that swept over the world of music affected the artistic destinies not only of composers of operas, but also those of composers of symphonies (Mahler and Bruckner, for example) and of songs (Hugo Wolf). In opera, the storm carried one of the greatest of German post-Wagnerian composers to greatness. He was Richard Strauss, who bore the Wagnerian torch into the twentieth century.

12

Dramatic Realism

Richard Strauss

It is truly paradoxical that Richard Strauss (1864–1949) should have inherited Wagner's mantle and worn it with such regal dignity. For Strauss was the son of a man who, during Wagner's lifetime, had been one of the master's most bitter antagonists in Munich. Richard's father, Franz, was a famous horn player who was a member of the orchestra of the Court Opera when Wagner's music dramas were introduced. Such contempt did the elder Strauss have for Wagner that he became the central force in all cabals and intrigues formed to destroy the master. Strauss made no attempt to hide his feelings from Wagner. In the middle of a rehearsal of a Wagnerian music drama, in Wagner's presence, Franz Strauss left his seat in the orchestra pit exclaiming acidly that he would never play such outlandish music.

For a time Richard Strauss echoed his father's vitriolic opinions about Wagner. As a boy, Richard heard *Tristan and Isolde* in Munich and expressed his own contempt in no uncertain terms. In his early career as a composer, Richard Strauss's music was deeply rooted in Brahms, and his compositions were performed and admired. He might have continued along this route permanently had not he gone to Bayreuth in 1882, and heard *Parsifal* the year in which it was receiving its world premiere. *Parsifal* was such an overwhelming experience for Richard Strauss that it compelled him to reevaluate his former prejudice against Wagner.

Then a few years later he became the friend of a man who was to be responsible for redirecting Strauss's artistic direction away from Brahms to Wagner. That man was Alexander Ritter—a musician, poet, and philosopher, who was married to Wagner's niece. Ritter regarded Wagner's work as the new truth in music that composers had to embrace if they were to advance themselves creatively. Ritter talked passionately to Strauss about Wagner's ideals and urged Strauss to adopt them. "His influence," Strauss later said about Ritter, "was in the nature of a storm wind. He urged me on to the development of the poetic, the expressive in music."

Strauss now lost interest in writing symphonies, concertos, and quartets in the manner of Brahms. The musical structure he first found most adaptable to his new way of writing—the Wagnerian way—was the tone poem, or symphonic poem for orchestra. This is a flexible and free kind of form that Liszt had devised and developed to carry to orchestral writing some of Wagner's principles and techniques. A tone poem is an orchestral interpretation of a poem, picture, or story, giving the composer the opportunity for the kind of pictorial, atmospheric, and literal writing with which Wagner had become identified. A tone poem is "program music" as distinguished from the "absolute music" of a symphony, which is usually devoid of all extramusical implications.

And so, beginning in 1887, and continuing to the end of the nineteenth century, Strauss completed a series of tone poems that shocked the world of music with their discords, massive orchestration, sensuous sounds, chromaticisms, and the literalness with which the details of a program were carried out in musical terms—be it Don Juan's amorous pursuits, Till Eulenspiegel's merry pranks, Nietzsche's philosophy as propounded by Zarathustra, the adventures of Don Quixote, or the career of a hero.

This is not the place for a discussion of Strauss's orchestral music nor, for that matter, of the no less remarkable art songs for voice and piano he was producing during the same period. In both these fields Strauss achieved world fame and notoriety, emerging as one of the most provocative and most influential composers in the post-Wagnerian period. Then he directed his energies to opera, to become one of its greatest composers in the twentieth century.

When he made his first attempts at writing opera, Strauss left no doubts as to who his musical god was. His first opera, *Guntram* (1894), was based on an old German legend from which Strauss wrote his own libretto. It embellished the theme of redemption, a subject once so close to Wagner's heart. Here not only the text but the music as well were influenced by the *Ring* cycle. Strauss's second opera, *Feuersnot* (1901), was his attempt to write another *Mastersingers*. Both of these operas were failures. In imitating Wagner, Strauss had failed to achieve either freshness or individuality.

It is with his third opera, *Salome,* that Richard Strauss speaks for himself, even though the language remains Wagnerian. A biblical text developed into a play by Oscar Wilde, *Salome* was a mold into which Strauss could pour his own brand of musical sensuality and eroticism. Oscar Wilde's text was lurid and decadent, and so was Strauss's music— by turns lush and passionate and sensuous and at other moments highly discordant, with shrieking outbursts of sonorities, piercing trills, and quivering glissandos. It had muscular power, but also sensitive nerves. Music and play become one and inextricable.

Since it comes out of the Bible, the story is known to most. Salome feels a lust for the prophet John the Baptist, who rejects her advances. Embittered, Salome is set on destroying the holy man. Her stepfather, King Herod, is in love with Salome and promises to grant her any wish if only she will dance for him. She performs the "Dance of the Seven Veils" (now a staple in symphonic literature), which opens with an orgiastic outburst of sounds and rhythms before subsiding into slow, sensuous music in which we can hear portrayed the sinuous contortions of Salome's body as she performs her dance. The mood becomes increasingly frenzied until it rises to a climax that is overpowering. The dance over, Salome demands the head of the prophet as the price for her performance. When it is brought to her on a tray she kisses its lips. In a hysterical narrative that closes the opera she addresses it with spent passion. King Herod becomes so revolted that he orders Salome's death.

Never before in opera had such sensuality and eroticism been interpreted with brutal frankness in both the libretto and the music. Most of the opera world of Strauss's day recoiled with horror. Vienna (where the opera was to have been introduced) turned it down by order of the censors. In Berlin, the kaiser himself prevented the opera from being performed. He finally relented, and when *Salome* was heard in Berlin in *192* 1906 the critics used words like "perverse," "depravity," and "repulsive" to describe it. For a while censors did not allow the opera to be given in London.

When *Salome* received its American premiere in 1907 it caused such a scandal—and inspired such an outcry in the newspapers, in pulpits and from subscribers—that it had to be dropped from the repertory after only one performance. As late as 1910, when Mary Garden was starred in *Salome* in Chicago, a reviewer called it "disgusting," and the hue and cry of the first-night audience against it compelled the directors to cancel all further presentations after the second. Strange to say, in view of this subsequent outraged response in so many different cities, *Salome* actually was an immense success at its world premiere—in Dresden on December 9, 1905; the composer was given twenty-five curtain calls.

Strauss's next opera was even more morbid, hysterical, psychoneurotic, and in many ways repellent in subject matter and treatment than was *Salome.* This is the first Strauss opera for which Hugo von Hofmannsthal—a distinguished Austrian poet and dramatist—provided the libretto. For two decades after that, Strauss and von Hofmannsthal worked on operas with a remarkable sympathy for and understanding of each other's problems, and a lofty regard for each other's ideas and individual genius. This harmonious partnership was the reason they were able to work together so long and for so many operas. Their first joint effort, *Elektra,* is one of their most celebrated.

For his libretto, von Hofmannsthal went to ancient Greece, specifically to Sophocles' tragedy *Elektra.* To Sophocles' story, von Hofmannsthal contributed his own extraordinary gift for dramatic interest and profound characterizations (with psychological insight not often encountered in opera). Elektra became the personification of evil; her mother, Klytemnestra, the essence of depravity.

The basic plot adhered closely to that of Sophocles. Elektra had been crazed by her torment over the death of her father, Agamemnon, who had been murdered by Aegisthus, lover of Elektra's mother, Klytemnestra. The mother is also agonized—but by a guilty conscience, which (as Elektra tells her bitterly) can only be soothed through the spilling of blood. Elektra enlists the aid of her brother, Orestes, in avenging the murder. He kills both his own mother and her lover. In a frenzy of madness and joy, Elektra dances on the grave of her father, then falls dead.

To heighten the sensuality of his writing, Strauss subdivided his strings into eight sections, gaining thereby a more luxuriant tone. Lower strings were emphasized in his orchestration to point up the grim psychoneurotic overtones of the drama and to penetrate deeply into the inner psyche of the principal characters. Shattering discords help portray the hatred of the demented Elektra for her mother and to emphasize the guilt that haunts and terrifies Klytemnestra. The melodic line frequently becomes a continuous vocal sweep of sound, like the cries of a wounded animal. Throughout the score, as one unidentified German critic said in reviewing the premiere performance, "the marvelous imitative effects of the orchestra are blood-curdling, drastic, and gruesome to the last degree. It is fortunate for the hearers that the piece is no longer, or else it would be too nerve-wracking." By the time Elektra performs her dance of death, frenzy seizes the entire orchestra. The dance of death is the shattering conclusion to the opera, a scene that, according to Alfred Kalisch, "betrays a creative power that is certainly without a rival in the present day."

Dresden, which had been so tolerant of and enthusiastic about the eroticism and sensuality of *Salome,* found Strauss's new opera *Elektra* thoroughly revolting when the premiere was given on January 25, 1909. So did the American audience that first witnessed *Elektra* in 1910 at the Manhattan Opera House.

But the passage of time and changing mores have robbed both *Salome* and *Elektra* of their capacity to shock and horrify audiences. On the contrary!—there is hardly an audience anywhere today that does not become spellbound at the compelling, throbbing, searing musical theater represented by both operas, each of which we now know is an enduring masterpiece.

In considering a new subject for their next opera, both von Hofmannsthal and Strauss agreed they would enjoy writing something strikingly different from *Elektra.* They were thinking of doing an opera that had sunshine and laughter, nostalgia and a gentle tenderness, sex interest and nobility. Von Hofmannsthal produced such a libretto in *Der Rosenkavalier (The Rose Cavalier),* and Strauss responded with a sparkling, lilting score partly suggestive of the waltz king, Johann Strauss II, and partly of Mozart. Waltz music courses throughout the opera; at the same time there are numerous other pages with Mozart's kind of grace, refinement, wit, and charm. But Wagnerian virtuosity and stylistic mannerisms are still apparent, as are Strauss's luscious orchestration and melodic gifts.

From the time of its premiere in Dresden on January 26, 1911, up

The Vienna State Opera House about 1890. The building was in use from its opening in 1869 until its destruction in 1945.

Salome (Birgit Nilsson) performs the "Dance of the Seven Veils" before King Herod (Karl Liebl). A Metropolitan Opera production.

A scene from Elektra *in a production of the Brussels Opera, May, 1942.*

Octavian, the Rose Cavalier (Gwyneth Jones), presents a silver rose to Sophie (Lucia Popp) in a Vienna State Opera production of Der Rosenkavalier.

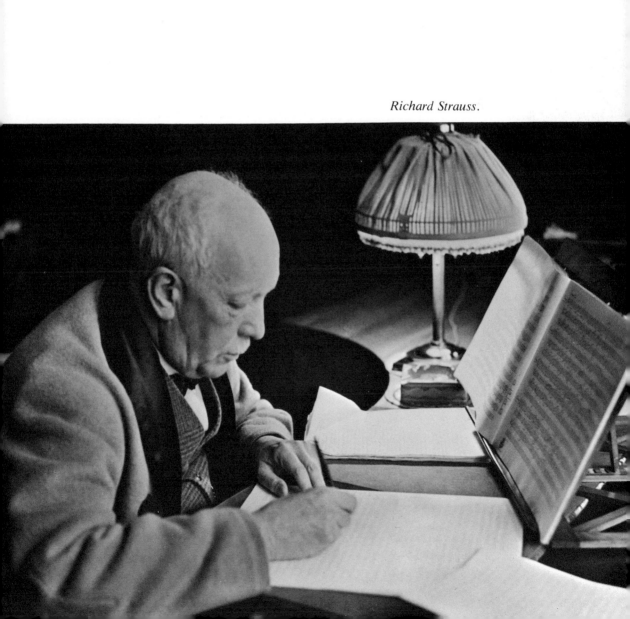

Richard Strauss.

to the present day, *Der Rosenkavalier* is Strauss's best-loved opera. If there is an opera comedy that equals or surpasses this one, we must go back to such hardy standards as *The Barber of Seville, The Marriage of Figaro, Falstaff,* and *The Mastersingers. Der Rosenkavalier* has a deserved place in such august company.

The most amusing character is a fat, lecherous nobleman, Baron Ochs, who is indefatigable in his pursuit of women. The noblest character is his cousin, the Princess von Werdenberg, known as the Marschallin. Though in her full mature years, she is in love with a seventeen-year-old boy, Octavian. All this takes place in eighteenth-century Vienna, when complicated love affairs and intrigues among the rich and powerful so fascinated pre-Wagnerian writers of comic operas.

The Baron is planning to marry an appealing young lady, Sophie. The custom of the times dictated that a silver rose be presented to the young woman as a symbol of a marriage proposal. Ochs comes to the Marschallin to ask her to find somebody to deliver the rose. He has come at an inopportune moment: Octavian and the Marschallin are exchanging tender sentiments. While Ochs is making his entrance, Octavian rushes off to disguise himself as the Marschallin's maid. The Baron proceeds to make advances to "her," even to suggest a rendezvous.

To rid herself of her cousin, the Marschallin promises to find a rose-bearer, which she does later on by dispatching Octavian (sans female costume). When Octavian, as the Rose Cavalier, presents a silver rose to Sophie, the two of them fall in love at first sight. This fact does not escape the Baron's notice. He challenges Octavian to a duel, in which the Baron is scratched. He howls with pain as if he had been butchered. But his anguish is immediately assuaged with the arrival of a letter from the Marschallin's "maid" (Octavian in disguise) suggesting a meeting. What Octavian plans is to humiliate the Baron.

The rendezvous takes place in a public tavern. Octavian has made arrangements to embarrass the Baron in various different ways until the poor man becomes sorely disturbed. When Octavian arrives, dressed in female clothes, the Baron is appeased, looking forward to a delectable evening. But Octavian soon reveals his true identity, which sends the Baron rushing out of the tavern in a rage. The Marschallin, aware that Octavian and Sophie are in love, comes to give the two young people her blessing. The opera ends with a wonderful trio and duet, both Mozartean in their delicacy and loveliness. In the trio, the Marschallin makes her noble renunciation of Octavian while Octavian and Sophie express

their joy. The duet is the wondrous love music of Octavian and Sophie.

That ending, and the various enchanting waltzes that flow in and out of the mainstream of the score, are not the only parts that made *Der Rosenkavalier* such a distinguished opera. One other episode deserves particular attention: the contemplative, tender, and at times pathetic monologue of the Marschallin in the first act when she must face the sad truth she is no longer young and therefore must soon lose Octavian.

Among the subsequent operas for which von Hofmannsthal served as Strauss's librettist are *Ariadne auf Naxos* (1912), *Die Frau ohne Schatten* (1919), and *Arabella* (1933). Von Hofmannsthal died just a few days after he had completed the text of *Arabella.* For his later operas Strauss had to work with other librettists. None of these operas comes even close to approaching the standards he had previously achieved with von Hofmannsthal.

By the end of World War I Strauss had become an international figure in music—not only as a composer but also as a conductor. He was one of the leading conductors of his age of his own works and of the music of Mozart and Wagner, with successful appearances in Europe's foremost opera houses, and at the Bayreuth Festival. He was also a frequent guest conductor of world-famous orchestras, usually in programs made up of his own orchestral music. He came twice to the United States: in 1904 with a visiting orchestra, and in 1921 as a guest of American orchestras.

He was an extraordinarily vain man who fed hungrily on the successes and honors showered on him. It was not in any spirit of levity that he made himself the hero of two of his works (the tone poem *A Hero's Life* and the early opera *Feuersnot*). In his own eyes he was a hero. He was violently jealous of any composer or conductor who threatened his august position in music; he spoke disparagingly of them with the hope of undermining their significance. He was greatly feared by his fellow musicians because he was a major power in German and Austrian music.

But in his own home he was a weakling. His wife was Pauline de Ahna, a singer who had appeared in Strauss's first opera, *Guntram,* and whom he had married on September 10, 1894. She was a strong-willed, domineering, snobbish woman. Like some overbearing mother to a recalcitrant child, she would dictate to Strauss when he should work and rest, and with whom he should socialize. He would meekly follow her orders without the slightest token of resistance.

When the Nazis first came to power, in 1933, Strauss supported the Third Reich by substituting for conductors who had been forced to flee from the country and by assuming the office of President of the Third

Reich Music Chamber of the German Federation of Composers, an office that laid down the law on Nazi musical standards.

But for all his vanity and inherent weaknesses, he soon became disenchanted with the Nazi leaders and displayed courage in defying them. He allowed his son to marry a Jewish girl. He had Stefan Zweig, a Jew, write the libretto for the opera *Die schweigsame Frau* (1935). The Nazis winced and might have preferred to ignore these indiscretions in view of Strauss's world fame, but obedience to their principles was inflexible. Three weeks after the premiere of *Die schweigsame Frau*, Strauss was forced to resign his positions in Germany and make a strategic retreat to his villa in Garmisch-Partenkirchen, a lovely mountain village near Munich. He continued writing music; his last works, *Four Last Songs,* were completed in 1948.

When Strauss raised his voice to protest Germany's invasion of Poland in 1939, he was placed under house arrest. None of his foreign royalties were now able to reach him. The only food he and his family had were the meager rations the Nazis doled out to them. Then came the German surrender, and the American occupation of Garmisch-Partenkirchen. When several American officers visited Strauss, the master identified himself by saying, "I am the composer of *Der Rosenkavalier."* He did not have to do so; they knew very well who Richard Strauss was, and they had come to pay their respects. Forgotten (and deservedly so) were his early musical activities under the Nazi government. On June 8, 1948, the American army made Strauss's denazification official when a court in Munich cleared him completely of charges that he had collaborated with the Nazis.

The rest of the world was very willing to accept Strauss as one of the musical giants of his generation. He went to London in 1947 to attend a Strauss festival and receive a hero's welcome. The major music centers of America and Europe celebrated his eighty-fifth birthday in 1949 with concerts, published tributes, and official honors. They came none too soon. Only three months after that Strauss was dead, the victim of uremia. He passed away in Garmisch-Partenkirchen on September 8, 1949.

Strauss lies buried in the garden of his villa in Garmisch-Partenkirchen. His three greatest operas—*Salome, Elektra,* and *Der Rosenkavalier*—are firmly entrenched in the repertory.

13

Nationalistic Opera

Opera in Russia, Modest Mussorgsky,

Folk Operas, George Gershwin

There was opera in Russia, too. In fact, Russia is the birthplace of a new important movement in opera: nationalism.

The beginnings of nationalism in Russian music go back to the first half of the nineteenth century, to Michael Glinka (1804–57), Russia's first important composer. Between his twenty-sixth and twenty-ninth years, Glinka traveled about Europe studying music and composing. Being away from Russia made him homesick. His nostalgia for things Russian led him to develop his musical writing into a Russian style (whereas all earlier Russian composers had been imitating the famous Europeans). This new style took advantage of Russian folk songs and dances, sometimes through quotation, sometimes through imitation. Glinka put it this way: "My most earnest desire is to compose music which would make all my beloved fellow countrymen feel quite at home, and lead no one to allege that I strutted about in borrowed plumes."

His first experiments in nationalism came with some instrumental works. But his all-consuming ambition was to write a Russian opera. He set about bringing this dream to fulfillment about two years after his return to Russia by completing *A Life for the Tsar,* heard in the year of its composition (1836) in Saint Petersburg. Its subject was taken from Russian history. The principal character, Ivan Susanin, is a hero who thwarts a Polish attempt to murder the young Russian czar and turns back in defeat the Polish army descending on Moscow. For this Ivan pays with his life.

While it is quite true that Glinka adopted the Italian operatic structure and methods of his time, *A Life for the Tsar* was something new in opera—a national opera. Many of Glinka's arias have the contours of Russian folk songs; Glinka's choruses are reminiscent of old Russian church music in their use of old modes instead of modern scales, and some of these choruses are hymns of praise to country and ruler. Most of the dances are of obviously Russian origin, though there were two Polish dances, a mazurka and a polonaise, in a scene calling for Polish characters. In one of the choruses Glinka used strings to simulate the sound of the balalaika, a native Russian instrument similar to a mandolin.

Six years later, Glinka's second and last opera—*Russlan and Ludmilla*—was produced in Saint Petersburg. Its story of the pursuit of lovely Ludmilla by three suitors, one of whom, Russlan, proves successful, came by way of a poem by Russia's great national poet Pushkin. Once again Glinka writes arias, choruses, and dances modeled after old Russian folk and church music. Here, however, the composer often combines his Russian identity with an oriental one, a practice pursued by many later Russian nationalists. For there is a good deal of the oriental in the Russian.

There was hardly a nineteenth-century Russian composer who was not influenced by Glinka. This included a group of five men who lived and wrote in the latter half of the nineteenth century. They came to be known as "the Mighty Five" or "the Russian Five." It is with these composers that Russian musical nationalism truly comes to prominence.

The founding father of this new "school" of composers was Mily Balakirev (1837–1910). It was he who clarified the aims and ideals of the nationalist movement: to mold music after the patterns and formats of Russian folk songs, dances, and church music; to derive programmatic subjects for compositions from Russian history, geography, and culture. It was Balakirev who stirred some of his composer friends to think and write as he did. These included César Cui (1835–1918), Nikolai Rimsky-Korsakov (1844–1908), Alexander Borodin (1833–87), and Modest Mussorgsky (1839–81).

204   On May 24, 1867, there took place in Saint Petersburg an orchestral

concert conducted by Balakirev made up of the works of these five composers. In his review, Stassov dubbed this quintet of composers "the
Mighty Five." (Only later on did it become a general practice with historians to describe this group as "the Russian Five.") These five composers
devoted their lives and works to the mission that had previously fired
Glinka: to create a thoroughly Russian musical art.

Balakirev did not write any operas. But the other four composers
did, and some of their nationalistic operas have earned an honored place
in musical history. Most important are *Prince Igor* (1890) by Borodin,
completed posthumously by Rimsky-Korsakov and Alexander Glazunov,
a young Russian composer. From Borodin's opera comes the exotic and
dynamic selection known as the *Polovtzian Dances,* familiar at symphony concerts. Also important are the most significant operas of Rimsky-Korsakov, including *The Snow Maiden* (1882), *Sadko* (1898); and
the most famous of all, *Le Coq d'or* (1909), produced posthumously.
Most opera lovers, however, know these three Rimsky-Korsakov operas
exclusively through excerpts: through "The Dance of the Tumblers"
for orchestra from *The Snow Maiden;* through "The Song of India"
from *Sadko;* and through "The Hymn to the Sun" and an orchestral suite
from *Le Coq d'or.*

One opera towers above all others on the Russian musical scene:
Mussorgsky's epic, *Boris Godunov.* To some musicologists, this is not
only the greatest Russian opera ever written, but one of the greatest folk
operas of all time.

Strange that so giant a work should have come from the hands of
Mussorgsky rather than from those of one of his colleagues! The others
were musically far more learned than Mussorgsky, far more cultured
and sophisticated. Mussorgsky's musical writing—like his appearance in
his last dismal years—was sloppy, uncouth, disheveled. But his native
genius gave him the wings to soar over his all-too-obvious technical and
stylistic shortcomings. His genius endowed his music with a power of invention, an individuality, and a strength of speech none of his four colleagues could match.

Modest Mussorgsky, son of a wealthy landowner, was born in Ka-
revo on March 21, 1839. Though he early showed unusual talent for
music and began composing in his boyhood, he was slanted by his parents toward a military career. In 1856 he was graduated from the cadet
school of the Imperial Guards and became an officer. All this time he
did not abandon composing. In or about 1857 he met Balakirev, who
was so impressed by the young officer's musical gifts that he accepted

him as a pupil in composition and theory. This was all the music instruction Mussorgsky ever received. By 1858 Mussorgsky decided that a military career was not for him. He abandoned his dashing uniform to concentrate on music.

Balakirev, with his ideals, aroused Mussorgsky to create Russian music. As a member of "the Mighty Five," Mussorgsky worked upon his first Russian-oriented and Russian-inspired composition—a tone poem for orchestra, *A Night on Bald Mountain,* upon which he labored between 1860 and 1866.

When the serfs in Russia were liberated in 1861, and the property of landowners was confiscated, Mussorgsky lost all his financial resources. He had to work for a living. Between 1863 and 1867 he was a clerk in the Ministry of Communications. It was during this period that a marked disintegration began to take place in his behavior and appearance—partly caused by his troubled nervous system, but mainly by the death of his mother, whom he had adored. Formerly as an officer he had been a handsome, well-groomed fop whose elegance of appearance matched his refined speech and courtly manners. After 1865, the year of his mother's death, he began indulging in heavy drinking to escape from his neuroticism and morbidity. At times he succumbed to delirium tremens.

Somehow he managed to continue writing music, though only by fits and starts. By 1868 he was working on his first opera, *The Marriage,* based on a story by Gogol. He never finished more than a single act, but this was enough for him to undertake successfully an experiment in a new kind of lyricism that he dubbed "the melody of life." He felt that melody should be molded after the inflections and patterns of speech. "What I want to do," he said, "is to make my characters speak on the stage as they would in real life and yet write music that will be thoroughly artistic."

His own brand of lyricism was one of the most important innovations, one of the strongest features of his masterwork *Boris Godunov.* Another was his ability to realize musical truth. He was convinced, as he put it, that "the quest for artistic beauty for its own sake is sheer puerility. It is art in its nonage." Mussorgsky was not interested in beautiful sounds, pretty melodies, elegant forms, and aristocratic styles for their own sake. He felt that music had to express human existence authentically and accurately. If the people, situations, and emotions in an opera were ugly and undisciplined, then the music for them should also be ugly

and undisciplined.

He explained: "To seek assiduously the most delicate and subtle features of human nature—of the human crowd—to follow them into unknown regions, to make them of our own; this seems to me the true vocation of the artist." In the process of realizing this musical truth he had to use discordant harmonies, harsh progressions, awkward modulations, barbaric rhythms. How well he succeeded is pointed up by the English critic Gerald Abraham when he wrote: "As a musical translator of words and all that can be expressed in words, of psychological states and even physical movements, he is unsurpassed."

Russian history, as unfolded in a drama by Pushkin, was the source of *Boris Godunov,* with the composer writing his own libretto. Mussorgsky wrote his libretto in prose instead of poetry, which was the usual practice, because he felt that prose was better adaptable to his unique kind of lyricism. There are several versions of *Boris Godunov.* Mussorgsky completed the first in 1869. This was an opera in seven scenes in which no relief is provided for the high tensions and the somber tragedy. This was an opera without audience appeal, and the directors of the opera house in Saint Petersburg rejected it. Mussorgsky then revised his opera to make it somewhat more popular. He interpolated some love interest and several arias with a melodic appeal greater than his own brand of speechlike lyricism. He rearranged the scenes and introduced episodes to dilute the grimness of the drama. This revised version met with favor when it was produced in Saint Petersburg on February 8, 1874. The audience responded enthusiastically. But world acceptance was still far away.

When *Boris Godunov* finally became universally popular, it was not through this revised version but through a third one, which, fifteen years after Mussorgsky's death, was adapted and polished by Rimsky-Korsakov. If Rimsky-Korsakov succeeded in refining Mussorgsky's crudeness, he also robbed the opera of much of its inherent elemental power. But Rimsky-Korsakov did succeed in making *Boris Godunov* thoroughly palatable to the ears of the opera world. His version was first given in 1896, starring Feodor Chaliapin, the greatest of all interpreters of the title role. Paris, London, and New York were some of the cities that expressed admiration for this folk opera during the next half dozen years or so. It is in this Rimsky-Korsakov edition that the opera is best known to most operagoers. However, Mussorgsky's own revised version has been intermittently revived both in Russia and elsewhere, since many critics became convinced that Mussorgsky's own version was far more striking in its originality and strength than Rimsky-Korsakov's mani-

Michael Glinka.

Modest Mussorgsky, a drawing by Alexandrovsky made in 1876.

A scene from a Metropolitan Opera production of Boris Godunov.

The crap-game scene from Porgy and Bess.

cured version. Several other adaptations of *Boris Godunov* have also been produced, including one by that eminent modern Soviet composer Dmitri Shostakovich (1906–   ).

Boris Godunov was Czar of Russia between 1598 and 1605. The opera opens with a prologue in which his colorful coronation takes place, following the death of his predecessor, Czar Feodor. Dmitri, Feodor's heir, had been assassinated by Boris. The first act takes place five years later. In a monastery cell, a monk describes how Czarevitch Dmitri had been murdered so that Boris might become Czar. One of the monks, Gregory, is deeply moved by the story. Since he bears a remarkable physical resemblance to the dead Dmitri, Gregory decides to assume Dmitri's identity, to spread the rumor that Dmitri is still alive, and then try to seize the throne from Boris. Gregory sets forth on this mission disguised as a peasant. The Russian masses rally around him, fervently believing he is truly Dmitri.

Word reaches Boris in his palace that the people headed by the false Dmitri are planning his overthrow. This uprising fills Boris with the delusion that Dmitri has risen from his grave, and the Czar has hallucinations that Dmitri's ghost has come to haunt and torture him. Horrified, Boris falls on his knees to pray to God for mercy. The revolt against Boris gains momentum; the masses, with the false Dmitri as leader, have reached the gates of Moscow. More and more agonized does Boris become, particularly after he has once again in one of his delusions seen the murdered Dmitri. Boris's monumental fears destroy his strength and reason. After saying farewell to his son and proclaiming him the new Czar, Boris falls to the ground, asks for his son's forgiveness, and then dies.

The love interest (introduced by Mussorgsky in his revision) takes place in what is known as the "Polish act." The love involves Marina, daughter of a Polish landowner, and Gregory (the false Dmitri). Since Marina aspires to be Czarina, she promises Gregory she will marry him after he becomes Czar. Some delightful music was introduced by Mussorgsky into this act, including a polonaise and a love duet.

The scene where Boris is tortured by fears and hallucinations and his death scene are overpowering episodes in which Mussorgsky's search for musical and dramatic truth is fulfilled. Musical truth is captured in many of the narratives, which gain in intensity and strength through Mussorgsky's use of his "melodies of life," and in a good many of the choruses for the Russian masses. The Coronation Scene provides stage glamour, as does the setting, costuming, and staging of much of the "Polish act." *211*

Mussorgsky wrote two more operas, *Khovanshchina* and *The Fair at Sorotchinsk,* neither of which he finished. This was done for him after his death by some of his compatriots, including Rimsky-Korsakov. In the first of these operas we find the beautiful first-act orchestral prelude that Mussorgsky named "Dawn on the Moskava River" and the exciting "Dances of the Persian Slaves," also for orchestra. A famous folk dance, the "Gopak," or "Hopak," is the best-known excerpt from the second opera.

Besides working on these two operas, in his last years, Mussorgsky also completed some important concert music, including two song cycles (*Sunless* and *Songs and Dances of Death*) and *Pictures at an Exhibition,* for piano, better known to us through the transcription for orchestra by Maurice Ravel. It is a wonder Mussorgsky could have accomplished all this. During this period he was bankrupt—physically, morally, and spiritually. He was now a chronic alcoholic. His nervous disorders were getting worse all the time. He neglected his personal appearance to a point where he was always dressed in shabby, dirty clothes, allowed his beard and hair to go unkempt, and gave the appearance of either a beggar or (if one noticed his stark, staring eyes) a madman. He avoided his musical colleagues and his friends, preferring to associate with disreputable companions. Somehow he managed to hold on to a job in the department of forestry for eleven years after he had assumed it in 1869, but most of the time he was incapable of performing his work, and time and again he failed to show up at his office. He never had enough money to buy the food he needed to sustain him properly, so his face and body became shrunken through undernourishment. More than once he was evicted from his lodgings for failure to pay rent.

He collapsed at a party one night in 1881 and had to be hospitalized. He had suffered an apopleptic stroke. There is good reason to believe that before his death he lost his sanity. His last request was for alcohol. Peace finally came on March 28, 1881, when he died in a hospital.

Russia was not the only country where some composers became obsessed with patriotic ardor and immersed themselves deeply in the traditions of their native lands. In other places, too, they reached into their country's history, backgrounds, lore, folk songs, and dances for operatic material. The only Polish opera that has gained an extensive hearing, for example (about fifteen hundred performances in Warsaw alone since its premiere, and hundreds of others elsewhere in Europe), is

Halka (1848 & 58), a folk opera, by Stanislaw Moniuszko (1819–72).

Leoš Janáček (1854–1928) was the composer of an extraordinary Moravian folk opera, *Jenufa* (1904). Moravia was a section of Bohemia (with its own customs, dress, and folk songs and dances) from all of which Janáček, who was his own librettist, drew copiously for a stark, grim drama. Jenufa's illegitimate child is murdered by Jenufa's foster mother so that the girl might be free to marry Laca. In his score, Janáček makes considerable and effective use of speechlike declamations, which he called "melodies of the language." Janáček's pronounced nationalism in *Jenufa* and his interest in having his melodies pattern themselves after speech earned him the sobriquet of "the Moravian Mussorgsky."

Of more recent date, national opera in Spain is represented by *La vida breve* (1913) by Manuel de Falla (1876–1946), best known to most through its intriguing Spanish dances; English national opera, by *Hugh the Drover* (1914) by Ralph Vaughan Williams (1872–1958).

From Prague, the capital of Bohemia (now part of Czechoslovakia), came one of the most amusing folk operas ever written. *The Bartered Bride* is its title; its composer, Bedřich Smetana (1824–84) is regarded as the founder of the Bohemian national school in music. Smetana wrote eight operas, most of them nationalistic. *The Bartered Bride,* which came early in his career, is his most famous, indeed the only one that remains in the permanent repertory of major opera houses.

Smetana's first opera, *The Brandenburgers in Bohemia* (1866), was severely criticized at its premiere for being an imitation of Wagner. To prove himself capable of writing in a way completely different from Wagner, Smetana asked Karel Sabina to write for him a light, frivolous, and thoroughly Bohemian libretto. What Smetana actually wanted was an operetta text for which he could concoct gay tunes and dances to fill in the gaps between spoken dialogue. This is what was accomplished in the first version of this opera, *The Bartered Bride,* and the Bohemians enjoyed the show immensely when it was first presented in 1866. This success encouraged Smetana to expand his successful operetta with additional choruses and dances. This version went over even better when it was heard in Prague in 1869.

Now convinced that *The Bartered Bride* had the makings of a folk opera, rather than an operetta, Smetana replaced the dialogue with recitatives. In this final and definitive form it was heard in Prague in 1870 and became Bohemia's best-loved and most frequently performed work for the musical stage. It has received almost two thousand performances in Prague since its premiere. During this period it has also been produced by virtually every leading opera house. In 1936, the Metropolitan Opera presented it in an English translation.

In *The Bartered Bride* we are in a light, gay, picturesque world—a Bohemian village in the 1860s. The characters, their customs and costumes, their way of life, are as indigenously Bohemian as are Smetana's fetching folklike melodies and native dance tunes. Particularly memorable are the peasant dances: the first-act polka; the furiant (a fiery type of peasant dance) in the second act; and "The Dance of the Comedians" in the third act.

The opera opens with a festival. Micha, a wealthy landowner, wants his stupid son Wenzel (who also stutters badly) to marry the lovely Marie. Micha calls upon Kezal, a professional matchmaker, to arrange the marriage. Marie is in love with a handsome stranger recently come to town —Hans. Kezal's job is to convince Hans to forget Marie. He offers Hans a bribe of three hundred gold pieces, which Hans accepts on the condition that the marriage contract specifies that Marie must marry Micha's son, without mentioning Wenzel's name. Marie, heartbroken that Hans has deserted her for gold, decides to marry Wenzel. But soon we learn that Hans is Micha's long-lost son. Hans can live up to his contract by marrying Marie while retaining Kezal's gold. Marie is delighted at this strange turn of affairs. But Wenzel (who is without a bride) and Kezal (who has been swindled out of his money) are desolate.

When American composers first tried writing national operas they usually chose the American Indians as characters, American Indian customs and mores as material for plots, and music imitating the chants and ritual dances of the American Indians. Two operas are typical: *Natoma* (1911) by Victor Herbert (1859–1924) and *Shanewis* (1918) by Charles Wakefield Cadman (1881–1946).

When an American finally achieved a national opera able to capture both the enthusiasm and the imagination of the civilized world, that work drew its inspiration not from the American Indian but from the Negro. This opera is George Gershwin's *Porgy and Bess*.

By the time George Gershwin (1898–1937) wrote *Porgy and Bess* he had already become famous as one of America's most successful composers of popular songs and scores for the Broadway theater and as a serious composer (*Rhapsody in Blue, An American in Paris,* Concerto in F for piano and orchestra). *Porgy and Bess* was Gershwin's last performance as a serious composer—and his best. It is the only American opera to have been heard in practically every major city in the United States and abroad, and to achieve extravagant acclaim in foreign lands. Between 1952 and 1956 an American Negro troupe toured with this opera through the United States, Latin America, Europe, the Middle East, and the Soviet Union and other countries behind the Iron Curtain. Wherever it was performed it was received triumphantly. During this period it became the first American opera ever given on the stage of the world-famous La Scala opera house in Milan. In 1965, *Porgy and Bess* entered the permanent repertory of the Volksoper in Vienna.

In the years that followed it was given by local opera companies in Turkey, Bulgaria, France, Budapest, Germany, Czechoslovakia, Sweden, and Norway. The year of 1970 began with its production by the Komische Oper in East Berlin and ended with a Danish production opening the season of the Copenhagen Opera. In the same year it added a significant chapter to American social history. It was given in the locale in which the opera is set—Charleston, South Carolina—in commemoration of the 300th anniversary of the founding of the city. On that occasion, for the first time in the city's history, both whites and blacks not only attended the performance but also were guests at a gala party following the premiere.

It is sad that Gershwin did not live to see his opera thus serve as a catalytic agent between blacks and whites in Charleston, for he himself never judged a man by the color of his skin. But it is tragic that Gershwin did not survive to learn that the opera (which he knew with finality was his masterpiece, and which he was convinced would endure) should have become the only American opera to achieve worldwide acceptance. For when *Porgy and Bess* had first been introduced in 1935, first in Boston for tryouts, then in New York, it was a failure. (It was not given in an opera house but in a theater.) Not until about five years after Gershwin's death did the opera first begin to make an impression, though some of its songs had already become popular. In 1942 it returned to New York to become the longest-running revival in the history of the American theater up to that time; it also captured the Music Critics Circle Award.

The opera begins with best foot forward. After an exciting and somewhat discordant overture we hear the wondrous lullaby "Summertime." The place is Catfish Row in the Negro section of Charleston, where a crap game is in progress. During the game a brawl erupts, during which Crown kills one of the players. Going into hiding to escape the law, Crown leaves behind him in Catfish Row his girl friend, Bess.

Deserted and alone, Bess is taken into the household of the gentle, loving cripple, Porgy, whose joyous outlook on life is reflected in "I Got Plenty o' Nuttin'." Porgy and Bess fall in love, as becomes obvious when they participate in the exultant love duet "Bess, You Is My Woman Now."

During a lodge picnic at Kittiwah Island, the people of Catfish Row are enjoying themselves. Sportin' Life, a gay blade who makes his living selling dope, expounds his cynicism about religion in the amusing "It Ain't Necessarily So." After the people start to leave the island for Catfish Row, Crown (who all this while has been hiding in the woods of the island) comes out of the shadows to snatch Bess and drag her off. A few days later Bess is back in Catfish Row. Porgy welcomes her back with love and tolerance, while Bess reaffirms her affection for him in "I Loves You, Porgy." Crown follows her to Catfish Row, where Porgy kills him. After Porgy is released by the police because nobody will testify against him, he discovers that during his absence Bess, stimulated by the dope Sportin' Life gave her, has run off with Sportin' Life to New York. Climbing on his goat cart, Porgy plans to go to New York to find and bring Bess back.

Porgy and Bess is a mighty American folk opera whose limelight is focused not only on the story of the hero and the heroine but on the Negro people and their environment. As this writer said in his biography of Gershwin, Gershwin produced "a musical art basically Negro in physiognomy and spirit, basically expressive of the heart and soul of the entire race. The pages that stir us most profoundly, and bring to the opera its artistic importance, are those most deeply rooted in Negro folk culture."

Gershwin's libretto was written by Du Bose Heyward, based on both the novel and the play *Porgy,* by Heyward and his wife, Dorothy. Du Bose Heyward collaborated with Ira Gershwin in writing the lyrics for the principal musical numbers of the opera.

14

The Twentieth Century

Claude Debussy, Alban Berg, Benjamin Britten,

Gian Carlo Menotti

Almost like ocean waves throwing about and scattering flotsam and jetsam on the seas, the music of the twentieth century has brought to the surface many different revolutionary techniques, materials, and systems that have changed opera.

Two new trends in music were impressionism and expressionism. The term *impressionism* brings to mind the name of Achille-Claude Debussy (1862–1918), its first and prime exponent. Debussy wrote only one opera, *Pelléas et Mélisande* (*Pelléas and Mélisande*), and it is the quintessence of his impressionist style.

Several composers are identified closely with the expressionist movement in music, most particularly Arnold Schoenberg (1874–1951), who developed its techniques and goals. The most frequently performed and artistically the most influential opera in the expressionist style is by one of Schoenberg's pupils and disciples, Alban Berg (1885–1935): *Wozzeck*.

In the first quarter of the twentieth century *Pelléas and Mélisande* and *Wozzeck* stood at opposite polar points, diametrically opposed in style, concept, and ideals. But each had this in common: a rejection of Wagner's grandiose architecture, extramusical concepts, pretentious aims, sensuous style, and massive techniques.

Let us first consider impressionism, Debussy, and *Pelléas and Mélisande*. Impressionism is a term taken from painting. In music, as in painting, an impressionist is not interested in recreating any given subject with photographic accuracy. The impressionist instead seeks to capture the moods and feelings the subject he is treating arouses in him. In music, as in painting, the emphasis is on color, sensation, mood, atmosphere. Subtle nuances, delicacy, exoticism replace romantic or dramatic writing and emphasis on structure and substance. To achieve this aim, Debussy devised new chords capable of evoking the most subtle colors and hues. He arrived at an exquisite and shimmering kind of orchestral sound by emphasizing woodwinds in low register, violins in high register, and the exotic sounds of delicate-toned percussion instruments.

The use of old church modes in place of traditional scales (something Debussy had learned from the Russians, whom he admired) and at times the employing of a five-tone oriental scale created exotic effects. Otherwise he relied extensively on the whole-tone scale. Debussy did not invent this—Glinka had used it sparingly—but he made it a functional, indispensable element of his impressionist music. The whole-tone scale is made up exclusively of notes at intervals of a full tone through the eight-tone scale, whereas the regular major and minor scales combine whole and half tones.

Though Debussy followed Wagner in using a continuous melodic line in his opera, his was more in the nature of recitative than was Wagner's, more atmospheric than dramatic, built up usually from fragments or repeated phrases. Debussy maintained this steady stream of sound not only in his melody but also in his rhythm, which he made to flow evenly by minimizing the importance of accentuations and pronounced beats and at times by dispensing with bar lines between measures.

Claude Debussy had been a musical rebel from his schooldays at the Paris Conservatory. He did, however, win a French competition, the Prix de Rome, which allowed him to live and compose in Rome for several years. Debussy did not arrive at impressionism until 1887, after he had returned from Rome. Back in Paris he looked for some creative haven for his rebellious musical nature. For a time he thought he had found it in Wagner—especially after visiting Bayreuth in 1888 and 1889. He became greatly enthusiastic about *Parsifal* and *Tristan and Isolde*. At first hearing he became a rapturous worshiper of Wagner, for that master's revolutionary techniques had struck a responsive chord in his own revolutionary tendencies.

But this idolatry of Wagner was short-lived. The bigness of Wagner's works, Wagner's propaganda, the mammoth musical forces Wagner employed, all soon began to repel Debussy's sensitive nature. A Frenchman, Debussy preferred clarity, emotional restraint, economy, refinement, delicacy—qualities that were the very opposites of those found in Wagner. Debussy now aspired to become a *French* composer (*"un musicien français,"* as he put it), just as Wagner was so unmistakably German.

He soon found a new hero to emulate: an eccentric Frenchman, Erik Satie (1866–1925) who rejected the old order and went his own way in his music with discords, unusual scales, barless notation, and esoteric and at times quixotic methods.

Two other important influences were brought heavily to bear on Debussy as he searched for a musical style best suited to his nature. One was the French impressionist school of painting, then come into vogue. Debussy used to meet Cézanne, Manet, Monet, and Degas in cafés. In listening to their theories about art, he recognized that their principles could also be applied to music.

A second major extramusical impact on Debussy at this time came from the symbolist poets, of whom Verlaine, Mallarmé, and Baudelaire were the most important. These poets were not interested in delivering a message or even having a meaning in their poems. They were concerned with the *sound* of their poetry, words being used for their effect on the ear in much the same way as composers used tones.

All these forces—Satie with his eccentric innovations, the impressionist artists, and the symbolist poets—acted on Debussy and helped him to evolve the means by which he could create music filled with dreams, mists, and mysteries; music with haunting moods and exquisite tone colors; music that sensitively reflected Debussy's responses to the subject he was treating musically. Thus he came to musical impressionism, first with his String Quartet (1893), then with his tone poem *Prelude to the Afternoon of a Faun* (1894), and after that with various orchestral and piano works and songs. Only when his impressionist style was fully matured did he embark on writing an opera.

For a text he chose Maurice Maeterlinck's play *Pelléas and Mélisande,* which had a kind of hazy quality as if the action were taking place behind a transparent curtain. The characters were more like shadows than human beings. The plot was projected so leisurely that for periods nothing was really happening. The enchantment in this play lay in its atmosphere, its air of mystery, its evocative moods and most of all in its flight from realism into a misty dream world.

Golaud is the grandson of King Arkel of Allemonde, a mythical kingdom in legendary times. One day he finds Mélisande in a forest; her beauty and sadness move him. He takes her back to the palace, where he marries her. There she meets Golaud's brother, Pelléas. Pelléas and Mélisande fall in love. Golaud soon discovers that his wife has betrayed him and he kills Pelléas. Mélisande, who has given birth to a child, lies on her deathbed where Golaud begs for her forgiveness, which never comes. The opera ends with Mélisande's death and Golaud's overwhelming grief.

Debussy's music represents a triumph of understatement. The dynamics are hardly more than a whisper (only four fortissimo passages appear in the entire score!). A major love scene comprises merely the simple exchange of the words "I love you" rather than the passionate outbursts of Wagner in *Tristan and Isolde;* the words are almost spoken, and at moments the orchestra remains completely silent.

Debussy's vocal writing largely consists of almost continuous declamation (sometimes only of repeated single tones), whose inflections caught the essence of the French language. The orchestral accompaniment projects sensitive, refined sounds as a background. When a more full-bodied lyricism is called for, which is not frequent, Debussy rises to the challenge: for example, in the unaccompanied song that Mélisande sings to herself as she combs her hair—the style that of an old French modal folk tune. When a more expressive orchestration is required, Debussy again rises to the occasion. In the closing moments, for example, when Golaud is led away from his dead wife, the orchestra comments with soft-spoken, surpassing tenderness, the final tones of which drop from the harplike tears. All of the vagueness, remoteness, and symbolic poetry of Maeterlinck were captured in this impressionist score. Play and music are one and inseparable. It is doubtful if there are many examples in opera where words and music are so inextricably intertwined.

The Opéra-Comique accepted *Pelléas and Mélisande*—but one problem followed another before that premiere took place. There was trouble with the censors, and with stagehands who insisted there was not enough time for them to make changes for thirteen scenes; there were complications with the musicians and the singers, who could not at first comprehend Debussy's kind of music and then were confused because a sloppy copyist had made a mess in writing out the parts.

These difficulties were finally straightened out. But the biggest one of all was not so easily disposed of. Maeterlinck had wanted his common-law wife, Georgette Leblanc, to appear as Mélisande. Debussy and the director of the Opéra-Comique insisted on using Mary Garden, who, vo-

cally and physically, seemed born for the part. When Miss Garden was
definitely chosen, Maeterlinck announced in the press that he had
washed his hands of the whole opera production, that he prayed for a resounding failure for it. Maeterlinck did everything he could to discredit
both the opera and the composer. He even thought of challenging Debussy to a duel. Instead he wrote a parody of the opera, which he had
distributed outside the opera house on the day of the dress rehearsal.
This piece of ridicule encouraged many attending the rehearsal to break
out in loud guffaws throughout the performance.

Nevertheless, *Pelléas and Mélisande* was finally produced on April
30, 1902. Maeterlinck's friends and followers were on hand to create a
disturbance. The rest of the audience seemed dazed at what it heard and
saw. Its reaction was echoed in the press. "All I heard," wrote Leon
Kerst, "was a series of harmonized sounds (I don't say harmonious)
which succeeded one another uninterruptedly, without a single phrase, a
single motive, a single accent, a single form, a single outline. And to this
accompaniment unnecessary singers drone out words, nothing but
words, a kind of long drawn-out monotonous recitatives, unbearable,
moribund." There were some favorable voices, but they were drowned
out by the raucous opposition.

But misunderstood, abused, laughed at, or hated, *Pelléas and
Mélisande* became the talk of the city. Talk inspired curiosity, and curiosity brought people to the box office. By its seventh performance the
Opéra-Comique was sold out. There were seven additional sold-out performances that season, and ten the season after that. By the end of the
second year, the opera was beginning to exert its curious spell on listeners. Even those who did not understand what the opera was trying to do
were beginning to succumb to its strange, exotic appeal. After four
years, *Pelléas and Mélisande* established itself as a success of the first
order both in and outside France. More than that, the opera, its composer, and impressionists were becoming a cult with the progressive elements among the younger musicians of the time.

Expressionism is also a term taken from painting. Undoubtedly, the
most celebrated expressionist painter was Kandinsky, while among the
foremost expressionist composers of opera were Arnold Schoenberg and
his pupil and disciple, Alban Berg. Where in impressionism painters and
composers conveyed their own subjective responses to the theme they
were writing about, the expressionist consciously divorced himself from
his subject matter, rid himself of all subjective feelings, and tried to get

to the essence, the inner soul state, of his subject through abstraction.

Design, reduced to its bare essentials, became all important. In music, the expressionist not only stripped his writing of human responses and relationships but also arrived at precision, brevity, an inexorable logic of thought, and the reduction of his musical means and materials to essentials. In short, what the expressionist composer sought to achieve was just the skeleton of a musical work—a body removed of heart, flesh, arteries, tissues, and muscle.

It is no paradox that the founder of musical expressionism—Arnold Schoenberg—should have begun his career as composer by imitating Wagner. For once Schoenberg, like Debussy, became saturated with Wagnerism, he grew tired of its romantic excesses. To free himself from Wagner's influence, Schoenberg, once again like Debussy, had to find a new style in violent opposition and contrast to Wagner. Expressionism, then, like impressionism, represents a revolt against Wagner.

But the expressionists broke ties not only with Wagner but with all the musical past. The basic element of music, as far as the expressionists were concerned, was *sound*. Music was no longer to be the means of expressing either emotion or ideas. For this reason the old concept of melody had to be replaced by a new kind of free lyricism that is called *Sprechstimme* ("song-speech"). This is a declamation in which the voice swoops freely to indicated pitches in a free rhythm, the melodic thought being reduced at the same time to fragments.

In expressionist music, no distinction exists between consonance and dissonance. Discords are to be used as freely as consonant, or harmonious, chords once used to be. Music, further, would no longer enslave itself to a basic tonality, but could roam about from one key to another without modulations, or transitions, and end up in any key it wished. This last technique is known as atonality. Atonality and song-speech are the two principal tools in the shop of the expressionist composer.

The first piece of completely atonal music ever written was the finale of Schoenberg's String Quartet No. 2, in 1908. The first significant use of song-speech is found in Schoenberg's song cycle *Pierrot Lunaire,* in 1912.

We come upon a truly historic milestone in musical expressionism with the most famous atonal opera ever written, *Wozzeck,* by Alban Berg. This work represents for opera a brave new unexplored world in much the same way that Wagner's music dramas had in the late nineteenth century and Debussy's *Pelléas and Mélisande* had in the first years of the twentieth.

Alban Berg had only one teacher—Arnold Schoenberg, between 1905 and 1912. Inevitably, the teacher molded Berg's musical thinking. As Schoenberg began charting his own course as an expressionist, and became increasingly involved with atonality, he encouraged Berg to accompany him in these musical adventures. And so Berg (whose early works had been highly romantic) began to turn his back to traditional music to embrace atonality.

The first piece of music Berg finished after completing his studies with Schoenberg was atonal: *Five Orchestral Songs,* in 1912. It caused a scandal when first performed in Vienna a year later. The scandal notwithstanding, Berg continued along the lines laid down for him by Schoenberg, producing other orchestral and chamber works, all in an atonal style, before undertaking the most ambitious project he had thus far assumed—the opera *Wozzeck*.

Berg first became interested in *Wozzeck* in 1914 when he saw a production of this remarkable play by Georg Büchner. Though written more than a century earlier, *Wozzeck* strangely anticipated some of the techniques of the expressionist movement in drama. This play obsessed Berg's thinking for several years. He worked out an opera libretto during the years of World War I, and it then took him about four years to complete his score.

Wozzeck is a curious libretto in which the action seems to be taking place in a distorted dream. Things happen not as they do in real life (though the basic plot is real enough), but as they might appear reflected by a cracked or misshapen mirror. The characters are for the most part caricatures; their abnormal behavior is often guided by their subconscious. Wozzeck is a poor, bedraggled soldier ridiculed by his regiment and a Doctor. Marie is his mistress, but he has a rival in the Drum Major. Wozzeck finds Marie wearing a new pair of earrings and then sees her dancing with the Drum Major. When Wozzeck refuses a drink offered him by his rival, the Drum Major gives him a sound beating. Marie takes pity on the humiliated Wozzeck. On his invitation she takes a walk with him; in a fit of jealous rage, he murders her with a knife. He rushes off to a tavern to relieve his tortured conscience through drink.

Suddenly he remembers he had left his knife with the body. Returning to the scene of his crime, he finds the knife. He throws it into a nearby pool. An impulse leads him to retrieve the incriminating weapon by jumping into the water, where he drowns.

As sensitively attuned as Debussy's music is to Maeterlinck's fragile text, so is Berg's powerful score wonderfully suited to Büchner's stark tragedy. The discordant sounds of Berg's atonal writing, the dramatic sweeps of the voice in his song-speech both help him to achieve high tensions. Sounds such as come from the orchestra and voices had never before been heard in opera, but they fit the text perfectly in achieving a harrowing, surrealistic effect new to opera at that time.

Thus what Berg realized is what Ernest Newman, England's great critic, called "the unique oneness of the dramatic situations, the psychology of the characters and the musical expression. . . . The non-technical listener . . . finds himself, perhaps for the first time in his life, taking a vast amount of non-tonal music and not merely not wincing at it but being engrossed by it. . . . He feels the music to be not only 'right' for the subject but the only musical equivalent conceivable for it."

So difficult is this opera to perform that it required 137 rehearsals before it could be produced the first time—in Berlin on December 14, 1925. Some critics were completely taken aback by this strange work. "I had the sensation of not having been in a public theater but in an insane asylum," reported the critic Zsorlich. Some critics acclaimed it as a landmark in twentieth-century opera as important as *Pelléas and Mélisande*. Because *Wozzeck* was so controversial it received performances throughout Europe, sometimes inspiring riots (as in Prague in 1926, where it had to be removed immediately from the repertory), sometimes arousing unusual enthusiasm (as in Leningrad in 1927, and in Philadelphia and New York in 1931). Since that time, *Wozzeck* has ceased to be a curiosity over which opposing factions exchange hot words. It has become a modern classic.

Berg wrote only more more opera, *Lulu*. Where *Wozzeck* is an atonal opera, *Lulu* is an opera in the twelve-tone technique. Schoenberg had been the one who had been responsible for developing the twelve-tone technique (or dodecaphony) into a highly important and functional system—in fact into the most revolutionary new system music had been subjected to in several centuries. Schoenberg first used the twelve-tone technique in 1923 in the last movement of his *Five Pieces,* for piano, and in the fourth movement of his *Serenade.* His *Suite,* for piano, in 1924 was his first work constructed throughout in the twelve-tone technique. For the next two decades Schoenberg used the system exclusively in all his works, including his only attempt at a full-length opera, *Moses und Aron (Moses and Aaron).*

The reason why Schoenberg passed on from atonality to the twelve-tone technique is that he began to feel the need of some controlling system if his writing were not to degenerate into total anarchy. The old systems and methods he was convinced were obsolete. And so he worked out a totally new method, using it with consummate skill. Before beginning to write a composition he created a pattern, or "row," of twelve tones of the chromatic scale—but one in which no note is repeated. A musical composition was then constructed by using this row in its original form and in various established formations permitting forty-eight variations.

A kind of inflexible logic, as rigid as a mathematical formula, now governed Schoenberg's writing. Discords now completely effaced consonance; the human equation was thoroughly eliminated; lyricism was replaced by either song-speech or a succession of the most fragmentary series of tones. The concoction of a piece of music became a kind of engineering process.

That this system, in spite of its rigidity of procedure, could be used for some extraordinary sound experiences has been proved by numerous composers besides Schoenberg. Several highly exciting operas have used the twelve-tone technique exclusively. Two of the most striking are Schoenberg's *Moses and Aaron* and Berg's *Lulu*.

Schoenberg began writing both the libretto and music for *Moses and Aaron* in 1932, completing two acts and some of the text for a third. He then abandoned the project. Toward the end of his life he tried to complete his opera, but death defeated him. He let it be known that if the opera were ever produced in an unfinished state, the first two acts should be given with the music, and the third act played as straight drama. This is the way the opera was first heard—in a concert version over the Hamburg Radio in Germany in 1954. This was also the way in which it was first staged (in Zürich in 1957). Even though it has never been finished, *Moses and Aaron* proved itself a work of great fascination and importance.

Schoenberg used the biblical story of Moses and Aaron to raise and answer questions about morality, religion, and idolatry. Moses (a song-speech role) is the symbol of spiritual values. Aaron (a singing role) represents the man of action. The third act points up the victory of the spirit over action.

The entire opera is based on a single twelve-tone row and its variants, used with such ingenuity, variety, and dramatic interest that monotony never sets in. The climax of the opera is an orgy before the Golden Calf. Schoenberg wanted this orgy to be staged with shocking realism. But his intentions have not been followed to the letter, even in this permissive age. Despite the necessary modifications, the orgy scene, both as a dramatic spectacle and a musical explosion, is one not easily forgotten. Here, as earlier, the continuous use of discords, the song-speech, the dissonant counterpoint, the orgiastic sounds at moments of climax, the unique screeching produced by voices and individual instruments, and the at times seemingly unrelated succession of thematic ideas develop an elemental force that is perhaps the outstanding characteristic of twelve-tone music.

Elemental force also sweeps through the pages of Berg's *Lulu,* which, like *Moses and Aaron,* is an unfinished work. The libretto was adapted from two plays by Frank Wedekind. The basic story is quite a sordid affair both in Wedekind and in Berg. Lulu is a disreputable, almost horrifying creature symbolizing human passions, agonies, and frustrations. She involves herself in promiscuous love affairs, drives one husband to suicide, murders a second husband, becomes a prostitute, and in the end is murdered by Jack the Ripper.

Berg translated stage action into music of an agonizing intensity and brutal strength that at times comes close to ugliness of sound. This is possibly the only kind of music that could treat the subject contained in the two Wedekind plays. *Lulu* is not an opera providing an evening of pleasurable relaxation or enjoyment. One emerges from the opera house feeling that one has just experienced a nerve-racking and at times gruesome production.

By the time Berg died in Vienna in 1935 he had finished two acts, 268 measures of a third act, and the complete finale. In such an incomplete state, the opera received its world premiere in Zürich on June 2, 1937. However, when the opera was given in Essen, Germany, in 1953, dialogue from Wedekind's plays filled out the third act (given with the music completed earlier for a symphonic suite) and this is how America first became acquainted with this opera at Santa Fe, New Mexico, in 1963.

If atonality is one step behind the twelve-tone technique, then the twelve-tone technique is a step behind serialism. Serialism is another system that has been responsible for important, provocative operas; indeed, serialism is probably the most influential of the avant-garde techniques evolved since the end of World War II. It is actually an extension of the twelve-tone technique. In the latter, only the pitch is controlled. In serialism other elements of music are equally systematized: tone color, tempo, rhythm, dynamics. Each element has a row of its own of twelve different markings. In this way the writing of music becomes *totally* controlled. A distinguished Argentine composer, Alberto Ginastera (1916–   ) is only one of many composers to have used serialism extensively in operas. His *Don Rodrigo* (1964) and *Bomarzo* (1967) have enjoyed exceptional success both in New York and other operatic centers. His *Beatrix Cenci* (1971) was one of the major attractions during the opening week of the Kennedy Center for the Performing Arts in Washington, D.C.

Some avant-garde composers since the 1950s have discovered that electronic sounds, reproduced on magnetic tape and transmitted through loudspeakers, could be utilized for very special and unique effects in a way traditional instruments cannot be used. This does not mean that the orchestra is dispensed with. What it does mean is that electronically reproduced sounds become a part of the orchestration. One of the earliest operas to explore the potential of electronic sounds was *Aniara* (1959) by Karl-Birger Blomdahl (1916–1968). This is the first opera ever written about space travel. "Aniara" is a spaceship filled with passengers en route to Mars after an atomic war on earth. The libretto describes what happens to the people when the mechanism of their ship proves defective and they must wander aimlessly in space as one passenger after another dies, while twenty years pass. The mounting tensions among the people, the atmosphere of outer space, the eerie sounds that float from vast distances, the suggestions of the supernatural—these are interpreted through electronic means to endow the opera with an altogether unique fascination.

Since *Aniara,* quite a number of composers have introduced electronic sounds into their operatic scores. Henk Badings (1907–   ) did this in *Martin Korda, D.P.* (1960), an opera about displaced persons in a camp; so did Boris Blacher (1903–   ) in describing the experiences of eleven survivors of a crash landing in *Incidents in Connection with a Crash Landing* (1966).

Generally speaking, the opera composers who have found the largest audiences in most parts of the world since the end of World War II have been those whose writing is an amalgamation of many different, varied idioms, techniques, and methods—allowing the changing incidents in their texts to dictate what idiom, technique, or method is most serviceable. These composers are known as eclectics. It is within this group that we encounter two composers who have dominated opera in our time: Benjamin Britten (1913–   ) and Gian Carlo Menotti (1911–   ). Both have written many operas that have been extensively performed and recorded; both are exceptionally articulate musically, and both have been most successful in tapping many different musical veins. Each has always found the appropriate music demanded by his text by traversing a wide gamut of styles from romanticism to modernism, and at times even to avant-gardism.

The first opera to make Britten a world figure in opera was *Peter Grimes* (1945), with a libretto based on George Crabbe's *The Borough*. Peter Grimes is a gruff, uncouth fisherman in a small fishing town on the English coast early in the nineteenth century. Though he is legally absolved of a crime for which he had been indicted (the murder of an apprentice) he is held in suspicion, and is regarded with antagonism, by his fellow townspeople. Virtually a pariah, Grimes becomes increasingly surly—even to the point of administering a beating to the woman he loves. Grimes hires a new apprentice. When this boy becomes the fatal victim of an accident, in which Grimes had no involvement, the townspeople become convinced Grimes is the murderer. They descend upon his hut in fury to take the law into their own hands. Rather than face an angry mob, Peter Grimes goes out into the sea to meet his death.

For this tragic drama, in which an innocent man's conflict with a ruthless mob is symbolized, Britten achieved an eclectic score combining declamation with fully developed lyrical pages; discordant writing with delightful sea chanteys and jigs; music of high tensions with moments of encompassing tenderness; romantic ardor with realistic tone painting. Yet, as Ernest Newman noted, "the whole texture, musical and dramatic . . . is admirably unified, in spite of the many genres it employs, ranging from almost naked speech to music at its fullest powers."

Britten's most famous opera after *Peter Grimes* was *Billy Budd* (1951), where once again the composer is concerned with injustice, with the victimization of an innocent man by the blind hatred of an evil enemy.

The text was taken from a novel by Herman Melville. Billy Budd is a likable, carefree young man—a sailor in the British navy during the French-British conflicts in the eighteenth century. He incurs the enmity of John Claggart, master-of-arms. Claggart invents a treason charge against Billy. In a fit of rage, Billy kills his accuser and for this is condemned by a court martial to die by hanging. The Captain wisely realizes that Billy has had sufficient provocation for committing his crime; but the Captain also knows that naval discipline must be upheld and Billy must die. The Captain's unaccompanied soliloquy about good and evil ends the opera.

As in *Peter Grimes,* Britten introduces sailors' chanteys within a score that is mostly declamatory, but occasionally erupts into tender or passionate song. One of the unusual features of this opera is that it calls for an all-male cast, hence its plot has no love interest. The center of importance lies in the tragedy that strikes down an innocent man. Since its world premiere at Covent Garden in 1951, Britten revised his opera to give it greater tautness and compression. The new version was heard at Covent Garden in 1964.

Both *Peter Grimes* and *Billy Budd* use large musical forces and are spacious in design. Britten has proved he could also write tragic operas with limited resources and economical means—chamber operas such as *The Rape of Lucretia* (1946) and *The Turn of the Screw* (1954), the latter from a novel by Henry James. He also proved himself thoroughly adept in comedy, in *Albert Herring* (1947); in writing an opera for children, *Let's Make an Opera* (1949), and another for television, *Owen Wingrave* (1971), once again based on Henry James; in creating a work full of Meyerbeer pomp and ceremony, *Gloriana* (1953), written for the coronation of Queen Elizabeth II of Britain; in combining humor with fantasy in *A Midsummer Night's Dream* (1960), an operatic version of the Shakespeare play, and in creating a new form that he called "parables," little operas intended for church performance: *Curlew River, The Burning Fiery Furnace*, and *The Prodigal Son*, written and produced between 1964 and 1968. The ease and flexibility with which Britten has been able to change his manner of writing have made him perhaps the most important opera composer of our day, and surely England's greatest opera composer since Henry Purcell.

There can be no questioning Britten's success. Yet if a computation were ever made of the number of people who have seen the operas of Gian Carlo Menotti in opera auditoriums, in theaters, in schools, with amateur groups, in motion pictures, and over television, it is more than probable that no twentieth-century opera composer has had a larger public.

Menotti's enormous appeal stems from the fact that his eclecticism leans more strongly toward sentiment, romanticism, and lyricism than to Britten's strong kind of declamation; more toward a tender melodic line in the vein of Puccini's *verismo* than to Britten's kind of tonal realism. As a man of the theater, Menotti is a master of the stage as few composers have been. He has filled the many roles he has assumed with the utmost competence—namely those of librettist, composer, stage director, casting director, and advisor in all other phases of production.

As a composer Menotti wears a coat of many colors; but the colors

A sketch of Claude Debussy conducting.

Alban Berg.

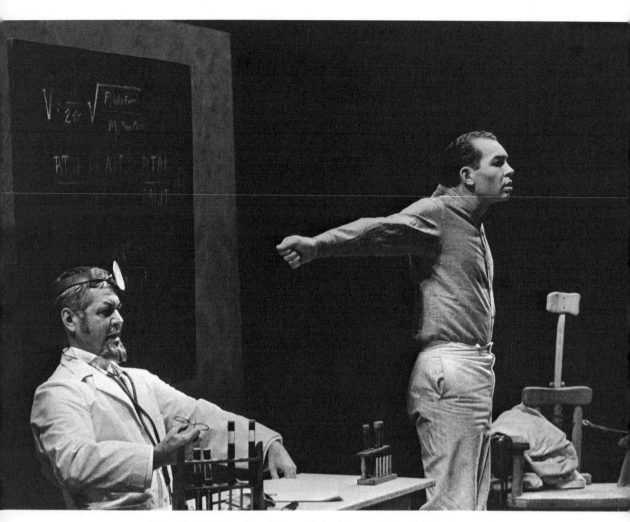

Wozzek (William Dooley) and the Doctor (Donald Gramm). A Metropolitan Opera production.

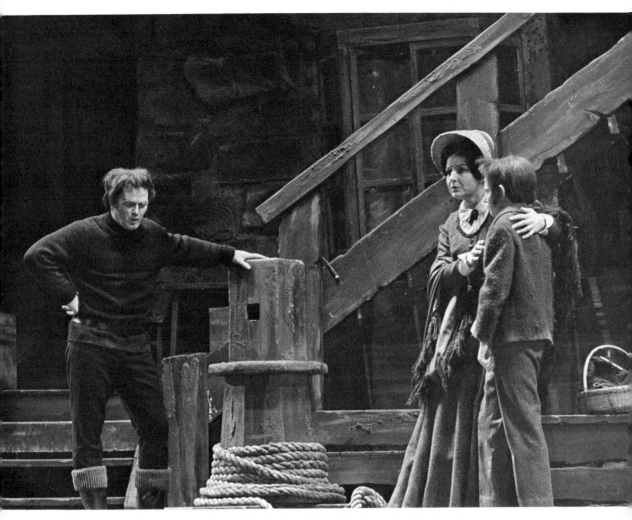

*Peter Grimes (Jon Vickers) and Ellen Orford (Lucine Amara) with the
Apprentice, John, in a Metropolitan Opera production.*

Benjamin Britten conducting the English Opera Group in a rehearsal of
The Turn of the Screw *in Berlin.*

A scene from Amahl and the Night Visitors.

are masterfully blended into a single design rather than suggesting patchwork. Give Menotti any textual situation and he will find the precise musical equivalent. He can be tragic and witty, sardonic and satiric; he can be, and often is, frankly and unashamedly sentimental, and he can be atmospheric; he can descend to the sordid and rise to the poetic. On the one hand he will imitate the *buffo* style and aria writing of the Italian masters; on the other, he can parody those old Italian styles for comic effect. He can employ modern idioms (discordant harmonies, polytonality, song-speech) for dramatic purpose, and at other times he is able to satirize the excesses of composers using these idioms. He is a traditionalist—and he is a nonconformist.

Far more than with any other contemporary opera composer, music is for Menotti a functional means with which a dramatic piece can be most faithfully projected. In fact, so consistently functional is Menotti's music that excerpts from his operas are rarely performed. In the opera house, or theater, or school auditorium, or television screen his music rarely misses aim; take parts of the score out of the opera and they sound contrived, uninspired, even lack musical interest. But if this is a weakness (and it is) it is balanced by Menotti's strength as a writer of music for the theater. He always manages to be wonderfully entertaining, whether he is tragic or comic, whether he writes for adults or children, whether he tries to be symbolic or realistic. This is why his operas have so often been produced in so many different places and through so many different media before such a varied audience.

Gian Carlo Menotti (1911–   ) is of Italian birth and citizenship. But he has been a permanent resident in the United States since 1927. After attending the Curtis Institute of Music, he wrote both the libretto and music for his first mature opera, an *opera buffa, Amelia Goes to the Ball* (1937). His theme was a frivolous one, ideally suited for *opera-buffa* treatment. In Milan, Amelia wants to go to a fancy ball, but is almost kept from attending it when her husband and her lover get into a fight. She smashes a vase over her husband's head and has her lover arrested as a burglar. She then goes gaily off to the ball—with the police officer. In his music Menotti captured the structure and spirit of Italian *opera buffa* most felicitously in a score overflowing with engaging and tuneful arias, duets, and ensemble numbers.

Menotti first emerged as a master of theatrical effect in *The Medium* (1946), a score that would henceforth be typical of his writing on tragic subjects. "It contains," as he said, "the potentialities of my style." Here, as later, his writing would change chameleonlike from one idiom to an-

Gian Carlo Menotti.

other, affected by every changing nuance or emotion or mood in the play. When the play is macabre, Menotti uses discord, song-speech, polytonality, and other modern techniques. When the play temporarily veers off to lightness, Menotti complies by writing a waltz in a popular style. There is also sprinkled through his score a good deal of sweetness and gentle lyricism in a Puccini vein. It may well be said that *The Medium* is an offspring of the *verismo* movement.

The composer found his subject while attending a seance, when he suddenly decided to write a tragedy about a fake spiritualist. In his libretto Madame Flora defrauds her clients with spuriously contrived seances—with the help of her daughter and a mute, Toby. At one of these sessions, Madame Flora experiences a pair of hands choking her. This leads her to confess to her clients that she is a fraud. Terror-stricken by this experience, she turns to drink, then begins to lose her reason. Disturbed by a noise behind a drawn curtain, she shoots wildly into it. Toby, who was hiding there, is killed. Over his dead body, Madame Flora entreats him to confess that it was he who had tried to strangle her.

The Medium was first heard at Columbia University in New York City on May 8, 1946. Two enterprising producers were so convinced that it had audience appeal that they brought it to Broadway, where it had a profitable run. Since then this opera has been given over one thousand times in America. It was made into a motion picture directed by Menotti in 1951, and in 1955 the opera was dispatched to Europe by the United States State Department. It has also been produced by leading European companies. It remains one of Menotti's most successful operas.

His best operas after that are also tragedies: *The Consul* (1950), *The Saint of Bleecker Street* (1954), and *Maria Golovin* (1958). The first, once again in a recognizable *verismo* style, also enjoyed an extended run on Broadway, where it was hailed by both the drama and the music critics. Here is what Olin Downes, the music critic of *The New York Times,* wrote: "He has produced an opera of eloquence, momentousness, and intensity of expression unequalled by any native composer." *The Consul* was awarded the Pulitzer Prize in music and the New York Drama Critics Award. It was extensively performed in Europe. When mounted at La Scala in 1951 it became the first American-written opera to be performed by that company.

The text has an unidentified European police state as setting. Magda
is trying to get a visa to leave the country and join her husband, who has

already made his escape. Totalitarian bureaucracy thwarts her every ef- fort. Tragedy piles on tragedy for poor Magda. She is unable to get a meeting with the consul (who is never seen on the stage). Her child dies. Her husband, who has returned to try to effect Magda's escape, is imprisoned. Completely distraught, Magda commits suicide.

The Saint of Bleecker Street has a religious story, set in our own time. Bleecker Street is in the Italian section of downtown New York. The heroine, Annina, is a sickly girl given to religious mysticism. She receives the stigmata (the marks of the crucifixion) on the palms of her hands, which forthwith endows her with holiness in the eyes of her religious neighbors. In an impressive ceremony, Annina is welcomed into the Church as the Bride of Christ. This experience so overwhelms her emotionally that she falls dead to the ground.

Religious feeling predominates in Menotti's music, particularly in the chants sung during the first-act ceremonial. Naturally, too, Menotti here, as elsewhere, yields to his weakness for writing arias in the Puccini style. But with these can also be found numbers with a wide popular appeal: a jukebox melody, for example; three wedding songs that combine florid writing with humor; and a catchy little ditty in the third act.

With *The Saint of Bleecker Street,* Menotti continued to gather accolades and honors. For the second time he was the recipient of the Pulitzer Prize and the Drama Critics Award. This opera also proved immensely successful at La Scala in 1955, in a telecast in London in 1956, and in numerous other European presentations.

In *Maria Golovin* (1958) Menotti returns to contemporary Europe for his background: to an unidentified frontier town some years "after a recent war." Maria's husband is still a war prisoner after four years of peace. During this period Maria has been living at the home of Donato, a blind man who makes bird cages. In time Maria and Donato become lovers. When Maria's husband is released from prison and comes to claim his wife, Maria bids Donato a permanent farewell. Aware he is losing the woman he loves, Donato fires a gun at Maria. He misses his aim, though he is not aware of this fact. He is happy with the thought that if he cannot have Maria, then neither can her husband.

Several years after the premiere of this opera, which had taken place at the Brussels World Exposition in Belgium, Menotti revised the opera extensively. The new and definitive version was first heard in Washington, D.C., in 1965.

Though he has achieved his prime importance with tragedies, Menotti has not deserted comedy. *The Old Maid and the Thief* (1939) is a slight escapade written for radio performance; *The Telephone* (1947) is a delicious bonbon calling for two characters—hardly an opera, but a brief, humorous little sketch with music suitable for a television variety program.

More ambitious both in structure and style, but still in a highly satirical and comic vein, is *The Last Savage,* introduced at the Opéra-Comique in Paris in 1963. Here, for the first time since *Amelia Goes to the Ball,* Menotti wrote his libretto in Italian; all his other libretti were written in English. For the Paris premiere, the Italian libretto was translated into French; for the American premiere, at the Metropolitan Opera in 1964, into English. The first time this opera was heard in its original Italian language was in Venice in 1964.

The attempt of Kitty, an American anthropologist, to find the Abominable Snowman (or "the last savage") in India offered Menotti many an opportunity, both in his play and in his music, to mock at some of our present-day social customs, foibles, and ways of life. Kitty's father, a millionaire, worries about the bureaucracy in Washington, D.C., frets over high taxes, is irritated by the power of American trade unions. The Maharajah of India falls in love with Kitty. His main concern, however, is the demand of his people for social reforms. Since Kitty refuses to marry the Maharajah until she finds her Snowman, the Maharajah contrives to have his stable boy assume the part.

Along the route of this plot, Menotti pokes fun at avant-garde painters and composers, American cocktail parties, American beatniks, and other facets and figures of American life in our times. Menotti designed this work not as an opera but as an *opéra bouffe.* In keeping with this medium he made extensive use of ear-caressing melodies and tuneful duets and ensembles, together with highly amusing vocal numbers.

Menotti's versatility reveals itself not only in the eclecticism of his style within any one opera but also in the resilient way in which he adapted his music to texts altogether different from any we have thus far discussed. In *Martin's Lie* (1964) he created a spare, intimate work for church performance whose setting is medieval England—a work not much different from a Britten church parable. In a television opera, *Labyrinth* (1963), he conceived a highly symbolical opera (Menotti called this work an "operatic riddle") with each character and event in the complicated and surrealistic text representing things, peoples, and ideas in the real world. Since he wrote this opera for television, Menotti made deft use of camera techniques, so that it is impossible to perform it in a theater or opera house.

In *The Most Important Man,* whose world premiere was given by the New York City Opera on March 2, 1971, Menotti involved himself with the racial problem. The "most important man" is black, Toime Ukamba, assistant to a distinguished white scientist in an apartheid community, probably in South Africa. Ukamba evolves a formula capable of revolutionizing society and making its owner the world's most powerful human being. Ukamba is willing to turn the formula over to his government under certain unspecified conditions. White scientists refuse to accept his terms, maintaining that a black man can never dictate policy in a government dominated by whites. In the bitter struggle that follows, Ukamba is shot, but not before he has had the formula destroyed.

Labyrinth was the second opera Menotti wrote expressly for television. The first time he did so he came up with another of his resounding successes: *Amahl and the Night Visitors.* Commissioned by the National Broadcasting Company, it was first televised over its network on Christmas Eve of 1951. Taking his inspiration from *The Adoration of the Magi,* a painting by the Flemish artist Hieronymus Bosch, Menotti relates the religious tale of a crippled boy, Amahl, who is visited by the Three Wise Men on their way to the manger in Bethlehem. When the crippled beggar boy offers them his crutches as a gift to the Holy Child, he becomes miraculously healed. For this simple religious theme, Menotti used dramatic recitatives extensively, providing contrast with eloquent choruses and ensemble numbers, and at times with engaging peasant dances. The little opera begins and ends with a haunting tune played on a pipe by the beggar boy. There is poignancy and beauty in the simple and unpretentious way Menotti tells his religious story through words and music.

Amahl and the Night Visitors has added several important footnotes to opera history. It was the first opera ever written directly for television. It was the first opera financed by the business world, through sponsorship. And it was the first American opera to become a holiday institution on television. For over a decade, *Amahl and the Night Visitors* was performed over the NBC network as a Christmas attraction. This practice was finally discontinued when Menotti insisted upon an entirely new production and the television producers refused to accede to his demand. This one-act opera, however, has often been staged in opera auditoriums.

Menotti described *Help, Help, the Globolinks!* as "an opera for children and for those who love children." Once again he resorted to comedy and satire. Globolinks are creatures from another world invading ours. They have the power to transform a human being into a Globolink. Surrounded by these strange creatures, a busload of schoolchildren tries in vain to frighten them away with the honking of the bus horn. This fails; a Globolink is not frightened by noise. But what finally succeeds in driving the Globolinks away is when music is played for them. You see, a Globolink just can't stand tonal music. Before they depart, the Globolinks transform only one person into their own shape. He is the school's principal, and the reason he is victimized is because he hates music.

In this one-act opera Menotti has used electronic sounds for the first time. They are heard soon after the orchestral prelude (which is interrupted with the announcement that the Globolinks have landed). Electronic sounds help create a weird background for the arrival of the creatures in their outlandish costumes, as many-colored lights flash about in psychedelic fashion from revolving towers.

Help, Help, the Globolinks! was introduced by the Hamburg Opera in Germany on December 21, 1968, before America first saw it, at Sante Fe, New Mexico, in 1969. As delectable in its levity and excursions into nonsense as it is unusual in its plot, *Help Help, the Globolinks!* has enchanted old as well as young, sophisticated operagoers as well as novitiates, Europeans as well as Americans. By 1970 it had received performances by seventeen professional opera companies, over twenty-five student and amateur organizations, over television in Germany, and in concert version by seven symphony orchestras.

Menotti wrote the libretto for a distinguished opera by another American: Samuel Barber (1910–   ). That opera is *Vanessa* which, following its world premiere at the Metropolitan Opera in New York on January 15, 1958, received the Pulitzer Prize and then became the first American opera ever produced at the world-famous Salzburg Festival in Austria. Barber is also an eclectic, but with an even stronger bent for romanticism and lyricism than Menotti. A stark drama, *Vanessa* takes place in a Scandinavian country in 1905. In a dreary manor, the heroine (Vanessa) has been waiting twenty years for her lover to return. She does not know he is dead. Her lover's son, Anatol, appears. He seduces Vanessa's niece, Erika, but then marries Vanessa. After Vanessa and Anatol depart, Erika is left alone in the bleak manor, nursing the same dream that so long obsessed Vanessa: that her lover would one day return to her.

This grim story is suited for dissonant and atonal writing, and there is a good deal of each in the score. But perhaps the most poignant pages are those that are melodic, notable examples being Erika's air, "Must winter come so soon?", Vanessa's song, "Our Arms Entwined," and an infectious little waltz, "Under the Willow Tree."

Vanessa was Barber's first opera. His second, *Antony and Cleopatra* (based on Shakespeare's play), was written on commission to open the new auditorium of the Metropolitan Opera at the Lincoln Center for the Performing Arts on September 16, 1966. It proved a dismal failure and did not return to the Metropolitan Opera repertory the following season.

It is perhaps the eclectics like Britten, Menotti, and Barber—and many others like them—who give us a clue to the future of opera. However new may be the language constantly being devised by avant-garde composers of today, and regardless of how many operas use that language, the operas that will probably have the widest appeal and greatest artistic importance are those utilizing every resource at the disposal of the composer that can help him make his text more meaningful.

Through the centuries, from its very beginnings, opera has always taken advantage of the technical and structural developments affecting other forms of music. This is why it has been able to remain a vital art form. Already we have seen that even such avant-garde idioms as the twelve-tone technique, serialism, and electronic music have made valuable contributions to opera. As still newer and even more revolutionary ideas and methods are devised, opera undoubtedly will continue to borrow what it will find most useful.

The history of opera—rich as it has been—can surely look forward to many new, vital chapters in the years to come.

Glossary

Accompagnato Accompanied. *See* Recitative.

Alto, or Contralto The lowest range of female voice, rising about two octaves from E·or F below middle C.

Aria An extended solo for voice in opera, sometimes characterized by lyrical beauty, sometimes by florid writing, sometimes by dramatic and emotional expression.

Arietta A short aria.

Assoluta *See* Prima Donna.

Atonality Absence of a basic key. See discussion in Chapter 14.

Bacchanale Named for Bacchus, the Roman god of wine. An elaborately mounted ballet, celebrating sensual pleasures.

Ballad Opera A popular operatic form in eighteenth-century England sometimes known as "the people's opera." It consists of spoken comedy (often timely and satirical in subject matter) with incidental music comprising tunes borrowed from the popular melodies of the times. The most famous ballad opera is *The Beggar's Opera* (1728), text by John Gay, music arranged by John Christopher Pepusch.

Ballet A dance production accompanied by music.

Foyer of the Metropolitan Opera House, Lincoln Center, New York.

Ballet-Opera An eighteenth-century French opera form in which ballet sequences are used extensively to develop the plot.

Barcarolle A piece of music in the style of the boat song of the Venetian gondoliers.

Baritone A male voice with the approximate range of two octaves upward from the A a tenth below middle C. The baritone range lies between those of the tenor and bass.

Bass, or Basso The lowest range of male voice, rising two octaves above E, an octave and a sixth below middle C. A singer with a slightly higher range is a bass-baritone; one with a lower range, a *basso profundo*.

Bel Canto "Beautiful song, beautiful singing." A type of aria and a style of singing emphasizing beauty of tone, purity of texture, elegance of phrasing, virtuosity, and agility. See discussion in Chapter 7.

Berceuse A cradle song or lullaby.

Bravura Brilliant and technically demanding vocal passage. A bravura aria is one with bravura passages.

Brindisi A drinking song.

Buffa, or Buffo Comic. An *opera buffa* is an Italian comic opera; a *basso buffo* is a basso specializing in comic roles in such operas.

Cabaletta A brief aria in operas by Rossini and some of his contemporaries. It has several repeats. With Verdi and his contemporaries, a cabaletta is the final, and elaborate, part of a long aria or duet.

Cadenza A virtuoso passage within an aria.

Cantilena A smooth and melodious vocal number.

Canzonetta A short, light, and cheerful song.

Castrato A male soprano (eunuch) with a sweet but powerful voice of high range and sensuous tone. See discussion in Chapter 2.

Cavatina A song simpler in style and structure than an aria.

Cembalo A harpsichord.

Chamber Opera An intimate form of opera of economical structural proportions requiring small musical forces and limited stage resources.

Chorus A group of singers performing ensemble music.

Claque A group hired to applaud a performer or performance to help arouse audience enthusiasm. Claques have also been hired to create a disturbance during an opera or a particular singer's performance.

Coloratura An aria featuring numerous runs and ornamentations. Also used for singers who perform this type of music.

Comic Opera A work for the musical stage, comic in subject matter

and treatment. Specific forms of comic opera are *opera buffa* and *opéra*
bouffe (but not *opéra-comique*).

Consonance   An agreeable combination of musical tones.

Contralto   *See* Alto.

Corps de Ballet   An ensemble, or ballet group, like a chorus, as opposed to solo dancers.

Da Capo Aria   An aria in three-part form. The middle part offers contrasting melody to the first and third parts. The third part repeats the melody of the first but with ornamentations. See discussion in Chapter 2.

Declamation   Vocal music—used for dramatic episodes in opera—that follows the inflections of speech and in which the text assumes greater importance than the melody.

Dissonance, or Discord   A discordant chord or chords that are not resolved into consonance.

Dodecaphony   *See* Twelve-Tone Technique.

Dramma Giocoso   A gay drama. This term was devised by Mozart for *Don Giovanni,* an opera combining comic and tragic elements. See discussion in Chapter 5.

Dramma per Musica   "Drama through music," a term used for the first operas written.

Duet   A vocal number for two voices.

Embellishment   Ornament, decoration, fioriture in a melody.

Entr'acte   French term for an orchestral interlude between acts.

Entrada   Spanish term for an orchestral prelude to an act.

Expressionism   A term borrowed from painting for music reduced to basic essentials and unmarked by human or emotional relationships. See discussion in Chapter 14.

Falsetto   Singing by a male performer in a high range with a quality and texture resembling that of a female voice.

Fanfare   A flourish for trumpets used in festive scenes or to attract attention.

Favola per Musica   "Fable in music," a descriptive term often used by composers of the earliest operas when the text was based on legend or mythology.

Finale   Extended conclusion to an act made up of arias, recitatives, and ensemble numbers.

Fioriture   Ornamentations and decorations either provided by the composer or improvised by the singer in an aria.

Gavotte   An old French dance in common time beginning on the third beat. This dance form appears often in operas by Rameau, Lully, Handel, and their contemporaries. Later operas sometimes used the gavotte style and form for arias.

Gebrauchsmusik   "Functional music." A term devised in twentieth-century Germany for music written for radio, motion pictures, use in schools, and so forth. Operas in a functional or popular style fall into this category. Examples are Kurt Weill's *The Threepenny Opera* and Hindemith's opera for children, *We Build a City.*

Heldentenor   *See* Tenor.

Imbroglio   A confused, complicated, or intricate scene with music that suggests confusion, though it has been carefully planned.

Impresario   Director of an opera company.

Impressionism   A term borrowed from painting. Music of this style suggests the sensation or impression aroused by any given subject. Subtle nuances, colors, effects, atmospheres are emphasized rather than structure or substance. See discussion in Chapter 14.

Intendant   German term for manager or director of an opera house.

Intermezzo   Originally a short comic play with music interpolated between acts of a serious opera. Later on the term was used for an orchestral interlude played with the curtain raised to suggest passage of time.

Intonation   Adhering to the correct pitch.

Intrada   *See* Prelude.

Kammeroper   German term for chamber opera.

Kammersänger   German term for "chamber singer," the highest honorary title for an opera singer in Germany and Austria. For female singers: *Kammersängerin.*

Kapellmeister   Current German term for conductor. Originally meant a choirmaster.

Leitmotiv   Leading motive. A rhythmic, melodic, or harmonic figure used throughout an opera to identify a character, object, mood, situation, or idea. The technique of using leitmotivs gained its highest degree of development and importance in Wagner's music dramas. See discussion in Chapter 11.

Lyric Drama   Synonym for opera.

Lyric Opera   An opera in which the lyrical element is more pronounced than the dramatic, or in which the vocal part assumes major importance.

Maestro di Cappella   An Italian term used in an earlier period, meaning "Master of the chapel." The leader of a choir, a conductor, a composer, or all three combined. The French equivalent term was *Maître de* *chapelle.*

March   Music in 4/4 time (sometimes in 2/4 time) for a parade or march. In opera a march can be a convenient device to get large groups on and off the stage.

Marionette Opera   Opera performed by marionettes. Various composers have written operas for this medium, an example being Manuel de Falla's *El retablo de Maese Pedro.*

Masque   An English form of theatrical entertainment made up of song, poetry, dancing, and pageantry popular between 1600 and 1800. Its subject was based on a mythological or allegorical story.

Mezza Aria   Literally, "half an aria." An aria that combines melody with recitative.

Mezza Voce   Literally, "half a voice." Singing with diminished volume.

Mezzo Soprano   The range of female voice between soprano and alto, usually rising about two octaves from A below middle C.

Monodrama   An opera with one character. Originating in the eighteenth century, the form was revived in the twentieth century by Arnold Schoenberg (*Erwartung*) and Francis Poulenc (*La voix humaine*) among others.

Music Drama   An operatic form devised by Richard Wagner, and used by his successors, for works in which the dramatic element is as important as the musical, and that represents the synthesis of these with other arts such as staging and costuming. See discussion in Chapter 11.

Naturalism   A movement in opera evolved in the twentieth century as an outgrowth of *verismo* (*q.v.*) in which life is presented more authentically and realistically than in earlier operas. Gustave Charpentier's *Louise* is a notable example.

Opera   A stage work of a text set either partly or wholly to music.

Opéra Bouffe   French comic opera with a light, frivolous, farcical, or satirical text partly spoken, partly set to tuneful melodies. See discussion in Chapter 8.

Opera Buffa   Italian comic opera. See discussion in Chapter 2.

Opéra-Comique   A genre of French opera, frequently on tragic subjects, distinguished from other types of French opera by the fact that dialogue is used in place of recitatives. See discussion in Chapter 8.

Opera Seria   Literally "serious opera." A stylized type of serious Italian opera following a rigidly set pattern popular in the seventeenth and early eighteenth centuries. See discussion in Chapter 2.

Ornament   *See* Embellishment.

Overture   An orchestral preface to an opera. Some composers preferred to designate such a preface a "prelude"; others preferred eliminating an overture or prelude altogether and substituting a few introductory chords.

Parlando, or Parlante   Literally, "speaking." An indication for a singer to simulate speech.

Portamento   Carrying the voice from one note to another while gliding over the intervening notes.

Prelude, or Vorspiel   An orchestral preface to an opera in place of an overture to set the mood or suggest the atmosphere of the coming drama. Gluck used the term *Intrada* for what later came to be called a prelude. Wagner and many subsequent opera composers often used preludes instead of overtures.

Prima Donna   Literally, "first lady." The leading female part in an opera. A *prima donna assoluta* ("absolute prima donna") is the most important female member of an opera company.

Primo Uomo   Literally, "first man." The leading male singer in an opera.

Quartet   A vocal number for four voices.

Quintet   A vocal number for five voices.

Recitative, or Recitativo   Declamation accompanied by music to advance the plot. In early operas, *recitativo secco* or "dry recitative" had a simple accompaniment of chords played on a harpsichord. It has less melodic or dramatic interest than *recitativo accompagnato* (sometimes also known as *stromentato*): recitative with a more extensive and elaborate accompaniment from the orchestra. See discussion in Chapter 2.

Register   The compass of a vocal range, and the colorations and voice production suitable for that range.

Répétition   French term for "rehearsal." A *répétition générale* is a dress rehearsal to which critics and guests are invited.

Rescue Opera   Operas in which the hero or heroine is saved after many complications, as in Cherubini's *Les deux journées* and Beethoven's *Fidelio*. See discussion in Chapter 3.

Ritornello   In early Italian opera a short instrumental passage between vocal parts of an aria or between scenes.

Romance, or Romanza   An aria romantic in feeling, or concerned with unfolding a narrative rather than with dramatic expression.

Roulade   Florid vocal passage.

Scena   A vocal number in an opera more extended and dramatic than an aria.

Serenade, or Serenata   A love song sung under a lady's window.

Sextet   A vocal number for six voices.

Singspiel   An early form of German comic opera of popular appeal that uses spoken dialogue instead of recitatives and whose music has the character of German folk or popular songs. See discussion in Chapter 5.

Song-Speech, or Sprechstimme   A kind of melodic line in atonal music resembling speech. See discussion in Chapter 14.

Soprano   Highest range of female voice, usually a little over two octaves from B-flat below middle C. Sopranos fall into three categories: lyric, dramatic, and coloratura.

Sotto Voce   Literally, "under the voice." Singing in an undertone, or in an "aside."

Stile Rappresentativo   Literally, "representative style." A vocal style developed by opera's earliest composers for declamations or recitatives in imitation of the sound of actual speech. See discussion in Chapter 1.

Stretta   An accelerated passage at the end of an aria, scene, or act.

Tenor   The highest range of male voice, extending two octaves above the C an octave below middle C. A *Heldentenor,* or "heroic tenor," has a large voice more suitable for dramatic than lyric roles.

Tessitura   Literally, "texture." The approximate range of a role or an aria.

Trio   A vocal number for three voices.

Twelve-Tone Technique, or Dodecaphony   A system developed and popularized by Arnold Schoenberg utilizing the twelve tones of the chromatic scale without repeating a note before using the others. Expressionist composers create a "row" of these twelve notes, which becomes the basis of their composition. See discussion in Chapter 14.

Unison   Singing of the same note or notes by more than one performer.

Verismo   A movement in Italian opera launched by Mascagni's *Cavalleria rusticana* that emphasizes realistic treatment of true-to-life situations. See discussion in Chapter 10.

Vorspiel   *See* Prelude.

Zeitkunst   Literally, "contemporary art." A cultural movement in Germany in the 1920s that encouraged writing operas with contemporary, often provocative or satirical texts and music with a popular appeal. Notable examples are Kurt Weill's operas of that decade and Ernest Křenek's *Jonny spielt auf!*

Zukunftsart, or Zukunftsmusik   Literally, "art" or "music of the future." A term conceived by Wagner to describe his musical-dramatic concepts. Battles over Wagner's aesthetics were fought bitterly for half a century utilizing this term.

Index